State of Virginia

Acts passed at a General Assembly of the Commonwealth of Virginia

State of Virginia

Acts passed at a General Assembly of the Commonwealth of Virginia

ISBN/EAN: 9783741105074

Manufactured in Europe, USA, Canada, Australia, Japa

Cover: Foto ©ninafisch / pixelio.de

Manufactured and distributed by brebook publishing software (www.brebook.com)

State of Virginia

Acts passed at a General Assembly of the Commonwealth of Virginia

ACTS

OF THE

GENERAL ASSEMBLY

OF THE

STATE OF VIRGINIA,

PASSED IN 1861-2,

IN THE

EIGHTY-SIXTH YEAR OF THE COMMONWEALTH.

RICHMOND:
WILLIAM F. RITCHIE, PUBLIC PRINTER.
1862.

PUBLIC OR GENERAL ACTS.

CHAP. 1.—An ACT imposing Taxes for the Support of Government.

Passed March 27, 1862.

1. Be it enacted by the general assembly, that the taxes on the persons and subjects in this chapter mentioned, or required by law to be listed or assessed, shall for the present year and thereafter be yearly as follows:

Taxes on lands and lots.

On tracts of lands and lots, with the improvements thereon, not exempt from taxation, sixty cents on every hundred dollars value thereof; and herein shall be included all tracts of lands and lots, with improvements thereon, not otherwise taxed or exempt from taxation, of incorporated joint stock companies, savings institutions and insurance companies. [*Tax on land* / *What included therein*]

On personal property.

2. On all the personal property (excepting provisions and wool of last year's clip; but this section shall not be so construed as to exclude from taxation any provisions purchased for sale by the holder thereof), moneys and credits, as defined in this section, including all capital, personal property and moneys of incorporated joint stock companies (other than rail road, canal or turnpike companies), and all capital invested, used or employed in any manufactoring, trade or other business, sixty cents on every hundred dollars value thereof. But property otherwise taxed, and property from which any income so taxed is derived, or on the capital invested in any trade or business, in respect to which a license so taxed is issued, certificates of stock, moneys and personal property that constitute part of the capital of any bank, savings institutions and insurance companies, whether incorporated by this or any other state, which have declared dividends within one year preceding the first day of February, of as much as six per cent. profits, shall not be taxed under the provisions of this section. The word "moneys" shall be construed to include not only gold, silver and copper coin, but bullion and bank notes. The word "credits" shall be construed to mean all bank, state or corporation stocks, claims or demands owing or coming to any person, whether due or not, and whether payable in money or other

thing. Moneys and credits owned by any resident of this state, whether such moneys or credits are within or without this state, shall be taxed at the rate prescribed by this section.

On free negroes.

On free negroes 3. On every male free negro who has attained the age of twenty-one years, one dollar and twenty cents; but no tax shall hereafter be assessed or collected on such male free negro under the act of the sixth of April eighteen hundred and fifty-three, establishing a colonization board.

On white males.

On white males 4. On every white male inhabitant who has attained the age of twenty-one years, not exempted from taxation by order of the court in consequence of bodily infirmity, one dollar and twenty cents.

On public bonds.

On interest on public bonds 5. On the interest or profit which may have accrued, and is solvent, or which may have been received by any person, or converted into principal so as to become an interest bearing subject, or otherwise appropriated, within the year next preceding the first day of February of each year, arising from bonds and certificates of debt of the Confederate States or of this or any other state or country, or any corporation created by this or any other state, whether the stock of such company be exempt from taxation or not, ten per centum. But such interest or profits derived from bank stock or shares of savings institutions and insurance companies which pay taxes thereon into the treasury, shall not be included herein, unless invested or otherwise appropriated, and if so invested or otherwise appropriated, the tax thereon shall be at the rate of sixty cents upon every hundred dollars value thereof. If no interest shall have been received within the year preceding the first day of February, then the value of the principal of such bonds shall be assessed and taxed as other property.

On bank dividends.

Bank dividends 6. On the dividends declared by any bank incorporated by this state, the tax shall be ten per centum upon the amount thereof, to be paid into the treasury by the bank. If the dividend be that of a bank incorporated elsewhere, the tax shall be ten per centum upon the amount thereof, to be assessed and collected as other taxes.

On dividends of savings institutions, telegraph, steam boat, insurance and such like companies.

On dividends of savings banks and insurance companies 7. On the dividends declared within the year preceding the first day of February, if the same be equal to or over six per centum on its capital, by savings institutions, telegraph, steam boat, insurance and such like companies, whether incorporated by this or any other state, or whether operating with or without a charter, to be paid by such institutions and companies into the treasury. respectively, ten per centum. If there be no dividend, or if such dividend be not equal to six per centum of such capital, then such institution and such company shall pay a tax on its capital at the rate of sixty cents on every hundred dollars of such capital; and herein capital shall consist of stock subscribed, money deposited, and bonds and other evidences of debt held or owned by such institutions and companies.

On dividends of companies not incorporated by this state.

8. On dividends of rail road or other like companies, not incorporated by this state, the tax shall be ten per centum upon the amount thereof, to be listed and charged to the recipient of such dividends, or those entitled to receive the same. If such dividend be not equal to six per centum of such capital, the stock so held shall be listed and taxed as other property.   *Dividends of companies not incorporated by this state*

On income.

9. On the income, salary, compensation or fees received during the year ending the first day of February of each year, in consideration of the discharge of any office or employment in the service of the state or of the Confederate States, or in consideration of the discharge of any office or employment in the service of any corporation, or in the service of any company, firm or person, except where the service is that of a minister of the gospel, one and one-half per centum upon so much thereof as exceeds five hundred dollars. The tax on a salary payable under this section by an officer of government receiving the same out of the treasury, shall be deducted at the rate chargeable on the annual salary, on the amount drawn from the treasury at the time the salary is audited and paid; and fees or other income of such officer shall be listed and assessed by the commissioners as in other cases, and at the rates prescribed thereon.   *On income or fees* *Exception* *Taxes of officers of government, how paid*

On toll bridges.

10. On the yearly rent or annual value of toll bridges and ferries, other than those toll bridges and ferries exempt by their charter from taxation, ten per centum.   *On toll bridges and ferries*

On collateral inheritances.

11. On the estate of a decedent, which passes under his will or by descent to any other person, or for any other use than to or for the use of the father, mother, husband, wife, brother, sister, nephew, niece, or lineal descendant of such decedent, there shall be a tax of two per centum of such estate.   *Collateral inheritances*

Estates passing under sequestration acts.

12. On all estate, which, under the effect or by the provisions of the sequestration act of the confederate congress, or any act amen-   *Sequestration act of congress*

datory thereof, may legally pass, otherwise than by purchase, to any person, there shall be a tax of two per centum on the value thereof.

Tax on estates passing

Internal improvement companies.

13. On every passenger transported on any rail road or canal in this state, one and a half mill for every mile of transportation; and on all freight transported on any such rail road or canal, three-fourths of one per centum of the gross amount received by the company controlling such rail road or canal, for the transportation of such freight, or for tolls thereon, or for privileges granted thereby, and it shall be the duty of every such company to collect for the state the tax herein imposed; and every rail road company or canal company, whether exempted from taxation by its charter or not, shall hereafter report quarterly, on the fifteenth day of March, June, September and December in each year, to the auditor of public accounts, the number of passengers transported, and the aggregate number of miles traveled by them within this commonwealth, and the gross amount received by such company for the transportation of freight over such road or canal, or any part thereof, or water or other improvement owned or connected therewith, during the quarter of the year next preceding the first day of the month in which such report is made. Such company, whose road or canal is only in part within the commonwealth, shall report as aforesaid such portion only of such amount received for transportation of freight, as the part of the said road or canal which is within this commonwealth bears to the whole of such road or canal. If the profits of such road or canal consist in whole or in part of tolls, the gross amount thereof shall, for the purposes of this act, be construed to be a part of the gross amount received for the transportation of freight. It is the intention of this act to abrogate and annul all exemptions from taxation of any such company contained in its charter, during the existing war, and to subject such company to the uniform rate of taxation prescribed by law, so far as the general assembly has power to do so.

Internal improvement companies.

Rail road and canal companies to report to the auditor quarterly
What to report

When only partly within the state

Statement of rail road officers.

14. Such statement shall be verified by the oaths of the president and the superintendent of transportation, or other proper officer. Every company failing to make such report, shall be fined five hundred dollars; and any company having a subordinate board, or any board managing any part of its works may, by its by-laws, create and enforce such penalties as will secure proper reports of such companies. At the time of making such reports, such company shall pay into the treasury the taxes imposed on passengers, freight, tolls and privileges as in this act is provided. Every such company paying such taxes, shall not be assessed with any tax on its lands, buildings, cars, boats or other property (owned but not hired) which they are authorized by law to hold or have. But if any such com-

Report made on oath
Penalty for failure
Tax on passengers
Tax on freight
To be exempt from tax on their lands
In case of failure

pany fail to pay such taxes at either of the times specified therefor, then its lands, buildings, cars, boats and other property shall be immediately assessed under the direction of the auditor of public accounts, by any person appointed by him for the purpose, at its full value, and a tax shall at once be levied thereon, as on real estate and other property, at fifteen cents on every hundred dollars value, on account of each quarterly default, to be collected by any sheriff whom the auditor may direct; and such sheriff shall distrain and sell any personal property of such company and pay such taxes into the treasury within three months from the time when such assessment is furnished to him. *(to pay, what is done)*

Express companies.

15. Every express company, in addition to the license tax on such company, on any express business, shall make a return to the auditor of public accounts, on the fifteenth day of June and December in each year, of the total receipts of such company, on account of its operations within the state of Virginia, within the six months proceeding the first day of June and December in each year. Such returns shall be verified by the oaths of the agent and chief officers of such company, at its principal office or offices in the state, in the manner and according to the form prescribed by the said auditor, whether collected within or without the state. Such express company shall pay on the total receipts so reported, a tax of one and a half per centum, except for the transportation of bank notes for brokers and for non-residents, for which the tax shall be one-fourth of one per centum upon the amount of bank notes transported; and for failure to make such report or pay such tax, a penalty of not less than one thousand dollars nor more than five thousand dollars, shall be imposed upon the company so failing, to be recovered as other penalties are; and to be paid into the general treasury in lieu of a tax: provided, however, that no express company, through any of its agents, shall transact any business appertaining to the business of a broker, unless it be for the commonwealth. Such principal officer shall require from the several agents employed by such company, a report of their transaction, on oath, which report, so sworn to, shall accompany the report of the chief officer to the auditor of public accounts. *(Express companies required to make semi-annual returns to auditor of receipts)* *(Returns to be on oath)* *(Tax on receipts)* *(Exception)* *(Penalty for failure to pay or report)*

On suits.

16. When any original suit, ejectment, attachment (other than on a summons to a suggestion sued out under the provisions of the eleventh section of chapter one hundred and eighty-eight of the Code), or other action is commenced in a circuit, county or corporation court, there shall be a tax of one dollar; if it be an appeal, writ of error or supersedeas in a circuit court, there shall be a tax of two dollars; if it be an appeal, writ of error or supersedeas in a district court, five dollars; and if in a court of appeals, five dollars. *(Original suits)* *(Appeals, &c.)*

FINANCIAL.—TAXES.

On seals.

Seals of courts, notaries or state Exemptions, Code, p. 216

17. When the seal of a court, of a notary public, or the seal of the state is annexed to any paper, except in those cases exempted by law, the taxes shall be as follows: For the seal of the state, three dollars; for any other seal, one dollar and fifty cents; and herein shall be included a tax on a scroll annexed to a paper in lieu of an official seal. But this section shall not apply to seals of courts affixed to bonds of any county executed for money raised to aid in equipping soldiers of such counties, or to aid in the support of the families of such soldiers; nor shall the tax provided in this section apply to any seal of a court affixed to any papers required in order to receive the arrearages of pay or allowances due to a deceased soldier, either from this state or the Confederate States.

On wills and administrations.

Wills and administrations

18. On the probate of every will or grant of administration, there shall be a tax of one dollar and fifty cents.

Deeds.

Deeds and contracts

19. On every deed admitted to record, whether the same has been recorded before or not, and on every contract relating to real estate, whether it be a deed or not, which is admitted to record, there shall be a tax of one dollar and fifty cents.

Taxes on bank corporations.

Bank corporations

20. On every law incorporating or chartering or rechartering any bank with a capital not exceeding two hundred thousand dollars, there shall be a tax of seventy-five dollars; with a capital of over two hundred thousand dollars and not exceeding four hundred thousand dollars, there shall be a tax of one hundred and fifty dollars; with a capital of over four hundred thousand dollars and not exceeding six hundred thousand dollars, there shall be a tax of two hundred and twenty-five dollars; with a capital of over six hundred thousand dollars and not exceeding eight hundred thousand dollars, there shall be a tax of three hundred dollars; and with a capital of over eight hundred thousand dollars, there shall be a tax of three hundred and seventy-five dollars.

Taxes on manufacturing companies.

Manufacturing companies

21. On every law incorporating or rechartering any oil, iron, coal or manufacturing company, if the maximum capital is one hundred thousand dollars or less, there shall be a tax of seventy-five dollars; and if it exceed that amount, there shall be a tax of one hundred and fifty dollars.

FINANCIAL.—TAXES.

Taxes on gas light and other companies.

22. On every law for the incorporation of any canal, rail road, insurance, gas light, express or telegraph company, if the maximum capital is one hundred thousand dollars or less, there shall be a tax of seventy-five dollars; and if it exceed that amount, there shall be a tax of one hundred and fifty dollars: provided, that the tax imposed by this section shall not apply to the Virginia canal company. Gas light and other companies

Tax on savings institutions.

23. On every law chartering, renewing or extending the charter of any savings institution, if the maximum capital is one hundred thousand dollars or less, there shall be a tax of seventy-five dollars each; and if it exceed that amount, there shall be a tax of one hundred and fifty dollars. Savings institutions

Tax on private corporations.

24. On every law chartering, renewing or extending the charter of any private corporation, other than those herein before mentioned, and other than acts for the incorporation of a college, academy, seminary of learning, or literary or charitable institution or cemetery, if the maximum capital is one hundred thousand dollars or less, there shall be a tax of seventy-five dollars; and if it exceed that amount, there shall be a tax of one hundred and fifty dollars. Private corporations Exceptions

Unorganized companies, how taxed.

25. All the acts of assembly creating or continuing corporations, mentioned in the twentieth, twenty-first, twenty-second, twenty-third and twenty-fourth sections of this act, which, since the third day of April eighteen hundred and sixty-one, have not been organized by accepting the charter granted to the corporators and paid the taxes thereon according to the provisions of the act entitled an act imposing taxes for the support of government, passed April third, eighteen hundred and sixty-one, shall hereafter, upon being organized, or upon accepting the charter, return a statement, verified by the oath of the president or other proper officer, to the auditor of public accounts, showing the amount of the capital of the company or corporation of which he is president, on or before the first day of July eighteen hundred and sixty-two, and those corporators omitting so to accept the charter and to return by that time, and afterwards accepting, shall, on or before the first day of July in the year next after such acceptance, make such report, and at the same time pay into the treasury the amount of tax imposed by this act. Tax on private corporations heretofore created

On Licenses.

Ordinaries.

Ordinaries and public entertainment

26. The taxes on licenses shall be as follows:

On a license to keep an ordinary or house of public entertainment, sixty dollars; and if the yearly value of such house and furniture, whether rented or kept by the proprietor, exceed one hundred dollars, and is less than two hundred dollars, the tax shall be seventy-five dollars; and if the yearly value thereof exceed two hundred dollars, there shall be added to the last mentioned sum, twenty per cent. on so much thereof as exceeds two hundred dollars; and if the license grants the privilege of retailing ardent spirits, porter, ale or beer, to be drank elsewhere than at such ordinary, there shall be added to said license a tax of seventy-five dollars in addition to the amount otherwise imposed; and if the business be continued, there shall also be a tax of one and one-half per centum upon the amount of such sales for the preceding year, in addition to the specific tax. But the privilege to sell ardent spirits hereby authorized, shall not be construed to authorize the sale of any other thing under cover of a license to keep an ordinary, and any sales not authorized at such ordinary shall be deemed to be sales made by the ordinary keeper without license.

Retailing ardent spirits

Ordinary keepers liable for sales made at taverns

Private entertainments.

Private entertainment and boarding houses

27. On a license to keep a house of private entertainment or a private boarding house, ten dollars. If the yearly value thereof and furniture exceed one hundred dollars, there shall be added to the last mentioned sum fifteen per cent. on so much thereof as exceeds one hundred dollars. But no house shall be deemed a private boarding house with less than five boarders.

Cook shops and eating houses.

Cook shops and eating houses

28. On every license to keep a cook shop or eating house, twenty-five dollars; and in addition thereto, twenty-five per cent. on so much of the yearly value thereof as exceeds one hundred dollars.

Bowling alleys.

Bowling alleys or saloons

29. On every license permitting a bowling alley or saloon to be kept for a year, seventy-five dollars; but if there is more than one such alley kept in any one room, twenty-five dollars each shall be charged for the excess over one.

Billiard tables.

Billiard tables

30. On every license permitting a billiard table to be kept for a year, one hundred and fifty dollars; but if there is more than one such table kept in any one room, seventy-five dollars each shall be charged for the excess over one table.

Bagatelle tables.

31. On every license permitting a bagatello or other like table to be kept for one year or any less time, thirty dollars for the first, and if more than one, fifteen dollars for each additional table. Bagatelle tables

Livery stables.

32. On every license to a keeper of a livery stable, one dollar and fifty cents for each stall thereof; and herein shall be included as stalls, such space as may be necessary for a horse to stand, and in which a horse is or may be kept at livery otherwise than for the purpose of feeding horses by one day only; and no exemption from this license shall be allowed to any person in consequence of such person being licensed to keep an ordinary or house of private entertainment, if any horses be kept, fed or hired for compensation by the proprietor thereof, except that no tax shall be required on such stalls as are kept exclusively and used for horses belonging to travelers or guests stopping at such house. Livery stables

License to distill ardent spirits from fruit, &c.

33. On every license to distill ardent spirits from fruit, vegetables, syrups, molasses, sugar cane or sugars, the tax shall be thirty dollars; if such distillery has been in operation for the preceding year or any part thereof, there shall be an additional tax of ten cents per gallon on the quantity of liquor manufactured at such distillery for the year next preceding or for any part thereof: provided, that thirty-three gallons of brandy shall be exempt from the operation of this tax, when made by the owner for his own use. A license for the business authorizing this section shall be obtained as other licenses are obtained, and with like penalties for a failure to obtain the same, notwithstanding the exemption provided for in the act passed March the 30th, 1860, entitled an act making regulations concerning licenses. Distilleries Tax for distilling

Licenses to rectify ardent spirits.

34. On every license to rectify ardent spirits, if the machinery be propelled by steam power, the tax shall be one hundred and fifty dollars, and if the machinery be not so propelled, the tax shall be seventy-five dollars; if such establishment has been in operation for the preceding year or any part thereof, and the same shall be continued in operation, there shall be an additional tax of twenty cents per gallon on the quantity rectified and sold in the next preceding year. Rectifying ardent spirits Tax
Additional tax if continued

Merchants.

35. On every license to a merchant or mercantile firm, where a specific tax is to be paid, ninety dollars; but if the capital employed and to be employed for the year, including as capital the cash so Merchant's specific tax

/ FINANCIAL.—TAXES.

When proportioned to sales

used, whether borrowed or not, and goods purchased on credit by said merchant or firm, be shown by affidavit to be less than five hundred dollars, the tax to be paid shall be fifteen dollars; but nothing contained in this section shall be construed to authorize any such person to sell wine, ardent spirits, or a mixture thereof; and when the tax is in proportion to the sales, if the taxable sales shall be under one thousand dollars, the tax shall be thirty dollars; if one thousand and under fifteen hundred dollars, thirty-six dollars; if fifteen hundred dollars and under twenty-five hundred dollars, forty-eight dollars; if twenty-five hundred dollars and under five thousand dollars, seventy-two dollars; if five thousand dollars and under ten thousand dollars, one hundred and fourteen dollars; if ten thousand and under fifteen thousand dollars, one hundred and forty-four dollars; if fifteen thousand dollars and under twenty thousand dollars, one hundred and sixty-eight dollars; if twenty thousand dollars and under thirty thousand dollars, two hundred and ten dollars; if thirty thousand dollars and under fifty thousand dollars, three hundred and twelve dollars; and if over fifty thousand dollars, fifteen dollars for every ten thousand dollars excess over the said sum of fifty thousand dollars. If any merchant is about to close out and discontinue his business, he may sell the same by auction, but under no other circumstances shall he sell by auction unless he obtain a license as auctioneer.

Merchant's permission to sell ardent spirits.

Liquor license on beginners

36. In every case in which the license to a merchant or mercantile firm includes permission to sell wine, ardent spirits or a mixture thereof, porter, ale or beer, by wholesale and retail, or by retail only, if such merchant or firm (commencing business for the first time) sell by wholesale and retail, or by wholesale only, an additional tax of *To continue business* one hundred and fifty dollars, and if by retail only, sixty dollars; and if such license be to a merchant or mercantile firm, to continue the privilege of selling wine, ardent spirits, or a mixture thereof, porter, ale or beer, if by wholesale, or by wholesale and retail, or by retail only, the tax shall be one and one-half of one per centum on the amount of such sales for the year next preceding the time of obtaining said license, in addition to the specific tax imposed on beginners; but said sales shall not be estimated in ascertaining the amount of a merchant's license.

Merchant tailors and others.

Other trades and callings taxed as merchants

37. Merchant tailors, lumber merchants, dealers in coal or wood, shall obtain licenses as merchants and be assessed and taxed thereon as other merchants are by the preceding sections of this act, and shall be subject to like penalties for conducting such business without a merchant's license, except that any captain or other person having the command or control of any vessel, shall not be required to take out a license to sell wood by retail from such vessel.

Commission merchants.

38. The tax on every license to a commission merchant, forwarding merchant, tobacco auctioneer or ship broker, shall be sixty dollars each, for commencing business; and if to continue such business after the same has been carried on for one year, the tax on such license shall be three per centum on the amount of commissions received; and this tax shall be in addition to such tax as may be imposed on a license to such merchant or firm, to sell goods, wares or merchandise. All goods consigned to any such commission merchant, forwarding merchant or tobacco auctioneer, whether such goods be agricultural productions or other articles exempted in the hands of the producer or owner from taxation, shall be included as subjects of taxation under the provisions of this section. *Commission merchants, tobacco auctioneers and ship brokers*

Auctioneers.

39. On every license to an auctioneer or vendue master commencing business, thirty-eight dollars; and if the place of business be in a town containing a population of three thousand inhabitants, forty-eight dollars; if the population exceed three thousand, an additional tax of twenty-three dollars for every thousand persons above that number, and at that rate for any fractional excess less than one thousand; but said specific tax shall in no case exceed five hundred dollars. On every license to an auctioneer who deals exclusively in real estate, five hundred dollars, and he shall have the right to sell real estate at auction or otherwise. On every license to an auctioneer or vendue master, in this section mentioned, to continue the business after the same has been carried on for a year, three-eighths of one per centum on the amount of taxable sales of such auctioneer or vendue master. But no sale shall be made at any place other than the house named in the license as the place of business, or at such other place as the person owning the property is authorized to sell the same; but this prohibition shall not apply to cargo sales or the property of persons closing out business for which they have a license; and no goods shall be consigned to such auctioneer for sale, unless the owner thereof has obtained a merchant's license for a period as long as one whole year. "Taxable sales" in this section shall be construed to embrace sales made by such auctioneer or vendue master, whether such sales be public or private: provided, that such tax on private sales shall not apply to cases where the merchant's tax is payable on said sales. *Auctioneers' scale of license in towns. Real estate auctioneers. When charged a per centage on sales. Where sale to be made. Exceptions. When goods may be consigned to auctioneer. Taxable sales.*

Common crier.

40. On every license to a common crier, if in a town of more than one thousand inhabitants, fifteen dollars; but he shall not be authorized to act in the sale of any property belonging to any person, unless such owner is authorized to sell such property without a license, or has obtained license to do so. *Common crier*

Sample merchants.

Selling goods by sample

41. On every license to sell goods by sample, card or other representation, three hundred dollars.

Express and telegraph companies.

Tax on express and telegraph companies

42. On every license permitting an express company to operate within the state, two hundred and fifty dollars; and on every telegraph company to operate within the state, one hundred dollars.

Patent rights.

Patent rights under laws of Confederate States

43. On every license to sell or barter the right to manufacture or use any machinery or other thing patented to any person or company, under the laws of the Confederate States, fifteen dollars in each county; and no merchant shall sell the same without an additional license and the payment of the tax prescribed by this section. But patentees who are citizens of Virginia shall not be subject to the tax imposed by this section.

Citizens of Virginia exempted

Quack medicines.

Quack medicines

44. On every license to sell patent, specific or quack medicines, if by retail, thirty-eight dollars, and if by wholesale, seventy-five dollars. A person having a merchant's license may sell such medicines without any additional license, unless the same be sold on commission; in which case the additional license and tax shall be imposed.

Book agents.

Book agents and print sellers

45. On every license to a person obtaining subscriptions to books, maps, prints, pamphlets, or periodicals, thirty-eight dollars for each county, city or town. On every license to sell, or in any manner furnish the same, thirty-eight dollars; if the person obtaining such license has not been a resident of the Confederate States two years, the tax shall be in each case three hundred dollars. But any person who has been a resident of the Confederate States for two years, desiring to distribute or sell any religious books, newspapers or pamphlets, may apply to the county or corporation court of each county, city or town in which he may desire to distribute or sell the same, and such court, upon being satisfied that such person is a proper person for such duty, may grant him a license without the imposition of any tax for the privilege; but this section shall not apply to books, newspapers or pamphlets written by citizens of, and published in, the Confederate States.

If non-residents

Residents selling religious books, &c

Agents for renting houses.

Renting houses

46. On every license to a person engaged as agent for the renting of houses, thirty-eight dollars.

Agents for hiring negroes.

47. On every license to a person engaged as agent for the hiring of negroes, seventy-five dollars. Hiring negroes

Stallions.

48. On every license to the owner of a jackass or stallion, for services of which compensation is received, three times the amount of such compensation, when the charge is for such service by the season; and when such services are for less than a season, then three times what a commissioner may judge to be a reasonable charge therefor. The tax, however, in no case to be less than fifteen dollars. Such license shall authorize the performance of such service in any part of the commonwealth. Jackasses and stallions

Theatrical performances.

49. On every license permitting the proprietor or occupier of a public theatre, or rooms fitted for public exhibitions, to use the same for a year, thirty dollars, if such room be in a town or city of more than five thousand inhabitants and less than ten thousand inhabitants, and ninety dollars in all other towns; and on every license permitting theatrical performances therein, in such towns for twenty-four hours, ten dollars; but a license may be granted permitting theatrical performances for the term of three months; in which event the tax shall be one hundred and twenty dollars during said last mentioned time; but if such house be in a city or town containing less than twenty thousand inhabitants, the license may be granted for a week, and the tax thereon shall be ten dollars per week. Nothing herein shall be construed to exempt the land and house so used, from taxation as other real estate. Theatres
Tax for twenty-four hours
When license may be for three months

Refreshments in theatres.

50. On every license permitting the sale of refreshments in a theatre during such performances, fifty dollars for each place of sale, and no abatement shall be made, if the privilege be exercised for a period less than one year. But such license shall not include the privilege of selling wine, ardent spirits, or a mixture thereof. Refreshments in theatres

Sales of ardent spirits in a theatre.

51. On every license permitting the sale of wine, ardent spirits, or a mixture thereof, porter, ale or beer at a theatre, to be drank at the place where sold, one hundred and fifty dollars for each place of sale; and no abatement shall be made, if the privilege be exercised for a period of less than one year. Sale of ardent spirits in theatres; tax thereon

Public shows, circuses or menageries.

52. On every license permitting any public show, exhibition or performance, other than the drama, whether in a licensed house or Shows

Circuses

Menageries

not, if in a corporate town, or within five miles thereof, for each time of performance, fifteen dollars; if elsewhere, eight dollars; and for every exhibition of a circus, if within a corporate town, or within five miles thereof, sixty dollars; if elsewhere, thirty dollars; and for every exhibition of a menagerie, if within a corporate town, or within five miles thereof, sixty dollars; if elsewhere, thirty dollars. All such shows, exhibitions and performances, whether under the same canvas or not, shall be construed to require separate licenses therefor, whether exhibited for compensation or not; and upon any such shows, exhibitions and performances being concluded, so that an additional fee for admission be charged, in lieu of a return check authorizing the holder to re-enter without charge, shall be construed to require an additional license therefor.

Manufacturers of porter, ale and beer.

Manufacture of malt liquors

53. On every license to manufacture porter, ale and beer, or either, seventy-five dollars.

Sale of porter, ale and beer.

Sale of malt liquors, how licensed

54. On every license to sell porter, ale or beer, by wholesale or retail, thirty dollars; and if the business be continued for more than one year, an additional tax of one and one-half per centum on the amount of sales of the previous year. But if the license be to retail, to be drank where sold, it shall be granted upon the certificate of the county or corporation court, in every respect as certificates are granted to ordinary keepers and merchants to retail ardent spirits.

Brokers.

Brokers; tax thereon

55. On every license to a broker, one thousand dollars, unless he deals exclusively in stocks; then the tax shall be three hundred and seventy-five dollars. A broker shall have the right to sell stocks at auction or otherwise; and any person who may sell stocks on commission, shall be regarded as a stock broker.

Insurance companies.

Insurance companies; tax thereon

56. On every license to an agent or sub-agent of any insurance company not chartered by this state, thirty-eight dollars; and in addition thereto, a tax of one and one-half per cent. on the whole amount of premiums received and assessments collected by such agent or sub-agent or company, within the state, as prescribed by law.

Physicians and others.

Physicians, dentists and lawyers

57. On every license to a physician, surgeon or dentist, eight dollars each; and on every license to an attorney at law, eight dollars. If the yearly income derived from the practice of any such callings or professions during the year next preceding the time of obtaining such license shall exceed five hundred dollars, there shall be an ad-

ditional tax on the excess, of one and one-half per centum; and this income shall be included in the license tax. A license to any such person shall confer on him the privilege of practicing such profession in any part of the commonwealth.

Daguerreian artists.

58. On every license to exercise the daguerreian art, or such like profession or performance, by whatsoever name it may be known or called, if in a city or incorporated town of less than five thousand inhabitants, thirty dollars; if more than five thousand inhabitants, sixty dollars; if elsewhere, fifteen dollars. And if the yearly income derived from the practice of said art exceed five hundred dollars in any county, city or town, an additional tax of one and one-half per centum on such excess for the year next preceding the time of obtaining such license; and such tax shall be imposed, whether an artist perform in a gallery or not. If more than one be engaged in the joint exercise of such profession or performance in the same gallery, the tax shall not be imposed upon each artist, but upon the gallery.

Horses brought into the state.

59. On every license to sell horses, mules, asses and jennets which are brought into this state for sale, fifteen dollars in each county; and the act making general regulations concerning licenses, shall be so far modified that the certificate for obtaining such licenses may designate the county or corporation as the place of sale; and horses so brought into the state, as often as they are sold, and the principal object of the sale is for profit, although previously sold in this state, shall subject the person so selling to the tax hereby imposed.

Horses, mules, &c. sold for profit.

60. On every license to sell for others, on commission or for profit, horses, mules, asses, jennets, cattle, sheep and hogs, or either of them, thirty dollars; and the sale may be made under such license in any county or corporation.

Carriages, buggies and other vehicles.

61. On every license to sell carriages, buggies, barouches, gigs, wagons, and such like vehicles, manufactured out of this state, seventy-five dollars in each county or corporation. If the business be continued after the same has been carried on for a year, the tax shall be on the amount of sales, in addition to the specific tax, as on merchants' licenses. But this section shall not be so construed as to exempt persons from taxation who may put together the principal parts of such vehicles as may be manufactured out of this state.

Slaves bought or sold for profit.

62. On every license to buy or sell slaves on commission or for profit, other than at public auction, twenty dollars in each county;

and on the yearly income of such business in all the counties (to be taxed but once), an additional tax of one and one-half per centum on such income. If the sale be made by an auctioneer, no additional license from him shall be required for that purpose.

General Provisions.

Tax on corporations.

<small>Certain private acts not to be published until tax is paid</small>

<small>Keeper of rolls to publish list of acts on which tax has been paid</small>

63. No private act of assembly on which a tax is imposed, shall be published, nor any copy thereof furnished to any person, until the party asking and requiring the same shall have paid into the treasury of the commonwealth the taxes prescribed by law; and it shall be the duty of the keeper of the rolls to publish, with the acts of assembly of each session, all acts upon which the tax prescribed by law has been paid into the treasury since the last publication thereof.

When tax tickets to be made out by commissioner.

<small>Commissioner and sheriff's duty when any person is suspected of being about to leave county before delivery of books</small>

64. After the first day of February and until the first day of July in each year, and until the delivery of the commissioner's books to the sheriff or collector of any county, if the same be delivered after the first day of July, it shall be lawful and the duty of every commissioner of the revenue to make out tickets showing the amount of taxes which will be chargeable on his books when completed, against any person whom he has reasonable ground to suspect is about to depart from his county before the first day of July or before the delivery of said books to said sheriff or collector. Upon the delivery of such tickets, the sheriff or collector shall be authorized to make immediate distress for the taxes therein specified, and to use all the remedies for the collection of such taxes, as are now given, after the first day of July, upon the delivery of the commissioner's books.

Penalty for failure to obtain license.

<small>When unlawful to engage in business without license</small>

65. Whenever a tax is imposed by law on a license to engage in any business, calling or profession, it shall be unlawful to engage in such business, calling or profession without obtaining a license therefor. Any person who shall in any manner violate this section, shall pay a fine of not less than twenty dollars nor more than one thousand dollars for each offence.

Limitation of license.

<small>Licensed privilege restricted</small>

66. No license shall be construed to grant any privilege beyond the county or corporation wherein it is granted, unless it be expressly authorized.

FINANCIAL.—TAXES.

Where licensed privilege to be exercised.

67. Every license granting authority to sell, unless the license be specially authorized by law for a county or corporation, shall be at some specified house or place within such county or corporation. *Licenses confined to county or corporation. Licensees to be at specified houses*

When forms for tax-payers to be furnished.

68. Commissioners of the revenue shall furnish or cause to be furnished, to every tax-payer to be found within his district, the forms prescribed by the sixty-fifth section of chapter thirty-five of the Code. He shall require answers according to said section, and with his books, shall transmit said forms to the auditor of public accounts, if required by him. *Forms to be furnished tax payer*

Market value of stocks to be taxed.

69. In all cases where this act imposes a tax on any public bond, or on any stock, in lieu of a tax on the interest or profits thereof, the commissioner shall assess the cash market value of such bond or stock. *Public bonds and stocks*

When double tax to be imposed.

70. Any person continuing business, after any license obtained by him shall have expired, without obtaining on or before the day his former license so expired, a license for the succeeding term, shall be assessed with twice the amount of tax otherwise imposed on such license. *Penalty when license is not renewed*

Deductions from commissioner's compensation.

71. If a commissioner shall, in his list of licenses to be furnished to the auditor of public accounts, charge or extend in any case a tax less than the law requires, the auditor of public accounts shall deduct the amount omitted to be charged or extended, from the compensation of the commissioner; and to enable the auditor to make an examination of such lists, the commissioner shall return to him, with his return of licenses, all interrogatories which may have been propounded by him, under the direction of the auditor of public accounts, and answered. *Amount undercharged by commissioner to be deducted from his compensation*

Slaves and similar subjects, how taxed.

72. The number of slaves and the value thereof shall be listed by the commissioners, and taxed according to their value, to the hirer or person in possession thereof on the first day of February; and all subjects of taxation required to be listed under the provisions of the thirty-fifth and thirty-eighth chapters of the Code, and not specially taxed herein, shall be listed and taxed as similar subjects, according to the forms furnished by the auditor of public accounts. *Slaves and other property, how taxed. Subjects not specially taxed how to be taxed*

Value of lands and lots not to be changed.

Value of lands and lots under certain assessments not to be changed

73. The value of lands and lots as ascertained by the assessment made under the tenth chapter of the acts of eighteen hundred and fifty-five and eighteen hundred and fifty-six, passed March tenth, eighteen hundred and fifty-six, under subsequent special acts, and under the thirty-fifth chapter of the Code in respect to new grants, shall be permanent and not be changed, except under the provisions of the said thirty-fifth chapter in case of a partition or conveyance;

When auditor may change land book

and the auditor of public accounts may so far change the form of the commissioner's land book as to show in one column the value of lands and lots, exclusive of buildings.

When agricultural productions are to be taxed.

When agricultural productions, goods and materials exempt from taxation, and when subject to license tax

74. Agricultural productions of this state in the hands of the producer, including pork and bacon, and in the hands of those who have purchased the same for the use of their own household, and not for sale, and goods and materials manufactured in this state, except ardent spirits, porter, ale and beer, shall be exempt from taxation as property, while remaining in the hands of the producer or manufacturer, and while such agricultural productions are held as aforesaid. Such productions and manufactured articles may also be sold by the producer or manufacturer without a license tax; but when once sold (with the exception named in this section), they shall be subject to a tax as other property, and to a license tax when sold. To give effect to this section, chapter first, entitled an act for the assessment of taxes on persons and property, passed March thirtieth, eighteen hundred and sixty, and chapter second, entitled an act making general regulations concerning licenses, passed March thirtieth, eighteen hundred and sixty, in cases where said chapters might be otherwise construed, shall be construed according to the provisions of this section: provided, that no person shall be required to take out a license or pay any tax for the privilege of buying his neighbor's produce to take out of the county in his own vessel or other conveyance to market, or for selling the same.

Domestic manufactures, how taxed.

How tax on sales of merchant tailors and others to be ascertained

75. Merchant tailors and all other persons manufacturing any production or material, except ardent spirits, porter, ale and beer, the sale of which material would be prohibited without a license, shall only be charged so much tax on the sales as the value of the material sold would bear to the whole value of the manufactured articles, to be ascertained upon the oath of the person, as in other cases.

Licenses, how granted.

How license to manufacture and

76. A license to manufacture porter, ale and beer, or either of them, may be granted by the commissioner of the revenue, as in

other cases, without any previous certificate or order of the court; *sell malt liquors granted* but a license to sell the same, or any of them, and the privilege of selling ardent spirits, shall only be granted, upon the certificate of the county or corporation court that the person to be licensed is sober and of good character.

Effect of the change of the name of a firm.

77. No change in the name of any firm of merchants, commission merchants, sample merchants, merchant tailors, auctioneers, or any other persons who are taxed upon the amount of business or sales of the preceding year, nor the taking into the firm of a new partner, nor the withdrawal of one or more of the firm, shall be considered as commencing, so as to allow, on that account, the payment only of the specific tax imposed by law for the privilege granted; but if any one of the parties remain in the firm, either as a general or special partner or otherwise, in interest, to be ascertained upon the oath of the party to whom the license is granted, the business shall be regarded as continuing. *What not to be considered as commencing business*

Insolvents; how collected.

78. A copy of every list of insolvents, whether of persons, personal property, licenses or militia fines, whether allowed by any court or board, or by the auditor of public accounts, under ordinance number seventy-two of the convention, entitled an ordinance for the relief of sheriffs of certain counties, passed June twenty-eighth, eighteen hundred and sixty-one, shall, in his discretion, as soon as practicable, be placed by the auditor of public accounts in the hands of any sheriff, collector or constable of any county or corporation for collection. Such sheriff, collector or constable shall receive and receipt for the same, and shall make return of delinquents thereon within one year from their receipt, in the same manner and under the same regulations as are prescribed for the return of other delinquent taxes. The amount appearing due after such return of delinquents, and the allowance of such commission as may have been prescribed by the governor, shall be paid into the treasury within one year from the time such copy of such delinquents may have been received by such sheriff or other officer. When such copies are received by such officer, he shall have the same powers of distress and other remedies for the collection of the amount appearing due thereby, as are allowed to sheriffs for the collection of taxes. Any officer failing or refusing to receive and execute a proper receipt for any such copy of delinquents, shall forfeit not less than one hundred nor more than five hundred dollars. *Insolvents; how sent out for collection* *What commission allowed for collection* *Penalty on officers failing to receive and receipt*

License to sutlers or other persons to sell goods, &c., within or near to a military encampment.

79. No license shall be granted to a sutler or other person to sell goods, wares and merchandise or other thing within or near to a *License to sutlers*

military post or encampment, unless the person desiring such license shall produce to the court or to the commissioner of the revenue, as may be required by law, a certificate of the commander of such post or encampment, approving of the issuing of a license to such sutler or other person; and any sutler or other person so selling without a license, at such places, shall be subject to all the penalties and liabilities imposed upon merchants and other persons selling without a license.

License to a merchant who is a beginner.

When license to merchants who are beginners, void
80. A license to a merchant who is a beginner, shall specify the value of goods to be sold by such merchant, and when goods to the value specified have been sold, the license thereafter shall be deemed to be void, and if such merchant fail to apply to a commissioner of the revenue for a new assessment and new license, and continue in business after his license is deemed to be void as aforesaid, he shall forfeit to the commonwealth, for the benefit of the general treasury, not less than one hundred nor more than two thousand dollars.

Commissions allowed for assessing and collecting revenue
81. The commissions and other compensation to commissioners of the revenue for the assessments to be made in pursuance of this act, and the commissions to be allowed to sheriffs and collectors for the collection of taxes so assessed, shall not exceed in the aggregate the amount that would have accrued to them if the assessments had been made under the act entitled an act imposing taxes for the support of government, passed April third, eighteen hundred and sixty-one, at the rates therein prescribed.

Repealing clause.

Repealing clause
82. That chapter one, entitled an act imposing taxes for the support of government, passed April third, eighteen hundred and sixty-one, be and the same is hereby repealed, so far as the same is not herein before re-enacted.

Commencement
83. This act shall be in force from its passage.

CHAP. 2.—An ACT amending and re-enacting the 39th chapter of the Code, in relation to Taxes on Dividends, certain Estates of Decedents, Process in Suits, Official Seals, Deeds, Wills, Administrations, and Foreign Insurance Companies.

Passed March 31, 1862.

Be it enacted by the general assembly, that the thirty-ninth chapter of the Code of Virginia shall be amended and re-enacted so as to read as follows:

Banks to declare dividends
1. Every bank of circulation incorporated by this state shall, in June and December of each year, by resolution, either declare a

dividend of profits arising out of the operations of said bank for the six months ending on the first day of June and December, or determine their inability to do so; and if a dividend be declared, the said bank shall cause a tax to be retained from the dividend on which it is payable. *When and for what period*

2. Immediately after the said dividend is declared, the cashier of said bank shall certify on oath to the auditor of public accounts the amount of such dividend, and the amount of tax payable on account thereof, or the inability of the bank to declare a dividend. If he fail to do so, he shall pay a fine of not less than one hundred nor more than one thousand dollars. *Cashier to report dividend to auditor. If no dividend is declared, report in like manner to be made. Penalty for failure to report*

3. The said bank shall, immediately after such dividend is declared, pay the state's dividend and the amount of tax into the treasury. If any bank fail to do so, it shall be liable not only for the amount of said dividend and tax, but also for ten per centum damages thereon, to be recovered by action or motion. *Dividends and tax to be paid into the treasury*

On certain estates of decedents.

4. Where any estate within this commonwealth of any decedent shall pass, under his will or the laws regulating descents and distributions, to any other person, or for any other use than to or for the use of the father, mother, husband, wife, brother, sister, nephew, niece, or lineal descendant of such decedent, the estate so passing, if of greater value than two hundred and fifty dollars, shall be subject to a tax of a certain per centum. *Tax on collateral inheritances*

5. Whenever such estate shall be paid or delivered, it shall be the duty of the commissioner to assess all such estates, not only with the annual tax prescribed by law, but a specific tax of two per centum, as a condition upon which the estate so devised or descending may pass. *Duty of commissioner to assess tax. Rate of tax*

6. The annual tax shall be placed in the body of the land or property book, as the case may be, and shall be charged to the estate of the decedent. *Where annual tax to be placed*

7. The specific tax shall be so charged, but entered at the back of the land or property book, as the estate may indicate. *Specific tax to be in back of commissioner's book*

8. After the tax has been so assessed, it shall be the duty of the sheriff or collector to collect and pay the same into the treasury as other assessed taxes; and he shall have the same powers of distress and the right to return the same delinquent for the non-payment of the tax, as he possesses in other cases: and it shall be the duty of the personal representative of such decedent to pay the whole of such tax, except on omitted taxes heretofore paid over on real estate, to sell which, or to receive the rents and profits of which, he is not authorized by the will: and the sureties of his official bond shall be bound for the payment thereof. *Sheriff to collect and pay tax. Exception*

FINANCIAL.—TAXES.

When estate deemed paid or delivered

Personal representative liable to damages

9. Such estate shall be deemed paid or delivered, and subject to the assessment hereby authorized, at the end of a year from the decedent's death, unless and except so far as it may appear that the legatee or distributee has neither received such estate, nor is entitled then to demand it. Any personal representative failing to pay such tax before the estate on which it is chargeable is paid or delivered over (whether he be applied to for the tax or not), and the same be returned delinquent by the sheriff, shall be liable to damages thereon at the rate of ten per centum from the time such estate is delivered over until the tax is paid, and shall forfeit one hundred dollars; which tax and damages, in such case, and forfeiture, may be recovered by the auditor of public accounts, in the same court, and in the same manner as if it were a debt due from an officer collecting the taxes.

Sheriff to collect

10. The taxes shall be collected by, and such payment shall be made to the sheriff or other collector of the taxes assessed in the county or corporation in which certificate was granted such personal representative for obtaining probate of the will or letters of administration.

The per centum of tax

11. The per centum shall be on every hundred dollars in value of the estate subject to such tax, which the personal representative may have to pay or deliver, and in proportion for a smaller sum. Where he has personal property to deliver in kind, and the same has been appraised, the value shall be ascertained from such appraisement.

Personal representative to sell property to pay tax

12. Such personal representative may, if necessary, sell so much of the property, subject to such tax, as will enable him to pay the same.

On process, seals, deeds and administrations.

Writ tax. Tax on seals, deeds, &c

13. There shall be a tax paid when an original suit, attachment (except attachments in the nature of suggestions) or other action is commenced. If the suit or action be commenced by attachment sued out by a justice, returnable to court, the tax shall be paid at or before the time the cause is docketed in court or at rules. A tax shall also be paid when an appeal, writ of error or supersedeas is commenced in a circuit court, and also when an appeal, writ of error or supersedeas is commenced in a district court or the court of appeals. A tax shall also be paid when the seal of a court, or of a notary public, or the seal of the state is annexed to any paper.

Tax on process to be paid to the clerks of courts

14. The said taxes on process and seals of courts shall be paid to the clerks of the courts respectively from which said process is issued, or the notice or attachment is returnable, or whose seal is used. The tax on the seal of a notary shall be paid to said notary, and that on the seal of the state, to the secretary of the commonwealth.

When tax on

15. No tax shall be charged when a seal is annexed to any paper

or document to be used in obtaining the benefit of a pension, revolutionary claim, money due on account of military services or land bounty, under any act of congress, or under a law of this or any other state, or when a seal is annexed by a notary public to an affidavit or deposition relating to a pension or revolutionary claim. *Seals not to be charged*

16. No deed shall be admitted to record, whether before recorded or not, until the tax thereon is paid to the clerk, except a deed conveying land as a site for a school-house or church. *Deeds not to be admitted to record until tax is paid*

17. No will shall be admitted to probate until the tax on such probate is paid to the clerk. *Will not to be admitted to probate until tax is paid*

18. There shall be no grant of administration or administration de bonis non on the estate of any decedent, until the tax on such grant is paid to the clerk, except where an estate is committed to a sheriff or other officer. *No administration to be granted until tax is paid*

How collecting officers account and pay.

19. The clerk of each court, every notary public and the secretary of the commonwealth shall make out an account of all taxes received by him on or after the first day of September in one year and before the first day of September in the next year. *How clerks and others to account and pay. When*

20. Each of the said officers shall swear to the correctness of the account; which shall be rendered to the auditor of public accounts, and the amount appearing due thereby paid into the treasury on or before the fifteenth day of December following, deducting thereout a commission of five per centum for receiving and paying out the same. *Correctness of accounts to be sworn to. Commissions for collecting*

21. If any of the said officers fail to render such account on or before the first day of October, there shall be a forfeiture therefor, as follows: A clerk so failing, shall forfeit six hundred dollars; a notary public, three hundred dollars; and the secretary of the commonwealth, one hundred and fifty dollars; and for every month that such failure may continue after the said first day of October, there shall be an addition to such forfeiture, of one-twelfth of the amount thereof. For any such failure, motions may be repeated from time to time so long as it continues. *Penalty for failure to render accounts. For continued failure*

22. None of the said officers shall receive any money from the treasury until he shall have rendered such account, and made such payment as is above required. *No money to be drawn by any clerk, &c. until report is made and money paid*

23. All sums received by any sheriff or collector under this chapter, after deducting a commission of five per centum thereon, shall be paid into the treasury on or before the fifteenth day of December next after the receipt thereof. In case of failure so to pay, proceedings may be had according to the forty-second chapter. *Where moneys to be paid. When*

24. If the taxes required to be paid under the provisions of this chapter be not paid at the time required, the auditor of public ac- *Judgment in case of default*

FINANCIAL.—TAXES.—APPROPRIATIONS.

How and where taken — counts shall, within three months after such failure, file in the clerk's office of the circuit court of the city of Richmond, with the clerk thereof, an accurate account of the amount with which any such she-
Judgment to be without notice — riff or collector may be chargeable on account of such taxes; and thereupon such clerk shall enter up a judgment against such officer and his securities for the amount wherewith he is so chargeable, with lawful interest thereon from the time of such failure until payment thereof, and fifteen per centum damages in addition thereto; which judgment shall have the same validity and be subject in all respects to the like proceedings thereupon as if it had been rendered by the court.

Commencement 25. This act shall be in force from its passage.

CHAP. 3.—An ACT defining the Persons who may obtain a License.

Passed March 31, 1862.

Who may obtain a license 1. Be it enacted by the general assembly, that no license shall be granted to any person except a citizen of the Confederate States, and except to such person as shall have declared on oath that it is bona fide his intention to become a citizen of the Confederate States, and that he shall have renounced forever all allegiance and fidelity to any foreign prince, potentate, state or sovereignty whatsoever; nor shall a license be granted to such person not a citizen, if such declaration shall have been made five years preceding the time of making application for such license, in any court of the United States or of the Confederate States, and such person shall have failed to become a citizen according to law. Any license or certificate for obtaining a license granted to any one not authorized to obtain the same, shall be absolutely void.

Commencement 2. This act shall be in force from its passage.

CHAP. 4.—An ACT appropriating the Public Revenue for the fiscal year 1861-62.

Passed March 26, 1862.

What appropriated 1. Be it enacted by the general assembly, that the public taxes and arrears of taxes due prior to the first day of October eighteen hundred and sixty-two, and not otherwise appropriated, and all other branches of revenue; and all public moneys not otherwise appropriated by law, which shall come into the treasury prior to the first day of October eighteen hundred and sixty-two, shall constitute a general fund, and be appropriated for the fiscal year to close on the

FINANCIAL.—APPROPRIATIONS.

thirtieth day of September eighteen hundred and sixty-two, as follows, videlicet:

For expenses of the general assembly for the session commencing on the second day of December eighteen hundred and sixty-one, one hundred and fifteen thousand dollars. *General assembly*

To expenses of representation, five thousand dollars. *Representation*

To pay expenses of the state convention for the adjourned session in November eighteen hundred and sixty-one, forty-five thousand dollars. *State convention*

For pay and mileage of electors of president and vice-president of the Confederate States, and their secretary, twelve hundred dollars. *Electors*

To the salaries and allowances of the officers of civil government, one hundred and eleven thousand dollars. *Officers government*

To defray criminal charges, including expenses of jurors, witnesses, and guarding jails, ninety-eight thousand dollars. *Criminal charges*

To pay for slaves condemned, and who are executed, transported or commuted, thirty-five thousand dollars. *Slave convicts*

For bringing condemned slaves from the counties where sentenced, to the penitentiary until sold or commuted, eight hundred dollars.

For support of convicts, fifteen thousand dollars. *Support convicts*

For transporting convicts to the penitentiary, ten thousand dollars.

For salaries to superintendent, assistant keepers, and so forth, at penitentiary, eight thousand one hundred dollars. *Penitentiary*

For contingent expenses of courts, thirty-five thousand dollars. *Courts*

To pay for printing records of the court of appeals and district courts, five thousand dollars. *Printing records*

For pay of adjutant general, two thousand dollars. *Adjutant general*

For the military contingent fund, including the amount appropriated by special act, one hundred thousand dollars. *Military contingent fund*

To the military school at Lexington, for support, independent of any appropriation made at the present session of the general assembly, thirteen thousand five hundred dollars. *Military institute*

To the public guard at Richmond, including the interior guard of the penitentiary, forty thousand eight hundred dollars. *Public guard*

For temporary quarters for the public guard, two thousand dollars.

For water rent for six and a half months to the fifteenth of July eighteen hundred and sixty-one, six hundred and ninety-three dollars and thirty-three cents. *Water rent*

To the armory, for repairs, eight hundred dollars. *Armory*

For repairs of arms, pay of artificers, and of their superintendence and tools, five thousand dollars. *Repair of arms*

For collection and transportation of arms, thirteen hundred and fifty dollars.

To commissioners of the revenue and clerks for examining commissioners' books, seventy-seven thousand dollars. *Commissioners of revenue, &c*

To the lunatic asylum at Staunton, for support, in addition to the pay patient fund, forty-five thousand dollars, and for transporting patients, three thousand dollars. *Lunatic asylum at Staunton*

FINANCIAL.—APPROPRIATIONS.

Lunatic asylum at Williamsburg
To the lunatic asylum at Williamsburg, for support, in addition to the pay patient fund, forty-five thousand dollars. For transporting patients, three thousand dollars; and for unexpended balance of twenty thousand dollars, appropriated by act of the twenty-fourth March eighteen hundred and sixty, for laundry, and so forth, ten thousand one hundred and eighty-seven dollars and fifty-four cents.

Lunatics
For maintenance of lunatics in jails, and so forth, nine thousand dollars.

Institution of deaf, dumb and blind
For the institution of the deaf and dumb and the blind at Staunton, for annuity, twenty-five thousand dollars.

Pensioners
To pensioners, two hundred and eighty-eight dollars.

Civil contingent fund
To the civil contingent fund, including the special appropriation made thereto at this session, one hundred thousand dollars.

Civil prosecutions
To civil prosecutions, ten thousand dollars.

Governor's house
For repairs and furniture for governor's house, five hundred dollars.

Capitol
For repairs and fixtures for capitol, five thousand dollars.

Messenger
For salary of messenger in the office of the auditor of public accounts, eight hundred dollars.

Grattan's Reports
For Grattan's Reports, one thousand copies of the sixteenth volume, fifteen hundred and fifty dollars, and five hundred copies of reprint of second, third and fourth volumes, twenty-five hundred dollars.

Leigh's Reports
For Leigh's Reports, five hundred copies of reprint of fifth volume, twelve hundred and fifty dollars.

Guaranteed bonds of James river and Kanawha company
For interest on bonds of the James river and Kanawha company guaranteed by the commonwealth, two thousand three hundred and thirty-one dollars.

Registration
For registration of births, deaths and marriages, three thousand dollars.

Commissions
For commissions to sheriffs and collectors of taxes, five thousand dollars.

Temporary loans
For redemption and interest on temporary loans, seventy thousand one hundred and fifty-five dollars and fifteen cents.

Chesapeake and Ohio canal
To pay interest on the bonds of the Chesapeake and Ohio canal company guaranteed by the state, and to be paid over to the second auditor by the auditor of public accounts for that purpose, pursuant to law, thirty thousand dollars.

Temporary clerks in first auditor's office
To pay for services of temporary clerks employed by the auditor of public accounts to copy and record lists of delinquent lands and property, and for other services to be performed in said office, four thousand two hundred and fifty dollars.

Pages
To each of the pages of the senate and house of delegates, the sum of two dollars per day for each day of service as such; to be paid upon the certificate of the clerk of the senate and of the clerk of the house of delegates respectively.

Porter to senate
To Alfred Thornton, porter to the senate, for his services as such, and also for his attention to the senate chamber and clerk's office of

the senate, and making fires in the same, two dollars and fifty cents per day; to be paid upon the certificate of the clerk of the senate.

To the further expenses of making fires and superintending furnaces in the capitol, the customary allowances to the several persons entitled to the same; to be paid upon the certificate of the superintendent of public buildings. *Services in capitol*

For the payment of interest on so much of the public debt as is not suspended, two million dollars. *Public debt*

To the secretary of the commissioners of the sinking fund, for his salary, three hundred dollars, and for expenses of advertising redemption of state debt, three hundred and seventy-five dollars. *Secretary commissioners of sinking fund Advertising*

For public printing, including printing for the general assembly, and for paper and books for public offices, forty-five thousand dollars. *Public printing*

2. Be it further enacted, that so much of the public revenue as may be received into the public treasury after the thirtieth day of September eighteen hundred and sixty-two, and the surplus of all other appropriations made prior to that date, unexpended within the fiscal year ending on the last day of September eighteen hundred and sixty-two, and all other moneys not otherwise appropriated by law, shall constitute a general fund, to defray such expenses authorized by law as are not herein particularly provided for, and to defray the usual allowances to lunatic asylums, and other current expenses of the commonwealth, in the fiscal year which shall commence on the first day of October eighteen hundred and sixty-two, and terminate on the thirtieth day of September eighteen hundred and sixty-three. And the auditor of public accounts is hereby authorized and required to issue his warrants in the same manner as if the same had been specifically mentioned, subject to such exceptions, limitations and conditions as the general assembly have prescribed or may deem it proper to annex and prescribe by law: provided, that nothing in this act contained shall be so construed as to authorize the auditor of public accounts to issue his warrant or warrants in satisfaction of any judgment or decree of any court of law or equity against the commonwealth, for a sum exceeding three hundred dollars, without a special appropriation by law. *General fund* *Disposal of general fund*

3. The payments to the military institute, for support, to the lunatic asylums, for support and transportation of patients, and to the institution for the education of the deaf and dumb and the blind, shall be made, one-fourth in advance, on the first day of October, one-half on the first day of January (if the visitors or directors so require), and the remaining one-fourth on the first day of April. *When payments made*

4. This act shall be in force from its passage. *Commencement*

FINANCIAL.—TREASURY NOTES.

Chap. 5.—An ACT authorizing the Issue of Treasury Notes.

Passed March 31, 1862.

Issue authorized 1. Be it enacted by the general assembly, that for the purpose of raising money to arm and equip the militia of the state, and for all defensive or offensive operations of the army and navy, growing out of the existing war, the governor is hereby authorized to direct the auditor of public accounts to issue treasury notes, to an amount *Amount* not exceeding in the aggregate one million three hundred thousand dollars, in addition to the sums heretofore authorized to be issued under the several ordinances of the convention heretofore passed, authorizing the same. The said notes hereby authorized to be issued *Denomination* shall be made payable on demand, to bearer, in sums not less than five dollars, and shall bear such rate of interest, not exceeding six per centum per annum, as may be deemed expedient, or may be *Receivable in payment of taxes* without interest. The said notes shall be receivable in payment of all taxes and other public dues, and may be reissued until otherwise provided by law. They may also, when presented at the treasury in sums of five hundred dollars, or any multiple of one hundred dollars above that sum, be converted into registered bonds of the state, bearing six per centum interest per annum.

Ordinances of convention 2. All the provisions of the several ordinances of the convention of Virginia in respect to the issue of treasury notes, shall be held to apply to the notes authorized to be issued by this act, except so far as they may be inconsistent therewith.

Commencement 3. This act shall be in force from its passage.

Chap. 6.—An ACT concerning Treasury Notes.

Passed February 12, 1862.

How signed 1. Be it enacted by the general assembly, that any clerk in the office of the treasurer, or of the auditor of public accounts, when designated for that purpose by the said treasurer and auditor respectively, shall be authorized to sign, for said treasurer and auditor, any of the treasury notes now authorized to be issued by authority of the several ordinances of the convention, and also any such notes which may be authorized by the general assembly; and the signature of any such clerk shall have the same effect, to all intents and purposes, as if the same had been made by the treasurer or the auditor of public accounts in person.

Commencement 2. This act shall be in force from its passage.

FINANCIAL.—LOANS.—SINKING FUND, ETC.

CHAP. 7.—An ACT providing for Loans to supply Temporary Deficiencies in the Treasury.

Passed March 29, 1862.

1. Be it enacted by the general assembly, that the governor be authorized to borrow from time to time, on the credit of the state of Virginia, such sum of money as may he needed to supply the temporary wants of the treasury. The money so borrowed shall be at a rate of interest not exceeding six per centum per annum; and certificates issued for the money so borrowed shall be signed by the treasurer, countersigned by the auditor of public accounts, and shall be made payable to the holder thereof by the commonwealth at such day as may be named therein. *Money, how borrowed*

2. That the fourth section of an act entitled an act appropriating the public revenue, and for other purposes, passed March seventh, eighteen hundred and fifty-one, so far as the same is inconsistent with this act, shall, from and after the passage of this act, be held inoperative and void. *Act of 1851 inoperative*

3. This act shall be in force from its passage. *Commencement*

CHAP. 8.—An ACT concerning the Sinking Fund.

Passed March 27, 1862.

1. Be it enacted by the general assembly, that until peace be declared between the Confederate States and the United States, no further investments shall be made by the commissioners of the sinking fund, nor shall any further redemptions of the debt of the state be made by them, except such certificates of debt as are absolutely payable without condition. The commissioners of the sinking fund shall semi-annually ascertain the amount of money due for redemption and the amount due for investment, and shall enter the said amounts upon their journal. *No further investments to be made*

2. This act shall be in force from its passage. *Commencement*

CHAP. 9.—An ACT making an appropriation to the Civil Contingent Fund.

Passed February 4, 1862.

1. Be it enacted by the general assembly, that the sum of ten thousand dollars be and the same is hereby appropriated as a civil contingent fund, to be expended in the manner prescribed by the twenty-eighth section of chapter seventeen of the Code of Virginia. *Amount appropriated*

2. This act shall be in force from its passage. *Commencement*

CHAP. 10.—An ACT making an appropriation to the Civil Contingent Fund.

Passed March 18, 1862.

Amount appropriated

1. Be it enacted by the general assembly, that the sum of ten thousand dollars is hereby appropriated to the civil contingent fund.

Commencement

2. This act shall be in force from its passage.

CHAP. 11.—An ACT authorizing the receipt of Confederate States Treasury notes in payment of Taxes and other Public Dues.

Passed March 22, 1862.

Confederate treasury notes, how receivable

1. Be it enacted by the general assembly, that the Confederate States treasury notes shall hereafter be receivable by sheriffs and other collecting officers in payment of taxes and other public dues to the state.

Commencement

2. This act shall be in force from its passage.

CHAP. 12.—An ACT to provide for the assumption and payment of the Confederate States War Tax.

Passed February 21, 1862.

Treasury notes, how issued

1. Be it enacted by the general assembly, that the auditor of public accounts be and is hereby authorized to borrow, with the approbation of the governor of the commonwealth, such amounts of the treasury notes of the Confederate States as may be necessary to pay the amount herein after authorized to be paid on account of taxes assessed against the citizens of this commonwealth, under an act of congress, approved on the nineteenth day of August eighteen hundred and sixty-one, entitled an act to authorize the issue of treasury notes, and to provide a war tax for their redemption; and the money so borrowed shall be paid into the treasury in the manner prescribed by existing laws.

Banks authorized to lend

2. For the purpose declared in the foregoing section, the several banks in the commonwealth are hereby authorized to lend to the commonwealth an amount, payable in the treasury notes of the Confederate States, not exceeding twenty-five per centum upon their respective capitals.

Auditor to issue his warrant pay

3. That the auditor of public accounts, so soon as the arrangements for the loan authorized in the first section are sufficiently

FINANCIAL.—WAR TAX.

matured, be and he is hereby authorized and directed to issue his warrants upon the treasury, payable in the treasury notes of the Confederate States, in favor of the secretary of the treasury of the Confederate States, for such sum or sums as in the aggregate may be equal to the amount agreed on by the auditor of public accounts, with the approval of the committees of finance of the two houses of the general assembly and the said secretary of the treasury, as sufficient to impose on the said secretary of the treasury the duty specified in the twenty-fourth section of the act of the provisional congress of the Confederate States, entitled an act to authorize the issue of treasury notes, and to provide a war tax for their redemption: provided, that the amount of such warrants shall in no event exceed the amount of taxes actually assessed by authority of the government of the Confederate States against the citizens of this commonwealth, after deducting ten per centum thereon. *(Able to secretary of the treasury. How approved.)*

4. That the auditor of public accounts be and is hereby authorized and directed to execute and renew, if so agreed, from time to time, an obligation or obligations committing the faith of the commonwealth to the repayment of the amount of such sum or sums of money as may be necessarily borrowed to execute the purposes of this act. Such obligations shall be renewable, in whole or in part, at the pleasure of the authorities of the commonwealth, for a period not exceeding the period for which the bonds of the state of Virginia may, under existing laws, be issued: and the negotiation of the loan shall in all cases be deemed a consent to the terms herein prescribed on the part of those lending the money. *(Faith of the commonwealth for redemption.)*

5. The interest on such obligations as may be issued under this act shall be paid as provided in the agreement for the loan. *(Interest.)*

6. During the session of the general assembly the auditor of public accounts, before doing any act herein authorized committing the faith of the commonwealth, shall submit his intended act to the committees on finance of the two houses of the general assembly, and obtain their approval. After the adjournment of the general assembly, or during a recess, he shall submit to the governor of the commonwealth, in lieu of the committees on finance, and obtain his approval. *(During session, whom auditor to consult. In recess.)*

7. Any obligation for money borrowed under the provisions of this act shall, when the day of payment arrives and the same is redeemed, be canceled, and preserved by the treasurer in his office. *(Obligations, when canceled.)*

8. This act shall be in force from its passage. *(Commencement.)*

CHAP. 13.—An ACT to provide for the payment of Interest to loyal citizens on certain Bonds guaranteed by the Commonwealth.

Passed March 13, 1862.

Interest on guaranteed bonds

1. Be it enacted by the general assembly, that the interest now due, or which may accrue hereafter during the present war with the United States, to any loyal citizen of the Confederate States, or to any corporation created by the laws of Virginia, on the bonds of the Chesapeake and Ohio canal company, and of the city of Wheeling, heretofore guaranteed by this commonwealth, shall be paid on the special order of the governor, out of any money in the treasury not otherwise appropriated, without waiting for formal protest for non-payment by said canal company and city, in all cases in which it can be made to appear to the governor that such bonds, on which said interest is claimed, were bona fide the property of such loyal citizen, or of some other loyal citizen of the Confederate States, or of such corporation, on or before the seventeenth day of April one thousand eight hundred and sixty-one, and have continued the property of some loyal citizen since said time, and not transferred by assignment or delivery since said time, from any disloyal citizen; which special order shall be made by the governor, on demand of payment of such interest, to the second auditor, who, on the receipt of the money, which shall thereupon be transferred to him by the auditor of public accounts, shall thereupon issue his warrants on the treasury for such interest, payable to those to whom the same is due: and the second auditor and the attorney general shall thereafter proceed against such company and city, as directed by the provisions of the act passed the tenth day of February eighteen hundred and sixty, entitled an act to provide for the prompt payment of the interest on the various bonds guaranteed by the commonwealth.

How paid

Corporations, how proceeded against

Proviso.

2. Provided, however, that nothing herein contained shall be construed as authorizing the governor to pay any interest as herein provided, to any corporation created by the laws of Virginia, which is located in a disloyal portion of the commonwealth, or the executive officers of which corporation shall be disloyal to Virginia.

Commencement

3. This act shall be in force from its passage.

CHAP. 14.—An ACT to authorize the transfer of certain Bonds of the State held in trust by the Government of the United States for certain Indian Tribes, and providing for the payment of Interest thereon.

Passed January 27, 1862.

Preamble

Whereas it is represented to the general assembly, by the secretary of the treasury of the Confederate States, that the secretary of the interior of the United States government holds in trust for the

Choctaw tribe of Indians the sum of four hundred and fifty thousand dollars of the registered bonds of this state, upon which one year's interest is now due: and it is further represented, that in the war now pending between the governments of the United States, and of the Confederate States, the said tribe of Indians have united themselves with the confederate government, and that government having assumed the "protectorate of the several nations and tribes of Indians occupying the territory west of Arkansas and Missouri, south of Kansas, north of Texas and east of Texas and New Mexico," embracing the country inhabited by the said tribe of Choctaws; and the said secretary of the treasury having applied to this general assembly for the payment of the said interest now due, and to become due hereafter: Therefore,

1. Be it enacted by the general assembly, that the second auditor be and he is hereby required to transfer on the books of his office the said sum of four hundred and fifty thousand dollars, standing in the name of the secretary of the interior of the United States, to the secretary of the treasury of the Confederate States, to be held by said secretary in trust for said tribe of Choctaw Indians, as provided by the treaty entered into by the authorities of said confederate government and of said tribe of Choctaw Indians; and thereupon the certificates of the registered bonds of this commonwealth, held by the said secretary of the interior of the United States, shall be deemed to be canceled and be void, and all payment of any interest due thereon, or to become due hereafter, shall be illegal. And it shall be the duty of the said auditor to issue like certificates of the registered debt of this state for the full amount so held by the said secretary of the interior of the United States, to the said secretary of the treasury of the Confederate States, to be held by him in trust for said Choctaw tribe of Indians, the said certificates of debt bearing date on the first day of January eighteen hundred and sixty-one: and the commissioners of the sinking fund of the state shall direct the said auditor to pay to said secretary of the treasury the semi-annual interest which was due on the first of July last, and on the first of January of the present year, to be disbursed according to the trust reposed in him; and thereafter to pay the principal and interest which may become due on said certificates of debt as is now or may be hereafter prescribed for the payment of interest on the state debt.

2. This act shall be in force so soon as the proper authorities of the Confederate States shall file with the second auditor an obligation, approved by the commissioners of the sinking fund, to indemnify the commonwealth against any loss or liability incurred by reason of this act.

CHAP. 15.—An ACT prescribing Penalties against Illegal Assessments and Collection of Taxes.

Passed March 28, 1862.

Penalty for assessing and collecting taxes

1. Be it enacted by the general assembly, that if any person holding any office or appointment under any usurped government, claiming to be established within the limits of this state, separate from the existing government, assess or collect taxes, or seize or convert property to the payment of such taxes or other claim, under such government, such person, so collecting such taxes or other claim, shall be liable to the person from whom such taxes or claim shall be collected,

How enforced

for ten times the amount of such taxes or claim; to be recovered, upon motion, before any court of record in this commonwealth, upon ten days' notice of such motion. In addition to the penalty incurred by any such collector, any person injured may recover from any such assessor, or other person making any such claim, by action, any consequential damages resulting from the seizure or sale of property or

Against whom

enforcement of the payment of such taxes. If the remedies hereby given shall prove unavailing, by reason of the insolvency of any person against whom judgment may have been rendered, any person who has held office, or who may be holding any office or appointment under such government, shall be liable therefor, upon like motion

Who exempt

and proof of the insolvency aforesaid: but this remedy shall not be given to any one who has been instrumental in establishing such usurped government, or who has held any office or appointment under it, or professes allegiance or fidelity to it, or to the government of the United States.

Commencement

2. This act shall be in force from its passage.

CHAP. 16.—An ACT to enforce payment of Balances due from Commissioners of Forfeited and Delinquent Lands.

Passed March 25, 1862.

Preamble

Whereas, by the tenth section of an act entitled an act to amend an act entitled an act to amend and explain the laws concerning western land titles, and for other purposes, passed March fifteenth, eighteen hundred, and thirty-eight, provision was made for enforcing the payment into the treasury of all balances in the hands of commissioners of forfeited and delinquent lands; which provision is deemed insufficient to secure the rights of the commonwealth: Therefore,

What done, on failure of commissioner

1. Be it enacted by the general assembly, that in all cases of the failure of a commissioner to pay into the treasury the amount appearing by the clerk's certificates required by said act to be in his

hands, or which from said certificates ought to be in his hands, the auditor of public accounts shall proceed, in the circuit court of the city of Richmond, by motion, upon thirty days' notice, against such commissioner and his securities, jointly or severally, in the same manner and to the same extent, in all respects, as he may now proceed against a sheriff for his default in paying the taxes assessed by virtue of the thirty-fifth chapter of the Code of Virginia, edition of eighteen hundred and sixty. In all such proceedings, the amount of the sales made by such commissioner (after deducting all amounts allowed him by the court under whose order the sales were made, for commissions and expenses attending the survey and sale of such lands, and all payments made thereon) shall be deemed to be the amount of money in the hands of such commissioner; but the right is reserved to any such commissioner, or his securities, to show, upon the trial of said cause, that he is not liable for the amount of his sales, after making the deductions aforesaid. *Notice* *Amount, how ascertained* *Reservation to commissioner*

2. Where personal notice cannot be given, the auditor of public accounts may give notice, by publication, of the time and place of the motion to be made by him against such commissioner and his securities; which publication shall be for thirty days, in some newspaper published in the city of Richmond. Upon the trial of said cause, the auditor of public accounts shall file an accurate account of the amount wherewith such commissioner is chargeable, under the provisions of this act; to be ascertained from the certificates of the clerk who certified said sales. The judgment against the principal remaining in default, shall be for the amount appearing by the auditor's account to be chargeable against him, with interest thereon, at the rate of twelve per centum per annum, together with fifteen per centum damages thereon; but the securities shall not be chargeable with any greater rate of interest than six per centum per annum, without damages. *Notice, how given* *Judgment, for what amount*

3. The act passed the twelfth of March eighteen hundred and sixty-one, entitled an act to enforce payment of balances due from commissioners of forfeited and delinquent lands, is hereby repealed. *Act of 1861 repealed*

4. This act shall be in force from its passage. *Commencement*

CHAP. 17.—An ACT authorizing the Auditor of Public Accounts to suspend the institution of Legal Proceedings against Sheriffs in certain counties.

Passed March 27, 1862.

1. Be it enacted by the general assembly, that in addition to the powers and duties required of the auditor of public accounts, by the ordinance of the convention, passed June twenty-eighth, eighteen *Power of auditor to suspend proceedings*

hundred and sixty-one, entitled an ordinance for the relief of sheriffs of certain counties, the said auditor is hereby authorized, in his discretion, to suspend the institution of any legal proceedings against the sheriffs of the counties referred to in said ordinance, that may be invaded and occupied by the army of the United States, for their failure to account for the revenue of their respective counties for the present year, and for any future year that the same may be occupied by the forces of the enemy.

Commencement

2. This act shall be in force from its passage.

CHAP. 18.—An ACT providing for the collection of Taxes and other public Dues in the hands of defaulting disloyal Officers, and in the hands of other persons disloyal to the State.

Passed March 25, 1862.

Preamble

Whereas it is represented to the general assembly, that the banks incorporated by this state, located in northwestern Virginia, have failed to make report of the taxes, dividends and bonus due to the state, and that many officers of this commonwealth, charged with the collection of taxes, have failed to account to the treasury thereof for their collections; but upon the contrary, the said banks and collecting officers have acknowledged allegiance to an usurped government claiming to be established within the limits of this state, without authority of the legislature thereof, and have paid such dividends, bonus and taxes into the treasury of such usurped government, in contempt of the laws of this state, and in violation of official duty and good faith: And whereas the said usurped government has appointed other collectors in counties and corporations where the regularly elected officers refused to collect and account to such government, who have proceeded to collect taxes, to the great oppression of the loyal people of this commonwealth: To provide a remedy for the speedy collection of all such public dues, and to guard against any injustice,

Remedies

1. Be it therefore enacted by the general assembly, that in addition to the remedies now provided by law for the recovery of taxes and other public dues in case any bank, sheriff, clerk, notary public or other collecting officer shall fail to report or pay the amount justly chargeable to such bank or collecting officer, in case of a bank, on or before the fifteenth day of January and the fifteenth day of July in each year; and in case of collecting officers, within the time or times prescribed by law, the auditor of public accounts may file in the office of the circuit court of the city of Richmond, with the clerk thereof, an accurate account of the amount with which such bank or collecting officer may be chargeable on account of any dividends,

Account, where filed

profits or bonus, whether the same be payable to the commonwealth proper, or any of the departments of the commonwealth, on account of the literary fund, fund for internal improvement, or on account of the bonus on the capital of such bank, or on account of any taxes; and thereupon, such clerk shall enter up a judgment against such bank, in its corporate capacity, and against such officer and his sureties, jointly or separately, or any one or more of them, for the amount of such account, with interest thereon, at the rate of twelve per centum per annum, from the fifteenth day of January and the fifteenth day of July, in case of a bank, on account of their semi-annual dividends, tax and bonus; and in case of a collecting officer, from the time payment is required by law to be made; subject to such abatement of interest as is now authorized by law. In addition to the interest to be included in such judgment, there shall be damages, at the rate of fifteen per centum, on the amount of such judgment, to be included therein. If the reports from banks, clerks and notaries public and the commissioners' books shall not have been received at the office of the auditor of public accounts, so as to prove the indebtedness of such bank or collecting officer, the said auditor, in case the books of commissioners and returns of licenses have been received, without showing a delivery to the collector, shall assume, as the basis of his account, that the books of the commissioners of the revenue and the lists of licenses were delivered to the collecting officers within the time required by law; and if reports, books and lists of licenses have not been received at the office of the auditor of public accounts within the time required therefor, the said auditor shall assume, as the basis of his account, the money appearing due from the last preceding assessments and from the last preceding reports: and the said auditor shall file an account, from such assessments and reports, against such bank, sheriff or other officer as he is satisfied was engaged in the collection of taxes; and the fact that any person was engaged in the collection of taxes, shall render him and his securities, if he has any, liable to a judgment; to be recovered in the same manner as against a sheriff or other collector, and to like interest and damages.

Judgment, how entered

Interest.

Time of computation

Basis of account

2. A lien shall exist on all the estate, real and personal, of any corporation or person liable to the judgment in this act authorized, from the time the taxes and other claims for which judgment is authorized, are payable into the treasury, or, as the case may be, from the time the auditor is authorized to assume that the taxes and other claims are payable; and such lien shall exist, whether the judgment shall be docketed in the county where the property is or not.

Lien of judgment

3. Any person aggrieved by any such judgment, may apply to the circuit court of the city of Richmond within five years after such judgment shall be entered up, or within two years after the time peace between the Confederate States and the United States shall be

Limitation for reversal

made and declared, to set aside such judgment; and for good cause, the said court may set aside said judgment, and proceed to try the cause upon its merits, and affirm the judgment already entered, or render such other judgment as the said court may consider right, in pursuance of the provisions of this act, making all the assumptions in favor of the commonwealth which the auditor of public accounts is authorized to make in filing the accounts aforesaid.

Proviso

4. Provided, that this act shall not be construed to extend to any officer loyal to the commonwealth, who, by reason of his loyalty, has been ousted from or hindered in the exercise of his office by said usurped government, or by the public enemy, and who has not recognized said usurped government, by voluntary payment thereto, or otherwise.

Commencement

5. This act shall be in force from its passage.

CHAP. 19.—An ACT for ascertaining and enrolling the Military Force of the Commonwealth.

Passed February 8, 1862.

Rolls, how obtained

1. Be it enacted by the general assembly, that immediately after the passage of this act, the governor shall procure from the commandants of the several regiments, battalions and detachments of the Virginia volunteers, complete rolls of the several companies now in service, to be returned forthwith to the adjutant general of the state, designating the name, age and residence of each volunteer, the time of his enlistment, and when his term of service will expire, and the company and regiment to which he belongs.

Requirements

Who enrolled

2. It shall be the duty of the governor to cause all the male citizens of the commonwealth, between the ages of eighteen and forty-five, not now in the active volunteer service, to be enrolled as soon as may be after the passage of this act, designating all exempts, and the cause of such exemption, including all refugees from districts in possession of the enemy, and designating such of them as have been in service, and the term of such service; and in all the tide water counties the enrollment shall also specify all sailors and watermen; and he is hereby authorized to prescribe such regulations, in addition to or in lieu of those now established by law, as will enable him promptly and efficiently to perform the duty hereby imposed upon him; and to that end, he may require the services of the commissioners of the revenue and sheriffs or sergeants of the several counties, cities and towns, or such other officers as to him shall seem expedient and necessary. In making such enrollment, it shall be

Exempts

Powers of governor

the duty of the governor to ascertain and state the time, if any, for which any of the militia shall have been in the service of the Confederate States or of the state of Virginia, during the existing war.

3. If any person liable to military duty shall fail to have his name enrolled by the officer appointed for that purpose, for ten days after the notice or proclamation requiring such enrollment shall have been posted or published at two or more public places in his ward or magisterial district, he shall, unless there be a sufficient excuse for such failure, be enrolled or drafted among the first levies to be drawn from such county or corporation. *What, in case of failure to enroll name*

4. If any officer shall fail to perform any duty required of him by the governor under this act, he shall be subject to a fine of not less than twenty dollars nor more than two hundred dollars. *Penalties on officers*

5. The officers enrolling the militia under this act shall be entitled to a compensation, to be fixed by the governor, not exceeding ten cents for each person enrolled; and the claims for such compensation shall be paid on the certificate of the governor. *Compensation to officers*

6. This act shall be in force from its passage. *Commencement*

CHAP. 20.—An ACT to raise Troops to meet the Requisition on Virginia by the President of the Confederate States.

Passed February 10, 1862.

Whereas the president of the Confederate States has ascertained the military quota of Virginia for the existing war to be sixty-five thousand eight hundred and forty-two men, and has made a requisition upon the governor for a portion thereof; and it is the purpose of this act to apportion the said requisition ratably among the several counties, cities and towns of the commonwealth, according to the white population thereof, and promptly to raise the same: *Preamble*

1. Be it therefore enacted by the general assembly, that as soon as may be after the passage of this act, the governor shall ascertain what number of men will be sufficient to raise the number of each volunteer company now in the confederate service from this state to the number of one hundred men, rank and file. He shall thereupon apportion the same among the several counties, cities and towns of the commonwealth, ascertaining the number to be furnished by each, upon the basis of its white population, after crediting to each the number of its resident citizens engaged as volunteers in the service of the Confederate States. *Number of volunteer companies to be raised to 100*

2. Having ascertained the quotas to be furnished by the several counties, cities and towns as aforesaid, he shall make proclamation *Proclamation*

thereof, and shall call for volunteers to fill such quotas. Every such volunteer shall report himself to the adjutant general by a day to be named in said proclamation, for enrollment in such company, containing less than one hundred men, as the said volunteer shall elect.

Quotas, how drafted After deducting from the number apportioned as aforesaid to each county, city and town the number of its volunteers under this call, the remainder shall constitute the number to be drafted therefrom; and thereupon the governor shall proceed without delay to cause the quotas so remaining due from the several counties, cities and towns to be drafted by lot from their enrolled militia, and to be assigned to their proper companies.

Levies, how assigned 3. If the number drafted from any county, city or town be required to fill the ranks of companies from such county, city or town, to the number aforesaid, they shall be mustered into the service in such company; and as far as practicable, the drafted levies from any county, city or town shall be assigned to companies from such county, city or town, or from counties, cities or towns nearest thereto.

Re-enlistment 4. At least thirty days before the day on which the term of service of each volunteer company now in the field shall expire, the governor shall cause such company to be mustered for re-enlistment by the officer commanding the same, who shall submit to each volunteer *Roll of company* the question whether he will re-enlist or not, and shall make out an accurate company roll, designating therein the name, age and residence of each volunteer who shall decline to re-enlist, the time his term of service shall expire, and the company and regiment to which he belongs, and return the same forthwith to the adjutant *Draft, how made* general; and thereupon the governor shall cause to be drafted, by lot, upon the principles and in the proportions prescribed in the foregoing sections of this act, from the enrolled militia of the respective counties, cities and towns of this commonwealth, a number of men equal to the number of those so refusing to re-enlist, including as a part of the militia of the several counties, cities and towns in which they reside, the volunteers so refusing to re-enlist.

Draft, how apportioned 5. Any draft under the provisions of this act shall, so far as practicable, not only be apportioned among the counties, cities and towns of the state (not in the possession of the public enemy, or in which from any cause a draft cannot be enforced), so as to give to each fair credit for the number of men theretofore furnished; but the same principle, so far as may be practicable, shall be extended to the apportionment among company districts in every county, city and town.

Artillery companies 6. Artillery companies, whether heretofore or hereafter organized, may be equipped as light batteries of six pieces each, containing not more than one hundred and fifty men, rank and file: and whenever any such company shall contain not less than one hundred and twenty men, rank and file, it shall be entitled to an additional second lieutenant, to be elected by the company and commissioned by the governor; and in any artillery company heretofore organized and accepted by the governor, he shall be authorized to commission the officers thereof of corresponding rank and grade with the same arm of the service in the Confederate States; and to effect this object, he may recall the commissions now held by the officers thereof, and issue in their stead commissions as of the same date, conferring the proper rank and grade.

7. On the day on which the term of service of any volunteer company shall expire, the men refusing to re-enlist and not drafted for service, shall be discharged; and thereupon the other members of the company, the volunteers re-enlisting, with the complement furnished by voluntary enlistment and by draft, shall proceed forthwith to reorganize the company and elect its officers. The commissioned officers shall be commissioned by the governor. The commissions of those elected to the same office shall be of the same date with their former commissions, and those not re-elected may retire from the service, and their names shall be reported for enrollment with those refusing to re-enlist, and their commissions shall be vacated. *Who discharged* *Companies, how reorganized* *Officers not re-elected*

8. Whenever a majority of the companies composing any regiment or battalion shall be reorganized under the provisions of the preceding sections, the commissions of the field officers of such regiment or battalion shall be vacated, and as soon thereafter as may be, the commissioned company officers shall elect for a regiment one colonel, lieutenant colonel and major; and for a battalion, one major. *Field officers, how elected*

9. Except in the cases mentioned in the sixth section of this act, there shall be for each company a captain and three lieutenants, who shall be elected by the company and commissioned by the governor. *Company officers*

10. The term of service of all persons drafted or volunteering under the provisions of this act, shall be three years, deducting therefrom the term of their previous service, during the existing war; nor shall any volunteer declining to re-enlist, who may be drafted under this act, be ordered to duty for the period of forty days from the expiration of his previous term of service, unless in the opinion of the governor the public exigences shall imperatively demand his services. And the general assembly recommend that a furlough of at least sixty days be granted to all volunteers who may re-enlist, at such time as the public exigences may allow. *Term of service* *Furlough*

11. Any person who may volunteer or be drafted under the provisions of this act, may, at any time before he shall be mustered into the service of the Confederate States, furnish an able bodied man, well clothed, who shall be accepted as his substitute; but the person *Substitutes, how furnished*

furnishing such substitute shall perform ordinary militia duty during the substitute's absence. Should such substitute, while thus engaged for another, be drafted, or called on to perform his own tour of duty, the person furnishing him shall be required to take his place, or to furnish another substitute on the same terms. No person (whether heretofore exempted or not by colonels of militia or others, on account of physical disability) who may be drafted under this act, shall be discharged from service by reason of such exemption; nor shall any discharge be granted by reason of alleged physical disability, unless the person claiming exemption be examined, and the disability certified to by the officers, and in the manner prescribed for obtaining similar discharges for men now in service.

If substitute be drafted

12. Whenever the governor shall be required to fill up companies under this act, he shall be authorized to accept volunteers in lieu of drafting.

Volunteers, how accepted

13. This act shall be in force from its passage.

Commencement

CHAP. 21.—An ACT to authorise the Governor to organise and call out certain Military Forces for the defence of the State.

Passed March 7, 1862.

1. Be it enacted by the general assembly, that in addition to the duties prescribed in the act passed February eighth, eighteen hundred and sixty-two, entitled an act for ascertaining and enrolling the military force of the commonwealth, the governor shall require the enrolling officers in the cities of Richmond, Norfolk, Portsmouth, Petersburg, Fredericksburg and Lynchburg, and in such of the towns of the commonwealth as he shall designate, to enroll separately all the white male inhabitants of the same, and within one mile of the city of Richmond, on the north side of James river, and within a half mile of the other cities and towns aforesaid, between the ages of sixteen and eighteen years, and between the ages of forty-five and fifty-five years, including in such enrollment all white male persons between the ages aforesaid, who may be sojourning in said cities and towns, and who may, by reason of the existing war, be refugees from their residences in this state, and are not elsewhere enrolled under the provisions of the said act of the eighth February eighteen hundred and sixty-two; and the enrolling officers of said cities and towns shall enroll all persons who are required to be enrolled under this section.

Who to be enrolled

2. The persons directed to be enrolled under said act of eighth February eighteen hundred and sixty-two, shall constitute the first military class, and those directed to be enrolled under this act shall

First class

Second class

constitute the second military class; and the governor shall have power to call into active service the whole or any portion of both or either of said classes, whenever in his opinion it may be necessary to the public defence; but nothing in this act shall be construed to interfere in any manner with the ratable draft on the first class aforesaid, under the provisions of the act entitled an act to raise troops to meet the requisition on Virginia by the president of the Confederate States, passed February tenth, eighteen hundred and sixty-two, or to authorize the governor to require the persons constituting the second class aforesaid to perform military duty elsewhere than in and near their respective cities and towns, nor for a longer period than thirty days at any one time.

3. The governor shall require all able bodied persons embraced in the first class, if not already, to be forthwith organized into companies, battalions and regiments, as nearly as may be, in pursuance of existing laws; and if by reason of drafts under said act of the tenth February eighteen hundred and sixty-two, or other cause, the strength of the companies, battalions or regiments shall be reduced below the minimum prescribed by law, the governor shall cause the companies to be rearranged; and if necessary, the battalions and regiments to be consolidated in pursuance of existing laws. Elections shall be held for company and field officers, and all other officers shall be appointed as now prescribed by law, on March fifteenth, eighteen hundred and sixty-two, or as soon thereafter as may be; and such new officers shall be at once commissioned by the governor; and thereupon the commissions of the old officers shall be vacated. But if any company shall fail to elect its officers for thirty days after its organization, the next succeeding court of the county or corporation in which such company is, shall appoint the officers for said company, who shall be commissioned by the governor. *Second class, how organized. Companies, how rearranged. Regiments, when to be consolidated. In case of failure to elect, how officers appointed.*

4. The able bodied persons composing the second class aforesaid shall be organized into companies, battalions and regiments. Each regiment of this class shall be composed of two battalions, and shall consist of at least five hundred men, rank and file. In every such battalion there shall be at least five companies. Every such company shall consist of not less than fifty nor more than one hundred men, rank and file. *Second class, how organized.*

5. For the purpose of properly training the forces hereby directed to be organized for active service, the governor may require those of such cities and towns as he may designate, and the population residing within one mile of the city of Richmond, on the north side of James river, and within half a mile of the other cities and towns, to be drilled, as he may deem necessary; and he may in like manner order the forces of the several counties of the commonwealth of the first class to be assembled for drill and instruction every alternate Saturday after they shall have been organized, at their usual places *When second class may be drilled.*

of muster, till the first day of June; and thereafter, on the last Saturday of every month; and shall order the commissioned officers only of each regiment of every such county to assemble and drill each intervening Saturday, at the usual places of muster of such regiment, till the said first day of June; and thereafter, on the third Saturday of every month: provided, however, that in any special case, when the public exigences shall in the opinion of the governor require, he may order more frequent drills of the said county forces.

Militia laws applicable 6. The laws applicable to the militia of the commonwealth shall in all respects apply to the persons composing the second class aforesaid, except so far as the same may be modified by the provisions of this act.

Exemptions 7. No person shall be exempt from service under this act, unless he he entitled to exemption from all military duties under laws now in force, or hereafter enacted; and the mode of exemption provided by law for persons of the first class, shall be applicable to those of the second class aforesaid; and in respect to persons in both said classes, the board of exemptions in each of said counties, cities and towns shall have power to grant partial or entire exemptions in cases of special and peculiar hardship, or when the public interest requires such exemption, subject to revocation by the governor.

Commencement 8. This act shall be in force from its passage.

CHAP. 22.—An ACT to authorize the repair, mounting and equipping of Artillery Pieces, and the purchase and repair of Small Arms, Accoutrements and Ammunition.

Passed March 24, 1862.

Cannon, how repaired 1. Be it enacted by the general assembly, that the governor be and he is hereby authorized to have repaired, mounted and equipped, with caissons and appropriate accoutrements, so as to be ready for service, such artillery pieces as may be in possession of the state, and to cause to be restored to the state any state arms in the hands **Small arms to be purchased** of individuals, withheld from the public service; and to purchase shot guns, rifles and other small arms, in this state, and to have them repaired and put in order for service as soon as practicable, and to purchase accoutrements and ammunition, or procure the making thereof.

Amount appropriated 2. That the sum of one hundred thousand dollars be and the same is hereby appropriated to carry this act into effect.

How contracts made 3. The repairing, mounting and equipping of artillery, and the repair of arms and accoutrements, by this act authorized, may be done by contract, or at the state armory, at the discretion of the governor.

4. This act shall be in force from its passage. <small>Commencement</small>

CHAP. 23.—An ACT amending and re-enacting the second section of chapter 22 of the Code of Virginia, respecting persons exempt from all military duties, and providing the mode of exemption.

<small>Passed February 18, 1862.</small>

1. Be it enacted by the general assembly, that the second section <small>Code amended</small> of the twenty-second chapter of the Code be amended and re-enacted so as to read as follows:

"§ 2. The following persons only shall be exempt from the per- <small>Who exempted</small> formance of all military duties, to wit: The vice-president of the Confederate States; the officers, judicial and executive, of the government of the Confederate States; the members of both houses of congress, and the clerk of each house; all custom house officers; the lieutenant governor, and all the members of the general assembly, during the term for which they were elected or appointed; the secretary of the commonwealth and his clerks; the clerks of the house of delegates and senate; the judges of the court of appeals and circuit courts; the clerk of each of said courts, and of each county and corporation court; judge of hustings court; the sheriff of each county, and the sergeant and the collector of taxes of each corporation having a hustings court, and the commissioners of the revenue; the attorney general, the treasurer, two auditors, register of the land office, superintendent of the penitentiary, and their clerks and assistants; every minister of the gospel licensed to preach according to the rules of his sect; superintendents of the public hospitals, lunatic asylums, and the regular nurses and attendants therein, and the teachers employed in the institution for the deaf and dumb and blind; one physician to each two thousand population, to be selected by the board herein after constituted; the president, the general superintendent and two local superintendents of the southern telegraph companies, in no case to exceed four persons; the president and superintendent of transportation of each rail road company; the president, secretary and chief collector of each canal company. No one shall be exempt from draft by reason of his being an agent of a commissary or assistant commissary, or quartermaster or assistant quartermaster, whether said commissary or assistant commissary, or quartermaster or assistant quartermaster be in the service of the Confederate States or of this state, or by reason of his holding any office or commission in the militia; and whenever any militia officer is drafted for actual service, his commission shall be vacated."

Officers of city, &c. how exempted

2. If the constituted authorities of any city shall, within twenty days after any draft has been made therefrom, apply to the governor for the purpose, he shall exempt from actual military service any drafted person, who may be at the time of the draft an officer of such city, or in its service in connection with its gas or water works or fire and police departments; and if, within twenty days after any draft, the president and superintendent of any rail road, canal and telegraph company shall certify upon their honor to the governor that the services of any drafted person, who is an officer or employee of such company, are necessary to the efficient operation of the said road, the governor may in his discretion exempt such person from actual military service: any person exempted under this section shall be deemed to be detailed for duty in the post or place he filled at the time he was drafted, without pay as a soldier; and in case he shall leave the service of such city or company, he shall at once be remanded to the military service for which he was drafted; and if any such person shall fail, for ten days after leaving such service, to report himself to the governor or to some military officer for duty as a soldier, he shall be proceeded against as a deserter. The governor shall promptly cause the places of all persons exempted under this section to be filled by further draft from the respective counties, cities and towns from which such persons were drafted. It shall be the duty of the president or mayor of the city, or company, as the case may be, promptly to report to the governor the name of any person so exempted, who may have left the service for which he was detailed.

When exempt remanded to service

How places of exempts to be filled

Board of exemptions, how constituted

3. Immediately after the passage of this act, the governor shall issue his proclamation, requiring the organization of a board of exemptions in each county and corporation, to consist of the presiding justice or recorder, and any two justices whom such presiding justice or recorder may associate with him. In case the presiding justice or recorder cannot for any cause act, the clerk of the hustings or county court shall summon any three justices, who shall constitute such board. Such clerk shall act as clerk of the board. In case there be no such clerk present and capable of acting, the clerk of the circuit court shall act; or if no such board should be organized, the governor may designate any three justices of the county or corporation, who shall constitute the board, and appoint their own clerk.

Powers of board of exemptions

4. The board shall have cognizance of all questions of exemption, and shall adjudge the sufficiency of the excuse given by any person, who, by reason of his failure to report his name for enrollment, as required by the act entitled an act for ascertaining and enrolling the military force of the commonwealth, passed February eighth, eighteen hundred and sixty-two, may have been enrolled among the drafted levies as prescribed in said act. For punishing contempts and compelling the attendance of witnesses, the board shall have the powers of a county court.

5. In no case shall the board grant a discharge upon a claim of exemption for bodily infirmity, unless at least two physicians of respectable standing, being duly sworn, shall prove before said board that the bodily infirmity is of a permanent character, and is such as will disqualify the claimant for discharging the duties of a soldier. *Discharge for physical infirmity, how granted*

6. Every claim for exemption, or excuse, shall be filed with the clerk of the board, who shall issue process for such witnesses as the claimant or enrolling officer may require: and within five days after a draft is made, and on a day to be designated by the board, the trial of cases of exemption and excuse shall commence; and the same shall be disposed of in a summary manner as speedily as may be. The clerk of the board shall promptly report to the adjutant general the name of each person exempted or excused by the board. *Exemptions, how tried*

7. For every failure to discharge any duty prescribed in this act, the members of the board and the clerk may each be fined not less than ten nor more than one hundred dollars. *Penalties for failure of the board*

8. All acts and ordinances and parts of acts and ordinances inconsistent with this act, are hereby repealed. *Repealing clause*

9. This act shall be in force from its passage. *Commencement*

CHAP. 24.—An ACT to declare the Powers of Boards of Exemption, and to impose penalties on members of such Boards for usurping powers not conferred on them, and to amend the 6th section of an act passed February 18th, 1862, entitled an act amending and re-enacting the 2d section of chapter 22 of the Code of Virginia, respecting persons exempt from all military duties, and providing the mode of exemption.

Passed March 11, 1862.

1. Be it enacted by the general assembly, that the true meaning of the act passed February eighteenth, one thousand eight hundred and sixty-two, entitled an act amending and re-enacting the second section of chapter twenty-two of the Code of Virginia, respecting persons exempt from all military duties, and providing the mode of exemption, so far as the powers conferred upon boards of exemption are concerned, is, that said boards of exemption shall have jurisdiction of the causes of exemption specially set forth in said act, and of no others, and shall pass on no case of exemption until the person claiming exemption has been drafted for actual service. *Act of Feb. 18 construed*

2. That in every case where a discharge is granted by a board of exemptions, the cause of exemption shall be entered of record, and the vote shall be recorded by yeas and nays; and if any such board shall usurp powers not conferred by said act, and shall grant a discharge from military service to any drafted person for a cause of *Discharge, how granted*

which such board has not jurisdiction specially conferred by said act, such discharge shall be void; and each member of such board voting for such discharge and exemption, or who shall fail to perform any duty hereby imposed, shall, for every such offence, be guilty of a misdemeanor, cognizable only in the circuit court of the county or city wherein such members reside, and shall be punishable by a fine not less than one hundred nor more than one thousand dollars, and by imprisonment, at the discretion of the court, in the county jail for a period of not less than one month nor more than twelve months.

Punishment of board of exemptions

Substitutes

3. In all cases where substitutes have been actually placed in service and certificates obtained, the board shall decide on the validity of the same.

Act of Feb. 18 amended

4. That the sixth section of an act passed the eighteenth February one thousand eight hundred and sixty-two, entitled an act amending and re-enacting the second section of chapter twenty-two of the Code of Virginia, respecting persons exempt from all military duties, and providing the mode of exemption, be amended and re-enacted so as to read as follows:

Cases of exemption, how tried

"§ 6. Every claim for exemption, or excuse, shall be filed with the clerk of the board, who shall issue process for such witnesses as the claimant or enrolling officer may require; and within five days after a draft is made, and on a day to be designated by the board, the trial of cases of exemption and excuse shall commence; and the same shall be disposed of in a summary manner, as speedily as may be. The clerk of the board shall promptly report to the adjutant general the name of each person exempted or excused by the board, and the cause of such exemption in each case."

Commencement

5. This act shall be in force from its passage.

CHAP. 25.—An ACT providing for the exemption of certain parties upon religious grounds.

Passed March 29, 1862.

Persons holding certain religious tenets to be exempted

1. Be it enacted by the general assembly of Virginia, that whenever, upon application for exemption to the board of exemption, it shall appear to said board that the party applying for said exemption is bona fide prevented from bearing arms, by the tenets of the church to which said applicant belongs, and did actually belong at the passage of this act, and further, that said applicant has paid to the sheriff of the county or collector of taxes for the city or town in which said applicant resides, the sum of five hundred dollars, and in addition thereto, the further sum of two per cent. of the assessed value of said applicant's taxable property, then the said board, on

Terms of exemption

the presentation of the receipt of said officers for said moneys, and after the said applicant shall have taken an oath or affirmation that he will sustain the confederate government, and will not in any way give aid and comfort to the enemy of the said confederate government, then the said board shall exempt said applicant: provided, *Proviso* that whenever such party may be unable, or shall fail to pay the said sum of five hundred dollars, and the tax of two per centum on their property, he shall be employed (when liable to militia duty) in the capacity of teamster, or in such other character as the service may need, which does not require the actual bearing of arms: and provided further, that the persons so exempted do surrender to the board of exemption all arms which they may own, to be held subject to the order of the governor, for the public use.

2. The sheriffs and collectors aforesaid shall account for all moneys received under this act, as they now account for license taxes. *Amounts, how accounted for*

3. Said board of exemptions shall certify to the auditor of public accounts lists of the persons so exempted, and copies of the sheriffs' or collectors' receipts for such commutation money, in order that the auditor may charge the officer with the amount so collected: provided the sheriff's commission shall be only two per cent. upon the amount paid under this act. *Duty of board* *Proviso*

4. This act shall be in force from its passage. *Commencement*

CHAP. 26.—An ACT to authorize the organization of ten or more Companies of Rangers.

Passed March 27, 1862.

1. Be it enacted by the general assembly, that the governor of this commonwealth be and he is hereby authorized to commission ten or more captains, and not exceeding twenty, and twenty or more lieutenants, and not exceeding forty, citizens of the counties in this commonwealth now in the possession of the enemy; with authority to raise ten or more companies, and not exceeding twenty, of one hundred men each, to be composed exclusively of men whose homes are in the districts overrun by the public enemy, within the limits of said counties, who shall enlist for twelve months in the service of this commonwealth, to act as rangers and scouts on our exposed frontier near the lines of the enemy, and in that part of the state overrun by the armies of the enemy, with the view of cutting off their marauding and foraging parties, and giving protection to the loyal citizens of the state. Whenever either of said captains and two of said lieutenants, to be commissioned first and second lieutenants, shall enlist seventy-five men, they shall be organized into a com- *Companies of rangers or scouts* *Companies, how organized*

pany, and the captain shall make report thereof, with a list or enrollment of his men, with the names of four sergeants and four corporals (to be appointed by him), to the adjutant general, who shall furnish the said company with such arms and ammunition as can be procured. When four of said companies shall be organized, the officers thereof shall elect a major; when six shall be organized, the officers thereof shall elect a lieutenant colonel; when ten shall be organized, the officers thereof shall elect a colonel. The officers so elected shall be commissioned by the governor as major, lieutenant colonel and colonel of said rangers and scouts. And the said officers and privates shall receive the same pay as is allowed to the privates and officers of the infantry by the Confederate States, from the return of the list and enrollment of said company to the adjutant general, and the time they shall be armed and equipped for and engage in active service.

Pay

Under command of governor

2. The said officers and rangers shall be under the command of the governor, and shall conform their operations to the usages of civilized warfare: provided the enemy on their part shall conduct the war according to the usages of civilized war. The commandants of companies shall report their operations to the officer in command, who shall report thereon to the governor.

When companies to act

3. The said companies shall be placed in such positions along our northern, western and northwestern frontiers from which they can give the greatest annoyance to the enemy, and the greatest protection to our loyal citizens, in such detached parties, of one or more companies or parts of a company, as will most promote the public interest.

When companies to be under confederate authority

Proviso

4. Whenever the said rangers shall be in the neighborhood of a confederate army, they shall be subject to the orders of the commandant of the same, and shall always co-operate with the movements of said army when ordered to do so: provided, however, that the provisions of this act shall not impair or interfere with the laws providing for the quota of Virginia to the confederate army.

Commencement

5. This act shall be in force from its passage.

CHAP. 27.—An ACT to amend and re-enact an act entitled an act to create an Ordnance Department, passed January 25, 1861.

Passed March 31, 1862.

Act amended

Be it enacted by the general assembly, that the act entitled an act to create an ordnance department, passed January twenty-fifth, eighteen hundred and sixty-one, be amended and re-enacted so as to read as follows:

MILITARY AFFAIRS.

1. Be it enacted by the general assembly, that an ordnance department be and is hereby created, to consist of one colonel of ordnance, to be appointed by the governor, by and with the advice and consent of the senate, and subordinate officers, not exceeding six in number, to be appointed in like manner; the said subordinates to hold such rank as may be prescribed by the governor, with the consent of the senate. The pay and allowances of all commissioned officers of the ordnance department shall be the same allowed to officers of the same rank in the artillery service of the Confederate States. *Ordnance department. Pay of officers*

2. This act shall be in force from its passage. *Commencement*

CHAP. 28.—An ACT to provide for having an accurate List and Record made of the Military Forces of Virginia.

Passed March 13, 1862.

1. Be it enacted by the general assembly, that the adjutant general be required to take such steps as may be necessary, to procure a correct and accurate list of the names of all the volunteer forces of the state of Virginia, which have been mustered into the service of the Confederate States since the commencement of the present war with the United States, and all the forces which may hereafter be mustered into said service, giving the names, ages, residence, and dates of being mustered into service of each of the officers, non-commissioned officers and privates of each company together, in the order in which it was mustered into service, and that he have the same recorded in the books of his office. *Lists to be made out*

2. This act shall be in force from and after its passage. *Commencement*

CHAP. 29.—An ACT to empower the Governor to have made out and filed in the State Department complete Lists of Virginia Forces.

Passed February 7, 1862.

Whereas it is the intention of this state to preserve for future reference, and to hand down to the latest posterity, the names of the valiant men who have rushed forward in the field to fight for southern independence: Therefore, *Preamble*

1. Be it enacted by the general assembly, that the governor be and he is hereby authorized and empowered to have made out complete and accurate lists of all the forces of Virginia, showing the time of service of each company, and whether they have voluntarily *Lists, how to be made out*

enlisted, or been drafted, who have been or may hereafter be in the field in defence of this state or Confederate States, and to have the same filed in the state department.

Powers of governor
2. Be it further enacted, that the governor is hereby empowered to do and to have done all things necessary to carry out the intent of this act; and the expense necessarily incurred in carrying out the same shall be paid out of the military contingent fund.

Commencement
3. This act shall be in force from and after its passage.

CHAP. 30.—An ACT to organize a Regiment of Pikemen for the Confederate Service.

Passed March 29, 1862.

John Scott authorized to raise a regiment of pikemen
1. Be it enacted by the general assembly, that Captain John Scott, Confederate States infantry, a citizen of Fauquier county, Virginia, be and he is hereby authorized to enlist a regiment of not less than six hundred nor more than twelve hundred men, rank and file, to be armed with pikes and other weapons; and as soon as the minimum is enlisted, the governor shall commission the said Scott colonel of the said regiment; and thereupon the lieutenant colonel, major and company officers shall be elected and commissioned in like manner as the like officers are elected and commissioned under the act of the tenth of February one thousand eight hundred and sixty-two, entitled an act to raise troops to meet the requisition on Virginia by the president of the Confederate States: provided, however, that to fill this regiment, volunteers may be enlisted from the forces now in the confederate service and furnished from this state, but not until their present term shall have expired, unless sooner released by the president of the Confederate States: and provided also, that this regiment, as soon as enlisted and organized, shall be tendered to the president, to constitute so much of the quota of this state, under the said act of the tenth of February one thousand eight hundred and sixty-two.

Officers, how elected

How to be enlisted

Appropriation
2. That a sum not exceeding fifteen thousand dollars be and the same is hereby appropriated to defray the costs of arming said regiment with pikes and other weapons; and so much of the said sum as may be expended in arming this regiment shall be considered by this state, and demanded by the accounting authorities thereof, as a just charge on the confederate government; but the same is not to be paid until the forces aforesaid shall be raised; and if less than the twelve hundred men be raised, then such part thereof as may be necessary to arm the same; and the pikes authorized to be made shall be made upon contract, to be awarded after public notice inviting bids.

3. No pay for services to the colonel or other officers and privates shall be made until the minimum of privates shall be mustered into service. *When pay to commence*

4. This act shall be in force from its passage. *Commencement*

CHAP. 31.—An ACT to constitute a Corps more effectually to collect the Arms of the State and Confederate States, not in actual service.

Passed February 12, 1862.

1. Be it enacted by the general assembly, that the governor of the commonwealth be and he is hereby authorized and requested to require the sheriffs and sergeants of the several counties and corporations forthwith to collect all the muskets, pistols, sabres and other arms belonging to the state of Virginia or the Confederate States, now in the hands of persons within their respective counties or corporations, not in actual service, and to transmit the same to the adjutant general of the commonwealth: provided this act shall not apply to such arms as have been recently furnished to the militia of any county, city or town for public defence, by order of the governor. *Arms, how to be collected*

2. For such services the said sheriff or sergeant shall be entitled to a compensation of twenty-five cents for each musket, rifle, sabre or pair of pistols so collected and transmitted; to be paid out of the treasury of the commonwealth, upon the production of the adjutant general's receipt for the said arms, with an order of the governor endorsed thereon. *Compensation to officers for collecting*

3. When required by the governor to proceed under this act, it shall be the duty of the several sheriffs and sergeants so called upon, to give public notice within their respective counties or corporations, requiring all persons having in their possession any of the arms referred to, forthwith to produce and deliver the same to such sheriffs or sergeants: and if any person having such arms in his possession shall fail to produce and deliver the same within twenty days from the day of the publication of said notice, he shall be liable to a fine of ten dollars for every such musket, rifle, sabre or pair of pistols; to be recovered before any justice of the peace: and if the person thus in default, without sufficient excuse therefor, be liable to military duty, he shall be forthwith drafted into the service for the war. *Notice, how given*

4. It shall be the duty of said sheriffs and sergeants, whenever such arms have been collected by them, forthwith to transmit the same to the adjutant general, at the expense of the commonwealth: and any such sheriff or sergeant, who shall fail or refuse to perform any of the duties that may be required of him under this act, shall be liable to a fine, not less than one hundred nor more than five *Arms, how transmitted* *Penalty*

hundred dollars; to be recovered against him, on the motion of the attorney for the commonwealth, upon ten days' notice, before the court of the county or corporation in which he may reside.

Commencement 5. This act shall be in force from its passage.

CHAP. 32.—An ACT authorizing Maryland Volunteers, who re-enlist in the Troops of Virginia, to be transferred to Maryland Regiments.

Passed March 7, 1862.

Preamble Whereas it is represented to this general assembly, that many of the citizens of Maryland now serving with the troops of Virginia, are desirous of re-enlisting in the army of the Confederate States, but at the same time are anxious to organize themselves together into regiments: And whereas, by re-enlisting into organizations to which they are at present attached, they continue their connection therewith, and are prevented from associating themselves together as they desire: Therefore,

Maryland volunteers, how transferred 1. Be it enacted by the general assembly of Virginia, that any citizen of Maryland, who shall re-enlist in the troops of Virginia, under the provisions of the act of the provisional congress of the Confederate States, approved December eleventh, eighteen hundred and sixty-one, and the act of the general assembly of Virginia, passed February tenth, eighteen hundred and sixty-two, shall, upon the expiration of the present term of his enlistment, if he desire it, be transferred to the first Maryland regiment in the provisional army of the Confederate States, or any other regiment of Marylanders which may be organized.

Commencement 2. This act shall be in force from its passage.

CHAP. 33.—An ACT to authorize the reorganization of the Culpeper Minute Men, and the Culpeper Rifles.

Passed March 13, 1862.

Volunteer companies from Culpeper, how reorganized 1. Be it enacted by the general assembly, that whenever, prior to the fifteenth day of March eighteen hundred and sixty-two, as many as thirty-five members of either of the volunteer companies from the county of Culpeper, called the Culpeper minute men, and the Culpeper rifles, whose terms of service recently expired, shall report themselves to the adjutant general for enrollment as volunteers in such company for three years, or for the war, subject to a credit for the period of service already rendered during the existing war, such company shall thereupon, for all the purposes of the act passed February tenth, eighteen hundred and sixty-two, entitled an act to raise troops to meet the requisition on Virginia by the president of the Confederate States, be proceeded with and be regarded as if it were a company now in the confederate service from this state.

2. That the governor shall designate the day on which the members of such company or companies, after the number of the same has been raised to one hundred men, rank and file, shall proceed to reorganize the company and elect its officers. *When company to be reorganized*

3. This act shall be in force from its passage. *Commencement*

CHAP. 34.—An ACT to reorganize the Seventeenth and Twenty-eighth Brigades Virginia Militia.

Passed March 13, 1862.

1. Be it enacted by the general assembly, that the county of Wise shall be attached to the seventeenth brigade Virginia militia; and one hundred and seventy-seventh regiment in the county of Russell to the twenty-eighth brigade, and that the officers of the one hundred and seventy-seventh regiment shall be trained at Aston's store in Russell county. *County of Wise attached to 17th brigade. Russell to 28th brigade*

2. This act shall be in force from its passage. *Commencement*

CHAP. 35.—An ACT to amend an Ordinance of the Convention to provide for the Organization of the Provisional Army for the State of Virginia.

Passed March 12, 1862.

Be it enacted by the general assembly, that the ordinance of the convention entitled an ordinance to provide for the organization of the provisional army for the state of Virginia, passed April twenty-seventh, eighteen hundred and sixty-one, be amended and re-enacted so as to read as follows: *Ordinance amended*

1. There shall be organized a provisional army for the state of Virginia, as the exigences of the service may require; which army shall consist of a major general, of four brigadier generals, two regiments of artillery, eight regiments of infantry, one regiment of riflemen and one regiment of cavalry. Each regiment of artillery shall consist of one colonel, one lieutenant colonel, one major, one adjutant, one sergeant major, one quartermaster sergeant, and ten companies; and each company shall consist of one captain, one first lieu- *Provisional army of Virginia Regiments, officers of*

Companies, officers of

tenant, two second lieutenants, five sergeants, four corporals, two artificers, two musicians and one hundred privates. Each regiment of infantry shall consist of one colonel, one lieutenant colonel, one major, one adjutant, one sergeant major, one quartermaster sergeant, two principal musicians and ten companies; and each company shall consist of one captain, one first lieutenant, two second lieutenants, five sergeants, four corporals, two musicians and ninety privates.

Cavalry regiment, officers of
Company, officers of

The regiment of cavalry shall consist of one colonel, one lieutenant colonel, one major, one adjutant (who shall be a lieutenant), one sergeant major, one quartermaster sergeant, one chief musician, two chief buglers and ten companies; and each company shall consist of one captain, one first lieutenant, two second lieutenants (exclusive of the lieutenant who is to be the adjutant of the regiment), five sergeants (one of whom shall act as quartermaster sergeant to the company), four corporals, two buglers, one farrier, one blacksmith and ninety privates. The regiment of riflemen shall consist of one colonel, one lieutenant colonel, one major, one adjutant, one sergeant major, one quartermaster sergeant, two principal musicians and ten companies; and each company shall consist of one captain, one first lieutenant, two second lieutenants, five sergeants, four corporals, two musicians and ninety privates: provided, that the governor is not authorized hereby to raise any more companies or battalions of troops for the provisional army, or to keep any officers of the same in pay, unless they have been assigned to duty, and are actually employed in the service.

Rifle regiment, officers of

Proviso

General and field officers, how appointed

2. The general and field officers shall be appointed by the governor, by and with the advice of the senate; and the governor shall commission the same. The governor shall appoint the company officers; but no officer shall be commissioned until the requisite command is raised. In the recess of the senate, appointments of such officers may be made and vacancies supplied by the governor; but the appointments shall be subject to ratification or rejection by the senate, at its next session; and the commissions of officers rejected shall be void.

Aid de camps

3. The major general shall be entitled to two aids de camp, who shall have the pay of a captain of cavalry. Each brigadier general shall be entitled to one aid, with the same rank and pay. To each regiment there shall be an adjutant, to be appointed from among the subalterns, by the commanding officer of the regiment.

Enlistments

4. The non-commissioned officers, musicians, artificers, farriers, blacksmiths and privates of the provisional army shall be enlisted for three years, unless sooner discharged, and the regulations for their enlistment shall be prescribed by the governor.

Commencement

5. This act shall be in force from its passage.

MILITARY AFFAIRS. 59

CHAP. 36.—An ACT for the relief of the Indigent Soldiers who have been or may be disabled in the military service of the State, and the Widows or Minor Children of Soldiers, who have died or may hereafter die in the service.

Passed March 10, 1862.

1. Be it enacted by the general assembly, that the county courts and the councils or boards of trustees of any city or town be authorized to make an allowance, for a period not exceeding one year, for the support of the indigent soldiers who have been disabled or may hereafter be disabled in the military service of the state, and the widows or minor children of soldiers who have died, or may hereafter die in the service. *[Allowance, how made]*

2. Such allowance shall be chargeable on the county, city or town, and provision shall be made for its payment in the manner prescribed by law for the payment of sums lawfully chargeable on counties, cities or towns. *[How chargeable]*

3. The county courts are authorized to make such allowance at any of their terms, but shall not at a term order the appropriation of an amount exceeding in the aggregate five hundred dollars, unless all the acting justices of the county shall have been previously summoned for that purpose, or a majority thereof be present. *[When] [Justices to be summoned]*

4. This act shall be in force from its passage. *[Commencement]*

CHAP. 37.—An ACT to amend and re-enact an Ordinance of the Convention entitled an Ordinance concerning the Office of Adjutant, passed June 23, 1861.

Passed March 29, 1862.

Be it enacted by the general assembly, that the ordinance of the convention entitled an ordinance concerning the office of adjutant, be amended and re-enacted so as to read as follows: *[Ordinance amended]*

1. The commandant of a regiment or battalion of volunteers or militia in actual service may appoint any white male person over eighteen years of age to act as adjutant, who shall be commissioned as such by the governor, with the rank of a first lieutenant, and receive the pay allowed adjutants in the confederate service. *[Who may be adjutant]*

2. This act shall be in force from its passage. *[Commencement]*

CHAP. 38.—An ACT to amend section 27 of chapter 24 of the Code (new edition), providing for a Clerk in the Adjutant General's Office.

Passed February 21, 1862.

Code amended 1. Be it enacted by the general assembly, that the twenty-seventh section of chapter twenty-four of the Code (new edition) shall be amended and re-enacted so as to read as follows:

27th section re-enacted "§ 27. The adjutant general shall receive for his services two thousand dollars, payable quarterly, as other salaries are paid, and to commence and be computed from the first day of January eighteen hundred and sixty. He shall appoint one clerk in his office, who shall receive a salary of twelve hundred dollars per annum, to commence on and be computed from the first day of January eighteen hundred and sixty-two; to be paid at the same times and in the same manner as other salaries are paid. He shall reside at or near, and shall keep his office at the seat of government; but when the public service shall render it expedient, the governor may direct him to remove with his office to any other place within the state."

Commencement 2. This act shall be in force from its passage.

CHAP. 39.—An ACT to authorise County and Corporation Courts to certify Insolvent Muster Fines in certain cases.

Passed January 30, 1862.

Muster fines, how certified 1. Be it enacted by the general assembly, that during the existence of the present war between the Confederate States and the federal government, it shall be lawful for the sheriff of any county or corporation, in which from any cause the officers have been or may hereafter be unable to hold courts of inquiry, to return delinquent lists of muster fines to the county or corporation court of such county or corporation; and upon the court being satisfied of the insolvency of the persons fined, it shall certify a list thereof, in the same manner in which regimental courts are required to certify such lists; and the same shall be allowed by the auditor of public accounts, and passed to the credit of such sheriff.

Commencement 2. This act shall be in force from its passage.

CHAP. 40.—An ACT exempting from taxation the Seal of Courts attached to papers or records for the recovery of the Wages or other Dues of deceased Soldiers, and to refund the Tax heretofore paid.

Passed February 5, 1862.

Tax on seals, &c., when not to be exacted 1. Be it enacted by the general assembly, that hereafter no state tax shall be imposed upon the seal of the court, where the said seal is required in the authentication of any paper or record necessary to the recovery of the wages or other dues of deceased soldiers, due to them as soldiers; nor shall such tax be imposed upon the grant of administration on the estate of any such decedent.

2. Be it further enacted, that the clerk of any county, corporation or circuit court, to whom such tax has heretofore been paid, and not by him paid into the treasury, be authorized to refund the same to the legal representatives of said deceased soldier. *When refunded*

3. This act shall be in force from its passage. *Commencement*

CHAP. 41.—An ACT to organize a Military Contingent Fund.

Passed March 15, 1862.

1. Be it enacted by the general assembly, that there shall be set apart, during the present war, a sum of money in the treasury to be called the "Military contingent fund;" out of which shall be paid all expenses attending the execution of the military laws, which are not otherwise provided for, or for which no special appropriations may have been or may be made, or any other military expenses which the government may deem necessary and proper. No payment shall be made out of the fund, except upon the written order of the governor, directed to the auditor of public accounts. *Military contingent fund*

2. That the sum of fifty thousand dollars is hereby appropriated and set apart for the present year to said fund. *Amount appropriated*

3. This act shall be in force from its passage. *Commencement*

CHAP. 42.—An ACT to amend and re-enact an Ordinance to provide for the enrollment and employment of Free Negroes in the public service, passed by the Convention July 1st, 1861.

Passed February 12, 1862.

Be it enacted by the general assembly, that the ordinance of the convention, passed July first, eighteen hundred and sixty-one, entitled an ordinance to provide for the enrollment and employment of free negroes in the public service, be amended and re-enacted so as to read as follows: *Ordinance amended*

1. The county and corporation courts which have not enrolled, shall enroll, as soon as practicable, all able bodied male free negroes between the ages of eighteen and fifty, residing within their respective jurisdictions at the date of this act; which said enrollment shall *Free negroes, how enrolled*

MILITARY AFFAIRS.

be deposited in the clerks' offices of the counties and corporations aforesaid, and a copy thereof transmitted by the clerk of each county or corporation court to the adjutant general of the state within five days after the same shall have been received by them.

Requisition, how made

2. That upon the requisition of the commanding officer of any post or department of the state or confederate forces for labor in erecting batteries, entrenchments or other necessities of the military service, addressed to the presiding justice of any county, or mayor or senior alderman of any corporation as aforesaid, he shall proceed forthwith to summon two other justices to assemble at the clerk's office as aforesaid; and any three justices shall constitute a board to carry out the purposes of this act.

Draft, how made

3. The said board, or a majority thereof, shall proceed to select from said list or enrollment such number of laborers as in their judgment may be proper and expedient, having reference to the condition and circumstances of the parties, and shall require the sheriff, sergeant or any constable to notify the free negroes thus selected to assemble at such time and place as may be agreed upon between said board and the military authorities as aforesaid, except those free negroes who may be in the employment of officers or soldiers in active service, and who are in the army: and any such sheriff, sergeant or constable failing to comply with any of the requisitions of this act, shall be subject to a penalty of not less than fifty nor more than one hundred dollars; to be recovered as in the case of other penalties.

Penalty on officers

Free negroes received in public service

4. That all free negroes thus detailed and appearing at the place of rendezvous, shall be received into the public service (under such officers as may be detailed by the commandant as aforesaid to receive them) as laborers, on condition that they be entitled to such compensation, rations, quarters and medical attendance as may be allowed other labor of similar character employed in the public service, and that they shall not be detained at any one time for a longer period than one hundred and eighty days, without their consent: provided, that the pay, rations and allowances provided for in this act shall be payable by the authorities of the Confederate States only, unless the services provided for in the act shall be rendered exclusively for the state, under the authority of an officer of the state.

Penalty

5. That any free negro duly detailed and notified as aforesaid, who shall fail or refuse to obey the requisition as aforesaid, shall be subject to the penalties provided by law for persons drafted from the militia, and failing or refusing to obey such draft.

Free negroes subject to articles of war

6. Such free negroes shall, whilst engaged in the public service as aforesaid, be subject to the rules and articles of war; which shall be fully explained to them by the officers aforesaid.

MILITARY AFFAIRS.

7. The county and corporation courts are authorized to accept and enroll as volunteers all such able bodied free negroes as may offer themselves for such service as is herein before provided for; and in case of any requisition for labor from any county or corporation, no draft shall be made until the list of volunteers shall be exhausted. And no requisition for slave labor from any such county or corporation shall be made till the free negroes, enrolled according to the first section of this act, shall be received into the public service as aforesaid. *Volunteer free negroes, how accepted*

8. Be it further enacted, that the clerk of this house forthwith send a copy of this act to each clerk of the county or corporation courts, and to each commandant of the different divisions of the Confederate States army in this commonwealth. *Copy, where sent*

9. This act shall be in force from and after its passage. *Commencement*

CHAP. 43.—An ACT to authorize the use of the Jails and Poorhouses of the State by the Confederate States, for the safe keeping of Free Negroes arrested by military authority.

Passed March 15, 1862.

1. Be it enacted by the general assembly, that any free negro who has been or may be hereafter arrested by authority of any military officer of the Confederate States, shall, upon the warrant of commitment of such officer, or any other military officer of the Confederate States, be received into his jail by the jailor of any county or corporation, and by him safely kept, according to the warrant of commitment, until discharged by due process of law; or such military officer may, upon a like warrant of commitment, require the overseers of the poor of any county, city or town to receive and keep such free negro until discharged as aforesaid. *Free negroes, when to be committed to jail or poorhouse*

2. The jailor or overseers of the poor shall, for the support of any such prisoner, be paid by the Confederate States, and for a failure of duty as to any such prisoner, shall be liable to the Confederate States in like manner as a jailor, in the case of a prisoner committed under the authority of the state, would be paid by or liable to the state: provided, that nothing herein contained shall be construed to impose a liability on the overseers of the poor for the escape of a prisoner received under the provisions of this act. *Duty of jailor and overseers of the poor*

3. This act shall be in force from its passage. *Commencement*

CHAP. 44.—An ACT to provide for the more effectual and speedy transportation of Freight and Travel through the Cities of Richmond and Petersburg.

Passed February 1, 1862.

Connection authorized

1. Be it enacted by the general assembly, that the Richmond, Fredericksburg and Potomac rail road company and the Richmond and Petersburg rail road company, or either of them, is hereby authorised to extend their roads, or either of them, through the city of Richmond, so as to connect with each other; and that the Richmond and Petersburg rail road company and the Petersburg rail road company, or either of them, is hereby authorized to extend their roads, or either of them, through the city of Petersburg, so as to connect with each other, and to use such connections for all their purposes of transportation in like manner as the rest of their road: provided, however, that in making said connections, or either of them, they shall not interfere with or use the line of the connections heretofore made by authority of the commander in chief of the confederate forces in this state, without his consent thereto: and provided further, that the government of the Confederate States and the state of Virginia shall be authorized to use said connections, made by said companies, in the transportation of troops, munitions of war, and all military supplies, in the same manner and upon the terms prescribed for the use of the rail roads of said companies, or either of them, as now established, or as may be hereafter prescribed by law.

Proviso

Government, power of, as to troops, &c

Assent of cities not required

Power of condemnation

Damages

Notice to common council

Surveys to be made

2. Be it further enacted, that in order to enable the said companies to make the extensions of their roads herein provided for, it shall not be necessary to obtain the assent of either of the cities herein mentioned, to carry out the objects and provisions of this act, but they are hereby authorised immediately to enter upon and occupy any real property, public or private, which may be needed to make said extensions, any law heretofore passed to the contrary notwithstanding, and to have the same condemned. The amount of any damages for entering upon and occupying any real property, to be ascertained as now provided for by law with regard to corporations generally: provided, however, that no dwelling house shall be taken for the purposes aforesaid, without the consent of the owner thereof. As soon as a route is located for either of the connections authorised by this act, through either of the said cities, notice thereof shall be given by the company making it, to the common council of such city, who, if they object to such location, may apply, within ten days thereafter, to the board of public works to change the same; and said board, if requested by the common council, shall cause surveys to be made to ascertain the practicability of making said connection by a route outside the limits of said city; and if, upon such surveys and other evidence, the board shall be of opinion that a suitable connection can be made without passing through the city, then said connection shall be made outside the limits thereof; but if the board

shall be of opinion that said connection ought to be made through the city, they shall cause the same to be located by such route as in their judgment will answer the purpose and cause the least injury to said city: provided, that before said connection shall be made through the city of Petersburg, the company proposing to make it shall obtain the consent of the confederate government to abandon the connection now existing through said city as soon as the one hereby authorized is completed, and when completed such existing connection shall be no longer used: provided, further, that the connections through the said cities of Richmond and Petersburg shall be located with a grade sufficient for the transportation by steam of freight and passengers, and be opened for trade and travel simultaneously; and a failure to use or operate one of said connections, shall render it illegal to use or operate the other. *Present connection in Petersburg, how abandoned* *Proviso*

3. The ordinances of the convention, passed on the twenty-fourth and twenty-sixth days of June eighteen hundred and sixty-one, so far as the same revoke the right of either of said companies to connect the said roads, and so far as the same are in conflict with this act, shall be and the same are hereby repealed. *Ordinances repealed*

4. This act shall be in force from its passage. *Commencement*

CHAP. 45.—An ACT releasing a Lien to the Richmond and Petersburg Rail Road Company.

Passed March 27, 1862.

Whereas, by an act passed on the thirtieth of March eighteen hundred and thirty-eight, entitled an act concerning the Richmond and Petersburg rail road, the board of public works was authorized to loan, on behalf of the commonwealth, to said company, the sum of one hundred and fifty thousand dollars, and the company was required to execute a mortgage upon its property and tolls to secure the payment of the principal and interest of said loan: And whereas, by an act passed on the twenty-fifth of March eighteen hundred and forty-three, entitled an act converting into stock the state's loan to sundry rail road companies, and for other purposes, the said company was authorized to increase its capital to the amount of the loan aforesaid, and the board of public works was authorized to subscribe on the part of the state for the said increased capital, and to take in exchange therefor, stock of the company to an amount equal to the principal of the debt, thus liquidating the principal, and leaving only the interest and the dividend which was then due to be paid, but the mortgage was retained to secure the payment of said interest and dividend: And whereas, by an act passed on the twenty-eighth of *Preamble*

February eighteen hundred and forty-six, entitled an act for the relief of the Richmond and Petersburg rail road company, the said company was authorized to issue bonds bearing interest, in lieu of dividends in money; which bonds were issued: And whereas, by an act passed on the ninth of March eighteen hundred and fifty, entitled an act in relation to the Richmond and Petersburg rail road, the said company was exonerated from the payment of dividends to the state until dividends were declared alike to the state and to other stockholders, and the collection of the dividend bonds then due was suspended during the pleasure of the legislature, but the mortgage which has been given by the company was retained to secure the payment of the whole of the said debt and interest: And whereas the company, as now appears by the books of the second auditor, has paid the full amount due for said dividend bonds, principal and interest, and thus the original loan has been repaid, the interest thereon has been satisfied, and the dividend bonds have also been paid, and there is no reason for the continuance of the lien upon the property of the company herein before mentioned, and it is therefore proper that the same be released: Therefore,

Lien released
1. Be it enacted by the general assembly, that the fourth section of the act entitled an act in relation to the Richmond and Petersburg rail road, passed March ninth, eighteen hundred and fifty, requiring said lien to be retained, shall be and the same is hereby repealed; and the lien of the commonwealth upon said rail road, for the debt and interest therein mentioned, shall be and is hereby released, and the said company exonerated from all claim of the commonwealth therefor.

Commencement
2. This act shall be in force from its passage.

CHAP. 46.—An ACT to authorize an alteration in the Line of the South Side Rail Road.

Passed January 26, 1852.

Line of road, how changed
1. Be it enacted by the general assembly, that it shall be lawful for the South side rail road company to change the line of their road, from some point of divergence at or near Rice's depot in the county of Prince Edward, to some point at or near the town of Farmville in said county: provided, that said alteration shall first be authorized by a vote of the stockholders of the said company, in general meeting.

Commencement
2. This act shall be in force from its passage.

CHAP. 47.—An ACT to provide for the Construction of a Rail Road Connection between the Orange and Alexandria and Manassas Gap Rail Roads and the Richmond, Fredericksburg and Potomac Rail Road.

Passed February 19, 1862.

Whereas it is of great importance to the military defence and to the internal commerce of the state, that a rail road connection be constructed between the junction of the Orange and Alexandria and the Manassas gap rail roads and the existing rail road from Richmond to Acquia creek: *Preamble*

1. Be it enacted by the general assembly, that the Richmond, Fredericksburg and Potomac rail road company be and they are hereby authorized, under the provisions of their charter, to extend their rail road from some point on the same, between Fredericksburg and Acquia creek, so as to form a junction of their rail road with the Orange and Alexandria and Manassas gap rail roads, at the junction of the said two last named rail roads, and passing through or with a branch of the said connection, extending to Evansport, or the mouth of Quantico creek. *Road, how extended*

2. For the purpose of effecting the object of this act, the Richmond, Fredericksburg and Potomac rail road company are hereby authorized to increase their capital stock in such manner as they may deem most advisable, to the extent of seventy-five hundred shares in addition to its capital hitherto authorized; or the said company, to such an extent as they may deem advisable to do so, may borrow money at a rate of interest not exceeding eight per centum per annum, and issue proper certificates or evidences of debt therefor, and make the same convertible into stock at the pleasure of the holder; and may secure the punctual payment of the principal and interest of such loans by a deed of trust on all or any portion of the property and franchises of the said company: provided, that the aggregate amount of stock and convertible loan issued under the authority of this act shall not exceed the sum of seven hundred and fifty thousand dollars: and provided further, that no certificate of loan convertible into stock, or creating any lien on or mortgage of the property of the company, shall be issued by the said company, unless the expediency of making a loan on such terms and of issuing such certificates shall have first been determined on at a general meeting of the stockholders, by two-thirds of the votes which could be legally given in favor of the same, and that no certificates of debt issued under this act shall be sold at less than eighty per cent. of the par value thereof: and provided further, that the said company shall not build any bridge across Acquia creek, or any other creek below the head of tide water, without sufficient drawbridges or openings thereon to admit of the complete navigation of such creek. *Capital stock, how increased* · *Company may borrow money* · *Amount* · *Meeting of stockholders* · *Stock sold, at what price* · *Proviso*

3. The common councils of the city of Richmond and the town of Fredericksburg are hereby authorized to subscribe for an amount not *Power of councils of Richmond*

68   INTERNAL IMPROVEMENTS.

and Fredericks-   exceeding one thousand shares each of the said increased stock, or
burg to sub-
scribe   to take an amount equivalent, at its par value, of such convertible
Terms of sub-   loan: provided, however, that no such subscription shall be made by
scription   either of the said common councils, until the expediency thereof shall
                  have been submitted to the vote of those persons qualified to vote at
                  the election of members of said common councils, and shall receive
                  the assent of three-fifths of the voters actually polled, after ten days'
                  public notice of the time and place of opening polls for the purpose.

When road to be   4. If the said Richmond, Fredericksburg and Potomac rail road
commenced   company shall not, within four months from the passage of this act,
                  bona fide commence the construction of said extension of their road,
                  or shall fail so far to complete the same, within fifteen months from
                  such commencement, as to admit through transportation thereon, or
                  shall neglect, at any time after such commencement, for two months
                  to prosecute the construction of said extension to completion, unless
Exemptions   prevented by the exigences of the war, then the provisions of said
from taxation,
when to cease   charter, so far as they exempt the property of said company from
                  taxation, shall be held and deemed inapplicable to the stock and
                  property created and acquired under the provisions of this act.

Subject to exist- 5. In all respects, except as to said exemption from taxation, the
ing laws   rights and franchises hereby granted shall be subject to the provisions
                  of chapters fifty-six, fifty-seven and sixty-one of the Code of Vir-
                  ginia, and to such further modifications as the general assembly may
                  hereafter determine.

Right of Ma-   6. If the Richmond, Fredericksburg and Potomac rail road com-
nassas gap and
Orange and Al-   pany shall not, within three months from the passage of this act,
exandria R. R.   accept the provisions thereof (notice of which acceptance shall be
company   forthwith communicated to the governor of this commonwealth), and
                  commence the work within four months from the passage of this act,
                  or shall neglect the prosecution of said work for two months, as
                  herein before provided, then, in any of these events, either the
                  Manassas gap rail road company or the Orange and Alexandria rail
                  road company shall be at liberty to accept the same within one
                  month thereafter (notice whereof shall be given in like manner):
                  and upon such acceptance by either of said companies, the company
                  first so accepting shall thereupon have authority to construct said
                  rail road connection, in like manner, and with the same privileges,
                  and under the same restrictions as are herein prescribed in reference
                  to the said Richmond, Fredericksburg and Potomac rail road com-
Time to com-   pany, except that such company so accepting said provisions, shall
mence work   have one month from the date of such acceptance to commence the
                  construction of said work.

How, in case of   7. And if the said Manassas gap rail road company or the Orange
partial construc-
tion   and Alexandria rail road company shall, as herein before provided,

accept the provisions of this act, and enter upon the construction of said extension, all the work done in the partial construction of said extension by the Richmond, Fredericksburg and Potomac rail road company, shall be deemed to have been done by the said Orange and Alexandria rail road company or the Manassas gap rail road company so accepting and entering upon said construction, and shall be held by it as its own property, upon payment therefor, to the said Richmond, Fredericksburg and Potomac rail road company, of such amount of money as the board of public works shall determine to be the value thereof. *Cost, how paid to Richmond, Fredericksburg and Potomac R. R. Co.*

8. This act shall be in force from its passage. *Commencement*

CHAP. 48.—An ACT to provide for the construction of a Rail Road for military purposes, connecting the Manassas Gap Rail Road, at or near Strasburg in the county of Shenandoah, with the Winchester and Potomac Rail Road, at or near Winchester in the county of Frederick.

Passed February 21, 1862.

1. Be it enacted by the general assembly, that the board of public works be and they are hereby authorized and directed, with as little delay as practicable, to construct a rail road, to connect the Manassas gap rail road, at or near the town of Strasburg in the county of Shenandoah, with the Winchester and Potomac rail road, at or near the town of Winchester in the county of Frederick: said road to be constructed in the most economical manner possible, so as to meet the military exigences of the present war. *Board of public works authorised to construct road*

2. To effect this object, the board of public works are hereby invested with all the powers and privileges, and subjected to all the duties and restrictions conferred and imposed by the Code of Virginia on companies incorporated for the construction of rail roads, except that they may take possession of and use any land or materials necessary for the construction of such road, previously to the institution and during the pendency of proceedings to condemn the same: and they are further authorized and empowered, if necessary for the construction of said road, to take possession of and use any rail road iron, cross ties and other materials belonging to or in the possession of either the Winchester and Potomac rail road company or the Manassas gap rail road company, which may have, at any time since the commencement of the present war, been removed by any parties from the Baltimore and Ohio rail road: provided, that no rail road iron or other materials shall be taken from the Manassas gap rail road company, which are intended for use in the completion of its road to Harrisonburg, and none shall be taken from either of said companies, the taking of which would in the opinion of the *Powers of board* *What may be condemned* *Military efficiency*

board of public works materially impair the military efficiency of either of said roads. It shall be the duty of the board of public works, within thirty days after they shall have taken possession of any land, rail road iron or other materials for the construction of such road, to institute proceedings in accordance with the provisions of the fifty-sixth chapter of the Code of Virginia, to have the same condemned for the use of the said road; and should they fail to do so, it shall be lawful for the proprietor or proprietors of such land, and the owner or owners of such rail road iron or other materials, to institute such proceedings: and provided further, that the proper compensation that may be allowed for lands and materials taken, including said rail road iron, cross ties, &c., shall be chargeable on the commonwealth, and paid for, upon the requisition of the board of public works, out of the fund hereinafter provided.

How condemned

Amount, how paid

Amount appropriated

3. For the construction of said road, and without reference to any compensation for lands or materials taken, the sum of one hundred and twenty-five thousand dollars is hereby appropriated, out of such funds as may be provided for the defence of the state, or out of the fund herein after provided.

Treasury notes, how issued

4. To provide funds for the purposes aforesaid, the governor is hereby authorized to direct the auditor of public accounts to issue treasury notes to an amount not exceeding in the aggregate the direct appropriation herein before provided, with the additional sums which may be required to pay the compensation for land and materials, as also provided for in this act. The notes hereby authorized to be issued shall bear interest at the rate of six per centum per annum, and be payable one year after the date thereof, in sums not less than twenty dollars. The said notes shall be receivable in payment of all taxes and other dues to the commonwealth, and may be reissued until otherwise provided by law. They may also, when presented at the treasury in sums of five hundred dollars, or any multiple of one hundred above that sum, be converted into registered bonds of the state, bearing interest at the rate of six per centum per annum. All the provisions of an ordinance of the late convention of Virginia, entitled an ordinance to authorize the issue of treasury notes, passed April thirtieth, eighteen hundred and sixty-one, shall be held to apply to the notes authorized to be issued under this act, except so far as the same may be inconsistent therewith.

Interest

How receivable

Ordinance to apply

Road, how transferred to Manassas gap R. R. Co.

5. When said road shall have been constructed and ready for use, the board of public works shall transfer the same to the Manassas gap rail road company, to be operated and held as the property of said last mentioned company, under the provisions of the general rail road law, and upon the same footing with their other road: provided, however, that said company shall have furnished towards the construction of said road not less than the sum of fifty thousand dollars, or its equivalent value.. Upon such transfer being made, the

Stock of com-

capital stock held by the commonwealth in said company shall be increased by the whole aggregate amount expended on the part of the state in the construction of said road; to be held by the state upon the same footing as preferred stock, and subject to all the provisions in that respect contained in the act passed on the tenth day of February eighteen hundred and sixty, entitled an act increasing the capital stock of the Manassas gap rail road company, and authorizing a further subscription thereto by the board of public works; and the capital stock of said company is accordingly hereby enlarged to that extent: and provided further, that the manner and terms upon which said road shall be operated in respect to the receipt from and transfer to the Winchester and Potomac rail road, of either freight, passengers or the mails, shall be under the control of the board of public works, or such other authority as may be prescribed by law. *monwealth, how transferred*

Road to be under control of board of public works

6. And in the event that the Manassas gap rail road company should not comply with the condition to furnish towards the construction of the said road the sum of fifty thousand dollars, or its equivalent value, then it shall be the duty of the board of public works to make such arrangements as may be practicable, either with the Manassas gap rail road company or the Winchester and Potomac rail road company, for operating the said road, giving preference in all cases to the military demands upon it. *When board authorised to make other arrangements*

7. This act shall be in force from and after its passage. *Commencement*

CHAP. 49.—An ACT to sanction an Ordinance of the State of North Carolina, entitled an Ordinance to incorporate the Piedmont Rail Road Company.

Passed March 27, 1862.

1. Be it enacted by the general assembly, that an ordinance of the state of North Carolina, entitled an ordinance to incorporate the Piedmont rail road company, which said ordinance was passed and ratified in open convention, in the state of North Carolina, the eighth day of February one thousand eight hundred and sixty-two, a duly authenticated copy of which ordinance was transmitted to the governor of Virginia by W. N. Edwards, president of said convention, by his letter to said governor, dated Raleigh, North Carolina, tenth February eighteen hundred and sixty-two, and by the said governor was submitted to the senate and house of delegates of Virginia, by his message of the thirteenth day of February eighteen hundred and sixty-two, be and the same is hereby sanctioned, and a right to construct the said road within the limits of this state, according to the provisions of the aforesaid charter, is hereby conferred on the company to be incorporated under the said charter: provided, that if the corporators to be organized under said ordinance accept the provisions *Ordinance ratified*

Proviso

of this act, it shall be upon the condition that the said Piedmont rail road company shall not have power to discriminate on either freight or travel, against the Richmond and Danville rail road, or any other rail road in Virginia connected therewith; and upon the further condition, that the connection of said Piedmont rail road with the Richmond and Danville rail road, hereby authorized, shall be made at some point south of Dan river, at or near the town of Danville, unless, in the opinion of the president of the Confederate states, the military interests of the country require such connection to be made elsewhere; in which event, such connection may be made at such point as the president of the Confederate States shall approve.

Further condition

2. This act shall be in force from its passage.

Commencement

CHAP. 50.—An ACT to improve the Navigation of New River.

Passed December 18, 1861.

1. Be it enacted by the general assembly, that the board of public works be and the same are hereby authorized and directed to adopt such measures as may be necessary to remove the obstructions to the navigation of New river by batteaux, and to improve the navigation of said stream by sluice, in such manner as will accommodate the transportation of military stores in batteaux, from some point at or near the Central depot, on the Virginia and Tennessee rail road, to the mouth of Greenbrier river, and in as perfect a manner as the appropriation herein after provided will admit of; and that they cause the said work to be completed at the earliest possible period.

Board of public works authorized to remove obstructions

When work to be completed

2. And be it further enacted, that the sum of thirty thousand dollars be and the same is hereby appropriated, out of any moneys in the public treasury not otherwise appropriated, to be used by the board of public works towards the completion of said work; and that for this purpose, they are authorized and required as soon as possible to employ a competent engineer to contract for, direct and superintend the construction of said work.

Amount appropriated

Engineer to be employed

3. Provided this act shall not be in force or take effect until the president and directors of the New river navigation company shall have transferred, and authority is hereby given them to transfer to the board of public works all the franchises, rights, title and interest of said New river navigation company in said improvement: and provided, that the board of public works shall pay or cause to be paid to the stockholders of the said New river navigation company, out of the appropriation here made, a sum of money equal to that which has been already subscribed and actually paid in for the purpose of organizing said New river navigation company.

Proviso

4. This act shall be in force from its passage.

Commencement

CHAP. 51.—An ACT to amend and re-enact the 4th section of chapter 10 of an act to incorporate the Virginia Canal Company, and to transfer the rights and franchises of the James River and Kanawha Company thereto.

Passed December 17, 1861.

1. Be it enacted by the general assembly, that the fourth section of chapter ten of the act passed March twenty-ninth, eighteen hundred and sixty-one, entitled an act to incorporate the Virginia canal company, and to transfer the rights and franchises of the James river and Kanawha company thereto, be amended and re-enacted so as to read as follows: *Act March 29, 1861, amended*

"§ 4. If the said Virginia canal company be not organized by the appointment of a president and directors, as required by this charter, on or before the twenty-ninth day of January eighteen hundred and sixty-three, this act shall be null and void: provided, that if no subsequent session of the general assembly be held before the said twenty-ninth day of January eighteen hundred and sixty-three, then the time within which the organization of said company may be effected shall be and the same is hereby extended to the twenty-ninth day of January eighteen hundred and sixty-four; and if said company shall not bona fide commence its works within six months after its organization, or if, after commencing its works, it shall suspend its operations for one year; or if it shall fail to comply with the provisions of the fifth chapter hereof, so far as the same refers to the fourteenth article of said provisional agreement, the general assembly may abrogate this charter, and declare that the corporate rights and privileges of the company shall cease; or it may allow said company such further time to complete the said works and to comply with its engagements, as to the legislature may seem just and proper." *How amended*

2. This act shall be in force from its passage. *Commencement*

CHAP. 52.—An ACT to amend the 9th section of an act entitled an act to amend the Charter of the James River and Kanawha Company, passed March 23d, 1860, and providing a Loan of Bonds to the James River and Kanawha Company to keep open the Navigation of the James River Canal, and to improve the Sluices upon a part of the River.

Passed March 18, 1862.

1. Be it enacted by the general assembly of Virginia, that the ninth section of the act entitled an act to amend the charter of the James river and Kanawha company, passed the twenty-third day of March eighteen hundred and sixty, be amended and re-enacted so as to read as follows: *Act amended*

"§ 9. Be it further enacted, that there shall be issued to, and placed under the exclusive control of the Kanawha board of direc- *How amended* tors of said company, or their successors, as constituted under the act of the general assembly entitled an act providing more effectual means for the improvement of the navigation of the Kanawha river, passed fifteenth of February eighteen hundred and fifty-eight, three hundred thousand dollars of the six per cent. registered stock of the commonwealth, to be issued in the mode now provided by law; and the said stock so issued shall be used by said Kanawha board of directors for the improvement of the navigation of said river, from the mouth thereof to Loup creek shoals: provided, however, said Kanawha board shall not dispose of said registered stock at less than par. And said registered stock shall not be issued for an amount exceeding one hundred and fifty thousand dollars in any one year, nor exceeding twenty thousand dollars in any one month. But before any of said stock shall be issued, the said James river and Kanawha company, by the president thereof, shall execute a deed of trust or mortgage upon the works, property and net revenue of said Kanawha line of improvement, from the mouth thereof to said Loup creek shoals, to the commonwealth, for the payment of the principal and interest of said three hundred thousand dollars: or upon the failure or refusal of said company to execute such deed of trust or mortgage, when required by the Kanawha board, then the said Kanawha board, by their president pro tempore, or other agent, may execute such deed of trust or mortgage; and the same shall be deemed to have the same effect as though it had been executed by said company: and such lien shall take precedence over any lien created by said company, to secure their bonds authorized to be issued by this act. The said Kanawha board shall pay into the treasury of the commonwealth three and one-half per centum on or before the fifteenth day of June and December of each year, on such amount of said registered stock as may be issued under this section, for interest and to provide a sinking fund. The said Kanawha board are hereby authorized and directed to prosecute the construction of said Kanawha line of improvement, free from the control or direction of the president and directors of said James river and Kanawha company, and which is known as the 'Eastern board,' and shall have the entire control and management of the same, free from such control and direction: provided, however, that the second auditor be and he is hereby directed not to issue any further sums or installments of the registered stock of the commonwealth, authorized by this section as originally enacted, during the present war, and not until, in the opinion of the board of public works, the work authorized to be done by this section can be resumed and prosecuted under the direction of the Kanawha board: and provided further, that the said auditor is further directed not to enter in his office or otherwise recognize any transfers or assignments of the stock heretofore issued to the Kanawha board, and not heretofore entered in his office, under this section, and to withhold payment of any interest on the seventy-six thousand dollars issued to said board and not yet en-

Powers of Kanawha board

tered as transferred in his office, during the present war and until, in the opinion of the board of public works, the work authorized to be done by this section can be resumed and prosecuted under the direction of the Kanawha board."

2. There shall be issued to the president and directors of the James river and Kanawha company, under the direction of the board of public works, registered stock of the commonwealth, not exceeding two hundred thousand dollars in amount, to enable said company, and the same is hereby appropriated, to keep open the navigation of the James river and Kanawha canal, and to improve the sluice navigation of the James and Jackson rivers from Buchanan in the county of Botetourt, to Covington in the county of Alleghany, and for no other purpose whatsoever; and the same may be issued at such times and in such amounts as the board of public works may deem expedient: provided, that such stock shall not be disposed of at less than par; but the said president and directors may, if they deem it advisable, deposit said stock, or a part thereof, with any of the banks of this commonwealth, as collateral security for any loan by such bank to said president and directors for the purposes aforesaid. *Registered stock, how issued* *Stock, how deposited*

3. The said registered stock shall not be applied to the purposes aforesaid until the James river and Kanawha company shall execute their bond, in the penalty of four hundred thousand dollars, with condition to return, in like registered stock of this commonwealth, such amount of the said stock as may have been applied, under this act, to keeping open the navigation of the canal and the improvement of the sluice navigation of the rivers, as herein before provided for, with interest thereon, within six years after the date of such bond; the interest to be paid semi-annually, on the first day of July and January in each year. *Bond, how executed*

4. This act shall be in force from its passage. *Commencement*

CHAP. 53.—An ACT to compel Turnpike and Plank Road Companies to keep their Roads in order.

Passed January 11, 1862.

1. Be it enacted by the general assembly, that in addition to the requirements of the several acts incorporating joint stock companies for the construction of turnpike and plank roads, every such company, heretofore or which may be hereafter incorporated, shall be required to cut down and remove all dead and dangerous timber liable to fall in the road; and for such failure shall be fined, at the discretion of a jury, not less than five nor more than one hundred *Dead timber, how to be removed*

dollars. And all such companies shall be liable to indictment by the grand jury of the counties in which their road is located, for failing to keep their roads in lawful condition, and fined, at the discretion of a jury, not less than five nor more than one hundred dollars.

Fines   2. All fines recovered under the first section of this act shall be paid into the treasury, and placed to the credit of the literary fund.

Commencement   3. This act shall be in force from and after the first day of April one thousand eight hundred and sixty-two.

CHAP. 54.—An ACT to repair the Road leading from the Warm Springs, by Huntersville, to Greenbrier River, at Marlin's Bottom.

Passed February 25, 1862.

Road to be repaired   1. Be it enacted by the general assembly, that the board of public works are hereby authorized and directed to have the road leading from the Warm springs in Bath county, by the way of Huntersville, to Greenbrier river, at Marlin's Bottom in Pocahontas county, repaired at the earliest possible period, for the transportation of military stores in wagons.

Amount appropriated   2. And be it further enacted, that the sum of six thousand dollars be and the same is hereby appropriated for that purpose, out of any money in the public treasury not otherwise appropriated.

Commencement   3. This act shall be in force from its passage.

CHAP. 55.—An ACT appropriating Money for the construction of a Road from Marlin's Bottom in Pocahontas County, to the Salt Works in Braxton County.

Passed March 29, 1862.

Road to be constructed   1. Be it enacted by the general assembly, that the board of public works cause to be constructed a road from Marlin's Bottom in the county of Pocahontas, by Webster courthouse, to intersect the Weston and Gauley bridge turnpike, at the Bulltown salt works in Braxton county, on or near the location made by Peter Scales, an engineer in the employment of this state: said road not to be less than twelve feet wide, and to be used for the transportation of military supplies for the army of the Confederate States during the present war with the United States, or hereafter.

Amount appropriated   2. And be it further enacted, that the sum of fifteen thousand dollars be and the same is hereby appropriated for that purpose, out of the fund for internal improvement.

INTERNAL IMPROVEMENTS.—CHANGES IN CODE. 77

3. *Provided, however,* that if before the completion of said road, the district of country in which it may lie shall fall into the hands of the enemy, the money hereby appropriated, or so much thereof as may not have been expended, shall be withheld until the possession of such district of country is recovered. *Proviso*

4. This act shall be in force from its passage. *Commencement*

CHAP. 56.—An ACT to repair the Road from Saltville to Tazewell Courthouse.

Passed March 28, 1862.

1. Be it enacted by the general assembly, that the board of public works be and they are hereby authorized and directed to have the road leading from Saltville to Tazewell courthouse repaired at the earliest possible period, for the transportation of military stores in wagons. *Road to be repaired*

2. And be it further enacted, that the sum of five thousand dollars be and the same is hereby appropriated for that purpose, out of the fund for internal improvement. *Amount appropriated*

3. This act shall be in force from its passage. *Commencement*

CHAP. 57.—An ACT to amend section 11 of chapter 29 of the Code, so as to exempt the property of persons in the military service of the State from distress for rent payable in money.

Passed February 19, 1862.

1. Be it enacted by the general assembly, that section eleven of chapter twenty-nine of the Code of eighteen hundred and sixty be amended and re-enacted so as to read as follows: *Code amended*

"§ 11. No proceeding shall be had in any suit at law or equity, or any distress warrant for rent, payable in money, or on any execution against the person or property of any one ordered into actual service, whether of this state or of the Confederate States of America, or against his surety, from the time such person shall be ordered to the place of rendezvous, until thirty days after his term of service shall have expired. This exemption shall not apply to any person who shall have received the money of another in a fiduciary character, nor as an officer of the commonwealth, or of any court, nor to any of his sureties, nor to any person who shall have employed a substitute to perform his tour of duty; nor shall it prevent the granting or reinstating of any injunction." *Legal proceedings against persons in military service* *Exception*

2. This act shall be in force from its passage. *Commencement*

CHAP. 58.—An ACT to amend and re-enact the 13th section of chapter 42 of the Code of Virginia, so as more effectually to regulate the Sales of Real Estate under executions in favor of the Commonwealth.

Passed January 28, 1862.

Code amended 1. Be it enacted by the general assembly, that the thirteenth section of chapter forty-two of the Code of Virginia shall be amended and re-enacted so as to read as follows:

"§ 13. The sale shall be upon six months' credit; and if the land be not purchased for the commonwealth, the officer shall take bond of the purchaser, with sureties, for payment of the purchase money to the commonwealth. Every such bond shall mention on what occasion the same was taken, and shall be made payable at six months from the day of sale. The bond shall be returned to the office of the court from which the execution issued, and the clerk shall endorse thereon the date of its return. For making such sale and taking such bond, the officer shall be allowed the same fees and commissions to which a sheriff is entitled for taking a forthcoming bond for the delivery of personal property; which fees and commissions shall be deducted from the amount of such sale, and the net balance be credited to the original judgment debtor; and any officer taking insufficient security in such bond, shall be officially liable to the commonwealth. For sales heretofore made, the sheriff or other officer who made the same, shall be allowed the commissions in this section provided, and the net balance shall be credited, at the time the bonds mature, to the judgment debtor."

Sale, how made Time of credit

Fees and commissions

When officer liable

Commencement 2. This act shall be in force from its passage.

CHAP. 59.—An ACT amending the 8th section of chapter 186 of the Code, concerning judgment liens.

Passed March 31, 1862.

Code amended 1. Be it enacted by the general assembly, that the eighth section of chapter 186 of the Code be amended and re-enacted, so that with the amendment the said section shall read as follows:

Lien of judgment "§ 8. No judgment, other than a judgment in favor of the commonwealth, rendered in the circuit court of the city of Richmond, shall be a lien on real estate as against a purchaser thereof for valuable consideration without notice, unless it be docketed, according to the third and fourth sections of this chapter, in the county or corporation wherein such real estate is, either within a year next after the date of such judgment, or ninety days before the conveyance of said estate to such purchaser. But a judgment in favor of the commonwealth, rendered in said court, shall be a lien as in the sixth section of this chapter, without the exception therein referred to." *How as to judgments in favor of commonwealth*

2. This act shall be in force from its passage. *Commencement*

CHAP. 60.—An ACT to amend the 14th section of chapter 15 of the Code, so as to authorize the enrollment of the Acts and Joint Resolutions of the General Assembly on parchment or paper.

Passed February 6, 1862.

1. Be it enacted by the general assembly, that the fourteenth section of chapter fifteen of the Code of Virginia be amended and re-enacted so as to read as follows: *Code amended*

"§ 14. The clerk of the house of delegates shall be keeper of the rolls. As such, he shall cause all the acts and joint resolutions of the assembly to be enrolled on parchment or paper. He shall have the custody of the acts and joint resolutions of the general assembly, and the records and papers of the house of delegates, and when required, shall make a copy of any of them; which copy, being certified by him, shall be evidence for any purpose for which the originals would be received, and with as much effect. He shall, as soon as practicable after the adjournment of the assembly, prepare the acts and joint resolutions of the previous session for publication, with an index and tables as prescribed by the sixteenth chapter, and furnish to the public printer the manuscript of such acts, resolutions, tables and index, arranged properly for being printed; and he shall superintend the publication thereof." *Keeper of rolls. Rolls, how made. Copies, how made. Publication of acts and joint resolutions*

2. This act shall be in force from its passage. *Commencement*

CHAP. 61.—An ACT to amend section 14 of chapter 163 of the Code, in relation to the Removal of the Records and Papers of Courts.

Passed February 13, 1862.

1. Be it enacted by the general assembly, that the fourteenth section of chapter one hundred and sixty-three of the Code of Virginia be amended and re-enacted so as to read as follows: *Code amended*

"§ 14. None of the records or papers of a court shall be removed by the clerk, nor allowed by the court to be removed out of the county or corporation wherein the clerk's office is kept, except on an occasion of invasion or insurrection, actual or threatened, where, in the opinion of the court, or in a very sudden case, of the clerk, the *When records may be removed* same will be endangered; after which, they are to be returned as soon as the danger ceases; and except in such other cases as are specially provided by law. Any clerk violating this section shall forfeit six hundred dollars."

Penalty

Commencement 2. This act shall be in force from its passage.

CHAP. 62.—An ACT to amend the 5th section of chapter 13 of the Code, in relation to administering the Oaths to be taken by the Members of the two Houses of the General Assembly.

Passed February 18, 1862.

Code amended 1. Be it enacted by the general assembly, that the fifth section of chapter thirteen of the Code be amended and re-enacted so as to read as follows:

Oaths, how taken "§ 5. The oaths to be taken by a person elected a member of either house of the general assembly, shall be administered by the clerks or presiding officers of the respective houses, a justice of the peace or a notary public. Those to be taken by any person elected an officer of either house of the general assembly, shall be administered in such manner as the house may prescribe by its rules. And the oaths to be taken by a person elected or appointed to any other office or post shall, except in cases in which it may be otherwise directed by law, be administered in a court of record, or by some judge or justice of such a court. A justice of another state may administer the oaths to be taken by a commissioner or other person residing therein."

Commencement 2. This act shall be in force from its passage.

CHAP. 63.—An ACT to amend 2d section of chapter 175 of the Code, so as to provide for the temporary appointment of Commissioners in Chancery.

Passed February 26, 1862.

Code amended 1. Be it enacted by the general assembly, that the second section of chapter one hundred and seventy-five of the Code be amended and re-enacted so as to read as follows:

Commissioners in chancery, how appointed "§ 2. Each court may, from time to time, appoint commissioners in chancery or for stating accounts, who shall be removable at its pleasure; there shall not be more than three such commissioners in office at the same time for the same court: provided, however, that if any one of such commissioners shall at any time be so engaged in the public service, as in the opinion of the court to prevent him from attending to his duties as commissioner, the court may appoint a special commissioner, who may continue in office until it be entered of record by the court that it is no longer necessary for him to do so." *Special commissioners*

2. This act shall be in force from its passage. *Commencement*

CHAP. 64.—An ACT amending and re-enacting the eighth section of the twenty-ninth chapter of the Code of Virginia (edition 1860).

Passed March 27, 1862.

1. Be it enacted by the general assembly, that the eighth section of chapter twenty-nine of the Code of Virginia (edition of eighteen hundred and sixty) shall be amended and re-enacted so as to read as follows: *Code amended*

"§ 8. No person shall absent himself from his regiment after the commandant thereof has received an order requiring a draft or detail to be made, and of which such person shall have been in any way informed, until such detail or draft shall have been made. Every person so offending, who shall be subsequently detailed to march, unless he join the detachment with which he is detailed, at its rendezvous, or show that he was prevented from so joining by unavoidable cause, shall be considered and treated as a deserter. Every person who shall refuse to give his name to the proper officer when called upon for enrollment, under the act passed February eighth, eighteen hundred and sixty-two, entitled an act for ascertaining and enrolling the military forces of the commonwealth, shall be considered and treated as a deserter." *Who treated as deserter*

2. This act shall be in force from its passage. *Commencement*

CHAP. 65.—An ACT to amend section 28 of chapter 52 of the Code of Virginia.

Passed March 6, 1862.

1. Be it enacted by the general assembly, that the twenty-eighth section of chapter fifty-two of the Code of Virginia be amended and re-enacted so as to read: *Code amended*

"§ 28. Every person appointed under either of the two preceding sections shall, either in person or by a sufficient substitute, when required by the proper surveyor, attend with proper tools, and work the road on such days as the surveyor may direct. But said surveyor *Who to work road*

Fines

may, in lieu of the labor of persons, require a force in working animals and suitable implements of equivalent value. For each person required to work and failing to do so, seventy-five cents a day shall be paid to the surveyor within twenty days thereafter, by the person in default, if a person of full age, or if he be an infant, by his parent or guardian; or if he be a servant or slave, by his overseer, if he be under one, otherwise by his master: and for failure to furnish animals and implements as aforesaid, the person required to furnish the same shall pay to the surveyor a sum equivalent to seventy-five cents a day for each of the persons in lieu of whom such animals and implements were so required to be furnished. If the money be not paid, it shall be recoverable by the surveyor, with costs before a justice; and any money received by a surveyor under this section, after the payment of costs, shall be applied to the improvement of the road of which he is surveyor."

How recoverable

Commencement 2. This act shall be in force from its passage.

CHAP. 66.—An ACT amending and re-enacting section 12, chapter 77, of the Code of Virginia.

Passed January 22, 1862.

Code amended 1. Be it enacted by the general assembly, that the twelfth section of chapter seventy-seven of the Code of Virginia be amended and re-enacted so as to read as follows:

Number of acres to be held "§ 12. Such trustees shall not take or hold at any one time more than two acres of land in an incorporated town, nor more than one hundred acres, exclusive of the church and burying grounds, out of such a town."

Commencement 2. This act shall be in force from its passage.

CHAP. 67.—An ACT to provide a Currency of Notes of less denomination than Five Dollars.

Passed March 29, 1862.

Authority to issue bank notes 1. Be it enacted by the general assembly, that the several banks of circulation of this commonwealth be and they are hereby authorized to issue notes of a less denomination than five dollars and not less than one dollar, including fractional amounts, between one and five dollars, to an amount not exceeding ten per centum of the capital of said banks respectively; and every bank or branch shall, after the expiration of ninety days from the passage of this act, pay

Notes redeemed

all sums less than five dollars, and redeem all notes of five dollars, either in specie or in its own notes of less denomination than five dollars, unless said bank or branch shall have issued and have in circulation notes of the denomination hereby authorized, to the amount herein before specified; and every bank or branch failing to pay in specie or in small notes as aforesaid, shall pay to the person demanding such payment or redemption, the sum of fifty dollars for each offence. The notes hereby authorized to be issued may be signed by such officer or officers of said banks as may be designated for that purpose by the board of directors; and any of said banks which may have preserved notes of less denomination than five dollars, heretofore issued under authority of law, shall be at liberty to circulate the same, so that their issue shall not exceed the amount authorized by this act. _{Forfeiture}

2. The banks whose issues are based upon a pledge of state stock may dispense with the signature of the treasurer, and issue such small notes in the same way as the other banks, but such banks shall not issue an amount of circulation larger than is now allowed by law.

3. Be it further enacted, that the lawfully constituted authorities of the city of Richmond be and they are hereby authorized to issue as currency, notes of a less denomination than one dollar, to an amount not exceeding five hundred thousand dollars; and the authorities of all the other cities, and the towns of the commonwealth containing a population of two thousand, and of the towns of Leesburg, Lewisburg and Warrenton, are hereby authorized to issue notes as currency, of a like denomination, to an amount double the amount of state tax assessed on property, real and personal, within such city or town for one year, taking therefor the average of the last preceding three years; and the notes issued as aforesaid shall be receivable in payment of all dues to the corporation issuing them; and the banks of the commonwealth are hereby authorized to receive and pay out the same. _{Delegated power to city of Richmond. Amount. Delegated power to certain towns.}

4. Be it further enacted, that the several cities, towns and counties of this commonwealth be and they are hereby authorized to issue as currency notes or bills of and under the denomination of one dollar, in sums equal to the amounts they may have respectively authorized to be appropriated, and which has been actually appropriated by them, for arming and equipping of their volunteers and supporting the families of those who are indigent and in service; but the amount authorized by this section to be issued by any city or town shall not be in addition to the amount authorized by the next preceding section.

5. Be it further enacted, that for the purpose of redeeming the notes issued by the counties, cities and towns of the commonwealth, under the provisions of this act, the courts of such counties, cities and towns as may issue such notes, are required at their annual levy

courts to levy upon the subjects of taxation mentioned in the fifth section of chapter fifty-three of Code of Virginia of eighteen hundred and sixty, an amount sufficient to redeem thirty-three and a third per cent. of the amount of such notes in circulation at the time of such levy in the years eighteen hundred and sixty-two and eighteen hundred and sixty-three; and at the time of the annual levy in the year eighteen hundred and sixty-four, the said counties, cities and towns shall levy upon said subjects of taxation an amount sufficient to redeem all such notes as may be then in circulation; such redemption to be made in such funds as are receivable in payment of dues to the commonwealth.

Quarterly returns to be made. 6. Be it further enacted, that the banks shall severally include in the quarterly statements now required by law to be transmitted to the governor, and the clerk of every county, city and town issuing notes under this act, shall make quarterly to the governor a statement under oath showing the amount and denominations issued, and the amount of each denomination then outstanding; which reports shall be laid before the legislature when in session.

Repealing clause. 7. That all laws now in force inconsistent with the provisions of this act, are hereby suspended as to the notes hereby authorized, and the banks and counties, cities and towns acting under its provisions, during the time this act shall remain in force; and the act passed the twenty-fourth January, eighteen hundred and sixty-two, entitled an act to authorize the banks of this commonwealth to issue notes of the denomination of one and two dollars, is hereby repealed.

Obligation on real and personal property. 8. The property, real and personal, of the people of the counties, cities and towns issuing notes under this act, shall be bound for the payment of the notes issued.

Commencement. 9. This act shall be in force from its passage.

CHAP. 68.—An ACT to release certain Corporations and Persons from forfeitures, penalties and rights of action incurred by issuing Notes as a Currency, contrary to law.

Passed March 19, 1862.

1. Be it enacted by the general assembly, that all forfeitures and penalties incurred before the passage of this act, under chapter sixty of the Code of Virginia, and the sixteenth, seventeenth, eighteenth and nineteenth sections of chapter one hundred and ninety-eight of the said Code, by any corporation, chartered company, county or savings bank, and the officers, agents and authorities thereof, acting for said parties, and by the sheriff of any county, and all rights of action given by the acts aforesaid against the said parties and per-

sons for a violation of said acts, be and the same are hereby released: provided, however, that none of said parties or persons shall have the benefit of this act, who shall, after the passage thereof, issue any note, bill or other writing, with the intent that the same shall be circulated as currency, or shall otherwise deal, trade or carry on business as a bank of circulation, contrary to law; or shall fail for ninety days to call in the notes, bills or other writings issued by them respectively in violation of said acts, and to redeem the same, when offered for redemption in sums of one or more dollars, by exchanging them for either gold and silver coin, or notes of the banks of Virginia, which are received by the bank or banks nearest to the place of such corporation, chartered company, or county. And if any of said corporations, chartered companies or counties fail, for the time herein prescribed, to call in the notes, bills or other writings issued as aforesaid, or to redeem the same, when presented for redemption, in the manner aforesaid, the attorney general, upon information of such failure, shall proceed to enforce the forfeitures and penalties aforesaid; but this proviso shall not be applicable to such of said corporations, chartered companies or counties as have been or shall be authorized to issue such notes, bills or other writing, if they shall confine their said issues within the limits prescribed by law.

Proviso

2. The act entitled an act to prevent the circulation of small notes, passed the third day of March eighteen hundred and fifty-four, is hereby repealed, so far as the same is in conflict with this act.

3. Provided, however, that this act shall not enure to the benefit of any chartered company, corporation, savings bank or individual who may have been indicted or presented in any court of this commonwealth for a violation of the provisions of said chapter sixty of the Code, and of the sixteenth, seventeenth, eighteenth and nineteenth sections of chapter one hundred and ninety-eight of the said Code, until the company, corporation, bank or individual against whom such prosecution is pending, shall have paid into court all the costs incurred by the commonwealth in such prosecution, and the fees of the officers of the court in such cases.

Proviso

4. This act shall be in force from its passage.

Commencement

CHAP. 69.—An ACT to authorize the Banks of this Commonwealth to issue Notes of the denomination of One and Two Dollars.

Passed January 24, 1862.

1. Be it enacted by the general assembly, that the several banks of this commonwealth be authorized and required to issue notes of the denomination of one and two dollars, to an amount not exceeding five per cent. of their respective capitals, which notes may be

Denomination
Notes, how issued
Limitation

signed by such officer or officers of said banks respectively, as may be designated for that purpose by the board of directors; and they are hereby prohibited, under the penalty of fifty dollars for each offence, to pay out the notes of any unauthorized corporations or individuals; and any of said banks which may have preserved the notes of the denomination of one and two dollars, heretofore issued under authority of law, shall be at liberty to circulate the same, so that their issue shall not exceed the amount authorized by this act.

2. The banks whose issues are based upon a pledge of state stock, may dispense with the signatures of the treasurer, and issue such small notes in the same way as the other banks; but no such banks shall be hereby authorized to issue an amount of circulation larger than is now allowed by law.

3. That all laws now in force prohibiting the receiving or passing of bank notes under the denomination of five dollars, are hereby suspended as to notes issued by the banks of Virginia, under this act, during the time this act shall remain in force.

Commencement 4. This act shall be in force from its passage.

CHAP. 70.—An ACT to amend and re-enact section 1, chapter 57, Acts 1861.

Passed March 1, 1862.

Certain sections of act of 1861 amended 1. Be it enacted by the general assembly, that section first, chapter fifty-seven, acts eighteen hundred and sixty-one, be amended and re-enacted so as to read as follows:

"§ 1. Be it enacted by the general assembly, that so much of all or any acts as now may subject any bank or banking corporation incorporated by the laws of this commonwealth, now in operation, or which may be put in operation whilst this act is in force, to the forfeiture of its charter, or to any other penalty, for failing or refusing to *Privilege suspended* pay or redeem its notes or debts in specie, shall be and the same are hereby suspended until the first day of March eighteen hundred and sixty-three, and until otherwise provided by the general assembly of *Forfeiture remitted* Virginia; and if any such bank or banking corporation shall have forfeited its charter by failing or refusing to pay in specie any notes or other debts due from such bank, the forfeiture thereby incurred shall be remitted, and the charter of such bank, with all the rights and powers thereby conferred, except such portions thereof as are herein before suspended, shall be and the same is hereby declared to be in full force and effect, to all intents and purposes, until the date *Proviso* before mentioned: provided, that nothing herein contained shall be so construed as to prevent the recovery of the amount of any note or debt due from any such bank, with legal interest thereon, in the mode prescribed by law."

2. This act shall take effect from its passage. *Commencement*

CHAP. 71.—An ACT to amend and re-enact the 63d Ordinance of the Convention, authorizing Banks to change their Places of Business.

Passed March 31, 1862.

1. Be it enacted by the general assembly, that the sixty-third ordinance of the convention of Virginia, entitled an ordinance authorizing banks to change their places of business, be amended and re-enacted so as to read as follows: *Authority to change place of business*

"That whenever the president and directors of any bank, or of any branch of any bank, shall consider the domicil of the bank unsafe, or that access thereto is interrupted by reason of the public enemy, and shall so enter on their minutes and appoint some other place for the custody of its books and effects and the transaction of its business, it shall be lawful for the board to remove thereto, and thereat to exercise its corporate rights, until the danger be over, when it shall return to its original domicil; and bills of exchange, checks and negotiable notes, payable at the domicil of such bank, shall be held and treated as payable at the bank in the place to which it is removed. The president and directors shall cause notice to be given of the removal of such bank, by advertisement and other means likely to make the fact public; and that whenever the domicil of any such bank or branch bank has been so changed, and the quorum of the board of directors shall fail to accompany such bank or branch bank to its new domicil (any one or more of such directors, or in case there be none present), the cashier, and such of the officers of the bank or branch bank as may be with him, shall have the power of a board of directors to transact its business and provide for its safety by further removals, whenever they shall consider such new domicil unsafe, that access thereto is interrupted; and the business transacted at such new domicil shall be as valid as if transacted at its original place of business. That when any city or town wherein a bank or branch bank is located shall be occupied, invested, or access thereto interrupted by the enemy, the parties to negotiable notes, bills and checks, payable in such city or town, shall remain bound after the maturity of such notes, bills and checks, without demand, protest or notice, as if the requirements of law in that behalf had been complied with." *Proviso* *Proviso*

2. Be it further enacted, that all the provisions of this act, in relation to banks and the branches thereof, shall apply to savings banks *Savings banks and insurance companies*

and insurance companies, as far as they may be applicable: and that the president and directors of said institutions shall have the same powers, exercise the same rights, and be subject to like provisions, and their acts and proceedings have the same validity, as are provided in the first section in relation to banks and their branches.

Commencement. 3. This act shall be in force from its passage.

CHAP. 72.—An ACT to amend and re-enact the 61st section of chapter 38 of the Code of 1860, being the first section of an act entitled an act to prevent the Circulation of Small Notes, passed March 3d, 1854.

Passed March 31, 1862.

Certain sections of act 1854 amended. 1. Be it enacted by the general assembly, that the first section of an act, entitled an act to prevent the circulation of small notes, passed March third, eighteen hundred and fifty-four, be amended and re-enacted so as to read as follows:

Duty of commissioners of the revenue. "§ 1. That it shall be the duty of commissioners of the revenue and courts, to whom application shall be made for license, to require from each and every person who shall apply for license, an oath that he will not pay out, within the limits of this commonwealth, notes of any denomination, issued by banks, corporations or individuals, without authority of law. And it shall be the duty of every commissioner of the revenue and court, to whom such application shall be made, to withhold the license until the oath aforesaid shall be taken."

Commencement. 2. This act shall be in force from its passage.

CHAP. 73.—An ACT concerning Bank Directors.

Passed March 13, 1862.

Provisions as to bank directors. 1. Be it enacted by the general assembly, that during the continuance of the present war, whensoever two or more directors of any bank, and whenever one or more of any branch bank of this commonwealth, shall be absent in the military service of the state, from the place where such branch or bank respectively may be situated, the business of such branch or bank may be conducted by three directors of any such bank or branch, in all respects as if the number now required were present. *Proviso.* And any bank of circulation in this commonwealth, in which the state is not a stockholder, may, by a vote of the stockholders thereof, in general meeting, fix the whole number of directors for such bank, so that the same be not less than five nor more than nine.

Commencement. 2. This act shall be in force from its passage.

BANKS. 89

CHAP. 74.—An ACT authorizing the Recovery of Money stolen from the Exchange Bank of Virginia at Weston.

Passed March 14, 1862.

Whereas, by an ordinance of the convention of Virginia, number *Preamble* seventy-three, entitled an ordinance concerning the Northwestern lunatic asylum and the West Liberty academy in Ohio county, passed June twenty-eighth, eighteen hundred and sixty-one, the work on said asylum was directed to be suspended until the general assembly should otherwise provide; that no further money should be drawn from the treasury on that account; and any surplus of the moneys theretofore drawn, after paying for work done, should be returned into the treasury: And whereas it is represented that four days after the time of the passage of said ordinance, an armed military force, as public enemies, entered the vaults of the Exchange Bank of Virginia at Weston, where the said money was deposited, and robbed the said bank of about twenty-seven thousand dollars of its specie, on account of the money deposited there by the treasurer of said asylum, by order of its board of directors, to the credit of said asylum: And whereas it is also represented that the said military expedition operated under and in pursuance of orders from an usurped authority claiming to be a government established within the limits of Virginia, without authority of the legislature: And whereas it is represented that the said money, after being so abstracted, was deposited in one or more of the banks of this commonwealth, located in the city of Wheeling, whose officers were co-operating with and professing allegiance to said usurped government, and had notice of the robbery and ownership of said money, and have become liable therefor; and to afford a speedy remedy to reclaim said money, and thereby enable the treasurer of said asylum to comply with the said ordinance of said convention: Therefore,

1. Be it enacted by the general assembly, that Jonathan M. Bennett, the treasurer of said asylum, may demand and have of any bank wherein the said money was so deposited, having notice of the ownership thereof, and of any person who at the common law would be liable therefor, the full amount of money so deposited in any such bank, or for which any other person may be liable as aforesaid, together with interest thereon at the rate of six per centum per annum from the time said deposit was made, or such other liability may have accrued, and such damages as may be equal to the reasonable costs of collecting the said money, and such additional damages as may be equal to the rate of exchange between currency and specie, which existed in Virginia, at the capital thereof, at any time within the year eighteen hundred and sixty-one, after the said robbery.

2. The proceedings for the recovery of said money may be brought *General provisions* in any court in this commonwealth, by motion, upon such regulations

90   BANKS.

consistent with this act, as are prescribed by chapter one hundred and sixty-seven of the Code of Virginia, except that proof of the robbery, the ownership of the money, and notice to any of the officers of such bank, either actual or constructive, shall be sufficient to fix the liability on such bank.

3. No person who has been guilty of any of the acts mentioned in the first section of chapter one hundred and ninety of the Code of Virginia, shall be capable of sitting as a juror upon the trial of the motion hereby authorized.

4. Any person who shall accept any appointment or office, or act in an official capacity, under authority of said usurped government, in the said Exchange Bank at Weston, or who shall protest notes as notary public therein, or do any other act in any manner to control the matters pertaining to said bank, under color of office or appointment emanating from said usurped government, shall be liable for the money so taken therefrom, to the same extent, and to be recovered in the same manner, as is authorized for the recovery from the Northwestern Bank, or other bank, as in this act is provided.

Commencement   5. This act shall be in force from its passage.

CHAP. 75.—An ACT to convert the Branch of the Northwestern Bank of Virginia at Jeffersonville into a Separate and Independent Bank.

Passed March 13, 1862.

Preamble

Whereas the armed occupation of northwestern Virginia, by lawless enemies of this state, has entirely destroyed all business intercourse and relations between the Northwestern Bank of Virginia at Wheeling and its branch at Jeffersonville, to the great detriment of the state and loyal stockholders, and it seems proper under the circumstances to dissolve the connection heretofore subsisting between said bank and its branch at Jeffersonville, and of authorizing the latter to transact business as a separate and independent corporation:

Bank incorporated

1. Be it therefore enacted by the general assembly, that the branch of the Northwestern Bank of Virginia at Jeffersonville be and the same is hereby constituted, created and incorporated a separate, distinct and independent bank, under the corporate name of

Name of bank

Graziers Bank of Virginia; and all the power, control, direction, supervision, relation and connection of said Northwestern Bank of Virginia over and with the said branch at Jeffersonville, are hereby dissolved, abrogated and annulled.

Assets

2. All the assets held by said branch (embracing all bills and notes discounted, whether the same be in suit, protested, due or ma-

turing, all judgments, balances due on accounts current, all money, either in coin or currency, all evidences of debt or other securities, all real estate, and every right and interest) are absolutely vested in the said Graziers Bank of Virginia; and in every case where suit has been instituted in the name of the Northwestern Bank of Virginia for the recovery of money or other thing, to which said branch is entitled, the suit so brought shall be prosecuted in the name of the Northwestern Bank of Virginia, for the use and benefit of said Graziers Bank of Virginia; and in every case where suit shall hereafter be instituted for the recovery of money or other thing belonging to said branch, the suit shall be in the name of said Graziers Bank of Virginia.

3. The said Graziers Bank of Virginia is subject to all the liabilities of the said branch, except so far as the said liabilities are modified by the following sections of this act. Liabilities

4. The said Graziers Bank of Virginia shall in no event be required to account to the said Northwestern Bank of Virginia for any portion of the net profits or contingent fund of the said branch, nor to contribute to the payment of, or pay out of the assets of said branch, or otherwise, to any stockholder, billholder or creditor of the said Northwestern Bank, any sum or sums of money which any such stockholder, billholder or creditor may be entitled to demand and have of said Northwestern Bank of Virginia. Proviso

5. At any time within three months from the passage of this act, any loyal holder of stock in the Northwestern Bank of Virginia, whose stock in said bank was purchased through the said branch, or whose dividends have usually heretofore been credited to him at said branch, may return and assign to said Graziers Bank of Virginia such stock, and demand and receive in lieu thereof a certificate for a like number of shares of stock in the said Graziers Bank of Virginia. Limitations

6. As soon as may be after the expiration of the said three months from the passage of this act, the governor of the state shall cause certificates of the stock held by the state in the said Northwestern Bank of Virginia, for an amount equal to the balance of the capital stock of said branch, not exchanged under the previous section, to be in like manner returned and assigned to said Graziers Bank of Virginia, for a like number of shares of the stock thereof. Proviso

7. The Graziers Bank of Virginia, hereby established, shall be required to redeem, from loyal citizens of the Confederate States of America, in notes of its own issue, all such notes of said branch as may be in their possession at the passage of this act: provided the same be presented in six months after notice of this provision shall have been published for one month in some weekly newspaper pub- Redemption
Proviso

lished in the city of Richmond: and provided further, the amount offered for redemption shall not exceed one hundred and eighty thousand dollars.

Proviso

8. The legislature reserves the power to provide, after the termination of the war with the United States, the extent, mode and time of redemption by said Graziers Bank of Virginia, of any outstanding notes of said branch, with which, according to the principles of equity, *Special deposit* justice and right, it is chargeable. But as it is represented to this general assembly that the said branch has a special deposit of twenty-four thousand dollars in gold with the said Northwestern Bank of Virginia, heretofore made by said branch to meet the redemption of its notes: and as notes payable at said branch may have been issued by the said Northwestern Bank of Virginia, which have not been reported to said branch, nor charged to said Northwestern Bank of Virginia, and which it would be evidently unjust to require the said branch to redeem, it is hereby expressly provided and enacted, that the whole amount of circulation of the said branch, which the said Graziers Bank of Virginia shall be required to redeem, under the provisions of this act, and of any subsequent act of the legislature, taken collectively, shall not exceed the balance of the circulation of said branch, after deducting therefrom the sum of twenty-four thousand dollars on account of said special deposit, and also any amount or amounts of circulation payable at said branch (if any such there be), issued by the said Northwestern Bank of Virginia, of which the said branch has not heretofore received notice from said Northwestern Bank of Virginia.

Delegated authority

9. The cashier shall forthwith, after the expiration of three months from the passage of this act, out of the surplus or contingent fund of the said branch, pass to the credit of the stockholders of the said Graziers Bank of Virginia and to the state, a dividend of ten per centum upon their stock issued under the provisions of the fifth and sixth sections of this act.

Location

10. The said Graziers Bank of Virginia shall be located and transact its business at the town of Jeffersonville.

11. The said Graziers Bank of Virginia may, by sales of new stock, increase its capital to two hundred thousand dollars.

Delegated authority

12. The present board of directors for the said branch shall continue to act as a board of directors for the said Graziers Bank of Virginia until a new board shall be appointed under the general law.

Proviso

13. Except so far as the same may be inconsistent with the provisions of this act, the general banking law of the state shall apply to the said Graziers Bank of Virginia: and the general law of joint

stock companies shall apply to the said Graziers Bank of Virginia, so far as the same is applicable to it, and not inconsistent with the provisions of this act.

14. This act shall be in force from its passage, but may be repealed, altered or modified, at the pleasure of the general assembly. *Commencement*

CHAP. 76.—An ACT to legalize the use of certain State Securities held by the Bank of Pittsylvania as part of its Capital.

Passed March 21, 1862.

Whereas it is represented to the general assembly, that by agreement between the directors of the Bank of Pittsylvania and certain subscribers to the capital stock thereof, state securities, Virginia, and others of the Confederate States, to the amount of fifty thousand dollars, were received by said directors in payment of the shares of said subscribers to said capital stock, under certain stipulations with said subscribers in regard to the redemption of said stock: And for greater certainty as to the right of said bank to hold and regard said stock as part of its capital paid in: *Preamble*

1. Be it therefore enacted by the general assembly, that the said payment so received by the said directors, under said agreement and stipulations as aforesaid, shall be held and deemed a legal and valid payment of said shares, according to the true tenor and import of said agreement; and that the said stocks, until paid or converted into money at their par value, shall be held and deemed a part of the capital of said bank, in like manner as if said shares had been, at the time of said agreement, paid in ordinary currency. *Legalizing acts of directors* *Proviso*

2. This act shall be in force from its passage. *Commencement*

CHAP. 77.—An ACT to prevent certain violations of the Sabbath.

Passed March 12, 1862.

1. Be it enacted by the general assembly, that if a free person shall hunt, range after or shoot any game or wild fowl on Sunday, he shall be fined not less than five nor more than twenty dollars, and such offence shall moreover be deemed a breach of good behavior. *Hunting, &c. prohibited on Sunday*

2. The proceeding to recover the said fine may be according to the provisions of the forty-third chapter of the Code of Virginia, and it shall moreover be the duty of any justice, upon affidavit being made before him of the violation of this law, forthwith to issue his *Fines, how recovered*

warrant for the apprehension of the offender. Any justice before whom such offender may be brought, shall proceed as soon as practicable to enquire into the case, and if it appear on the proof that the person charged has violated this law, such justice may impose such fine upon him, or may recognize him, with security, to appear at the next term of the county or corporation court, as he may determine, to answer for the said offence and to satisfy the judgment which may be rendered against him therefor.

Recognizance, how given

3. Any person convicted of the above offence shall, in addition to the fine imposed upon him, be required by such court or justice to give a recognizance, with good security, for his good behavior for one year; or if he fail to give such security, be committed to jail for thirty days, unless it be sooner given. Such recognizance shall be forfeited if such person offend as aforesaid within the time limited therein.

Fines, how recoverable

4. One-half of any fine imposed and recovered under this law shall go to the informer, and the other half to the commonwealth.

Restraining clause

5. Nothing in this act shall be construed so as to prevent any person from shooting or otherwise killing, on Sunday, on or near his premises, any wild beast or bird destructive to domestic animals.

Commencement

6. This act shall be in force from its passage.

CHAP. 73.—An ACT to amend and re-enact the 8th section of an Ordinance entitled an Ordinance to provide against the Sacrifice of Property, and to suspend proceedings in certain cases, passed by the Convention of Virginia on the 30th day of April 1861.

Passed December 19, 1861.

Ordinance extended

Be it enacted by the general assembly, that the eighth section of the ordinance entitled an ordinance to provide against the sacrifice of property, and to suspend proceedings in certain cases, passed by the convention of Virginia on the thirtieth day of April eighteen hundred and sixty-one, be amended and re-enacted so as to read as follows:

Commencement

"§ 8. This ordinance shall remain in force until repealed."

MISCELLANEOUS.

CHAP. 79.—An ACT to suspend Sales and Legal Proceedings in certain cases, and to repeal an Ordinance to provide against the Sacrifice of Property, and to suspend proceedings in certain cases, passed on the 30th day of April 1861, by the Convention of Virginia.

Passed March 29, 1862.

1. Be it enacted by the general assembly, that except in cases herein after provided, no writ of elegit, fieri facias or venditioni exponas, other than in favor of the commonwealth, or against persons not residing in the commonwealth, shall hereafter be issued until otherwise provided by law. Nor shall there be any sales under deeds of trust executed prior to the thirtieth day of April eighteen hundred and sixty-one, or decrees, until otherwise provided by law, except in cases in which the parties interested consent thereto, and in cases in which any of said parties being incompetent, by reason of infancy or other disability, to give such consent, a court of competent jurisdiction shall determine that the interests of the parties would be promoted by such sale: provided, that this section shall not be construed to require the consent of persons not residing in this state, as necessary to any such sales: and provided further, that this section shall not apply to any attachment, or proceedings thereupon, authorized by chapter one hundred and fifty-one of the Code of Virginia (edition of eighteen hundred and sixty), except that no order of the court or justice against a resident garnishee for the payment of money due to, or the effects of the principal defendant, shall be enforced until otherwise provided by law. *Execution not to issue / Infancy or disability / Proviso*

2. On affidavit filed with the clerk of the court in which a judgment or decree for money has been rendered, or to which the justice belongs, when the judgment was rendered by a justice, setting forth the amount due thereupon, and the affiant's belief that the person against whom such judgment or decree has been rendered is removing or intends to remove his own estate, or the proceeds of the sale of his property, or a material part of such estate or proceeds, out of this state, the clerk of such court in which such judgment is, or the justice rendering such judgment, shall issue an execution of fieri facias upon such judgment or decree for the amount thereof, endorsing such credits thereon as by the said affidavit may be admitted. Upon the motion of the defendant in such execution, the said court, if it be of opinion that said execution was issued upon false suggestions, or without sufficient cause, shall quash the same: provided the plaintiff in such execution has had at least ten days' previous notice of such motion; and such notice, when given to the said plaintiff and to the officer in whose hands the execution is, shall stay any sale under such execution until the said motion is determined; but this stay shall not continue beyond the day specified in the notice for the motion, unless the motion be duly made to the court. Any property seized under this section may be retained by *Execution, how issued / How quashed / Property seized, how retained*

or returned to the defendant, on his giving bond with condition to abide by and perform the order or judgment of the court on the motion to quash the execution; or in case no motion be made, to pay the plaintiff the sum due on such execution. The bond shall be taken by the officer levying the execution, with good security, payable to the plaintiff, in a penalty double the sum appearing to be due on the execution.

<small>Exceptional cases, which may be tried by a jury</small>

3. Except in prosecutions on behalf of the commonwealth, actions of detinue, unlawful entry or detainer, and suits wherein attachments shall be sued out under the provisions of chapter one hundred and fifty-one of the Code of Virginia (edition of the year eighteen hundred and sixty), in which said prosecutions, actions, suits and at-

<small>Other cases not to be tried</small>

tachments, trials may be had as heretofore, there shall be no trial of any cause requiring the intervention of a jury, nor of warrants upon small claims before a justice of the peace or other officer, except with the consent of the parties thereto: provided, however, that the court for the probate of a will may, as provided by the said Code of Vir-

<small>Issues out of chancery Writs of ad quod damnum</small>

ginia, order a trial by jury, and that issues may be ordered by courts of equity and tried, and writs of ad quod damnum awarded and executed, as now authorized by law.

<small>Cases of misdemeanor</small>

4. In cases of misdemeanor, juries may be summoned from the bystanders or vicinage; and with the consent of the party prosecuted he may be tried by the court.

<small>Limitation</small>

5. The time which has elapsed since the thirtieth day of April eighteen hundred and sixty-one, and the time during which this act is in force, shall not be computed in any case where an action is required to be brought or other proceedings to be had, or acts to be done within a certain time now prescribed by law.

<small>Liabilities of public officers</small>

6. This act shall not apply to liabilities on the part of public officers or their sureties, or to causes of action which have arisen since the thirtieth day of April eighteen hundred and sixty-one, or which may hereafter arise, or to debts or liabilities to the commonwealth,

<small>Interest, when collected</small>

nor to the annual collection of interest now due or hereafter accruing on any debt or obligation which existed on the said thirtieth day of April eighteen hundred and sixty-one; and the courts are authorized and empowered to hear and determine all claims or demands for such interest, and to enforce the same by ordinary process of law; and no bond, note, bill, acceptance, obligation or undertaking, the consideration of which in whole or in part is a debt, obligation or undertaking which existed on the thirtieth day of April eighteen hundred and sixty-one, shall be held or considered as a cause of action there-

<small>Interest and alimony</small>

after arising; and nothing in this act shall be held to apply to any provision by will, deed, judgment or decree, for the payment of interest or alimony for the support or benefit of infants or females, so as to require the parties entitled thereto to apply to the court in any case where they have an existing remedy by execution, enforcement of the deed of trust, or otherwise.

7. The payment of such interest for which no adequate remedy has been provided, may be enforced by petition or motion before a court or justice of competent jurisdiction, upon ten days' notice from the plaintiff to the defendant, and the clerk of the court or the justice of the peace rendering such judgment, shall issue an execution for such amount of interest and cost of recovery, without affecting the principal of the debt. The officer to whom such execution may be directed shall make due return of the said execution to the clerk's office of the county or corporation of such court, or of the county in which such justice may reside, in sixty days from the day on which it was issued. The clerk or justice of the peace shall endorse on such execution "No security to be taken." There shall be no formal pleadings in such cases, and the issue, if there be any, shall be whether the interest be due or not, and the same shall be determined by the court; and such petition or motion may be repeated from time to time, as further interest may become due. In rendering which judgment the instrument, on the interest of which said judgment was rendered, shall be specially described in said judgment. *Payment of interest, how enforced* *Execution, how directed* *No security to be taken*

8. Be it further enacted, that the ordinance entitled an ordinance to provide against the sacrifice of property, and to suspend proceedings in certain cases, passed by the convention of Virginia on the thirtieth day of April eighteen hundred and sixty-one, and all acts amendatory thereof, be, and the same is hereby repealed; but such repeal shall not affect any right established, accrued or accruing under, or remedy or relief provided by the second, third and seventh sections of said ordinance; nor shall this act be construed to repeal or in any wise affect the eleventh section of chapter twenty-nine of the Code of Virginia, edition of eighteen hundred and sixty. *Ordinance repealed*

9. Be it further enacted, that no creditor shall have the benefit of the provisions of the exceptions of this act, who shall refuse to receive payment of his debt, or of any interest which may have accrued thereon, the recovery of which is herein before permitted, when the same has been tendered prior to the institution of the suit, in such currency as is receivable in payments to the state.

10. This act shall be in force from its passage. *Commencement*

CHAP. 80.—An ACT to provide for the Trial of Persons charged with Offences committed in Counties in possession of the Enemy or threatened with immediate Invasion.

Passed March 27, 1862.

When county in possession of or threatened by enemy

1. Be it enacted by the general assembly, that whenever any county or corporation in this state shall be in the possession of the enemy, or shall be threatened with invasion, so as to make it probable that the jurisdiction of the courts thereof cannot be safely exercised therein, it shall be the duty of the judge of the circuit to which such county belongs, and any judge of the state, if there be no judge of such circuit, or he shall refuse, or be unable to act, shall be empowered to cause all persons charged with felony in such county or corporation, to be brought before him, by warrant directed to any officer in the commonwealth, to be by him executed, and to commit him for examination before an examining court of some county or corporation not in the possession of the enemy, or threatened with invasion, the most convenient to that where the offence shall have been committed.

Powers of judge of circuit

How person charged with crime, to be committed

Examining court

2. The said examining court shall proceed in the cases of all such persons in like manner as if the offence had been committed in the county or corporation wherein the said examining court shall be, and may remand any such person for trial in the circuit court of said county or corporation, and the said circuit court and its officers shall proceed therein in the same manner as in other cases remanded for trial in the said circuit court under existing laws.

Venue, how changed

3. In all cases of felonies, the judge of the circuit court of any such county or corporation as shall be in the possession of the enemy, or shall be threatened with invasion, so as to make it probable the jurisdiction of the courts thereof cannot be safely exercised therein, or the said court in vacation or in term, upon motion of the commonwealth's attorney or of the defendant, or for good cause, may order the venue for the trial of any such case to be changed to some other circuit court.

Where confined

4. When any such action shall be taken as is provided for in either of the foregoing sections, the person charged with the offence shall be thereafter confined in the jail of the county to which the case shall be removed.

Commencement

5. This act shall be in force from its passage.

MISCELLANEOUS.

CHAP. 81.—An ACT to extend the time for the exercise of certain Civil Rights and Remedies.

Passed March 14, 1862.

1. Be it enacted by the general assembly, that the period between the seventeenth day of April Anno Domini one thousand eight hundred and sixty-one, and four months after the ratification of a treaty of peace between the Confederate States of America and the United States of America, shall be excluded from the computation of the time within which, by the terms or operation of any statute or rule of law, it may be necessary to do any act or to commence any action or other proceeding to preserve or to prevent the loss of any civil right or remedy. *Act of limitation*

2. This act shall be in force from its passage. *Commencement*

CHAP. 82.—An ACT to amend and re-enact an Ordinance extending the Jurisdiction of the County Courts in certain cases, passed by the Convention on the 26th day of June 1861.

Passed March 10, 1862.

1. Be it enacted by the general assembly, that an ordinance passed by the convention on the twenty-sixth day of June eighteen hundred and sixty-one, be amended and re-enacted so as to read as follows: *Ordinance amended*

"When the court of any county shall fail to meet for the transaction of business, or the people thereof or any of them shall be prevented from attending thereupon by reason of the public enemy, the court of the county next thereto, where such obstruction does not exist, and the clerk thereof, or the circuit court of the city of Richmond and the clerk thereof, shall have jurisdiction of all matters, and authority to do and perform all acts which, as the law now is, are referable to the court or to the clerk of the county so obstructed." *Courts, jurisdiction of*

2. This act shall be in force from its passage. *Commencement*

CHAP. 83.—An ACT to protect Loyal Citizens whose property may be sold by Officers under illegal process.

Passed March 5, 1862.

Whereas it is represented to the general assembly of Virginia, that certain persons have established, since the adoption of the ordinance withdrawing the state of Virginia from the government of the United States, a usurped government within the limits of Virginia, *Preamble* separate from the existing government, and that certain persons are holding the offices of sheriffs, clerks, constables and justices of the peace, under color of authority from such usurped government, or under elections by its authority, or have otherwise recognized its authority by taking an oath to support such usurped government, or otherwise adhering to or supporting its authority: And whereas levies and sales of property have been made, by virtue of executions and other process issued by such clerks and justices, and the same sold by such sheriffs and constables, to the great prejudice of good and loyal citizens of Virginia: And whereas other like execution and process may be issued by such clerks and justices, and other sales of property may hereafter be made by virtue thereof, by such sheriffs and constables, to the like great prejudice of good and loyal citizens of Virginia:

Penalty for issuing process

1. Be it therefore enacted by the general assembly, that any such clerk or justice who may have issued, or may hereafter issue, any such execution or other process, by virtue of which property may have been or may be hereafter sold, and any person for whose benefit such sale may have been or may be hereafter made, and any such sheriff or constable who has made such sale, or may hereafter make such sale, and the sureties of any such clerk, sheriff or constable, and any or all purchasers of property so heretofore or hereafter sold, and the personal representatives of such person, officer or purchaser, shall be jointly and severally liable to any citizen of Virginia, loyal to the existing and true government thereof, and to the government of the Confederate States, whose property has been or may hereafter

Penalty on sheriff or constable

be so illegally sold, or to his personal representatives, for double the value of such property, with interest thereon at the rate of six per centum per annum from the time of the seizure or sale of such pro-

Judgment, how obtained

perty: and judgment may be obtained therefor in any court of record in this commonwealth, against such clerks, sheriffs, constables and justices as may have issued such executions or other process and

Sureties liable

executed the same, and the sureties of such clerks, sheriffs and constables and beneficiaries, or purchaser or purchasers, or any one or more of them, upon motion in such court, upon ten days' previous personal notice, or upon thirty days' notice published in any newspaper published in Richmond city, or any other newspaper published in this state. But in no case shall there be more than one satisfaction for the same money or thing.

Rights of loyal citizens protected

2. The remedy hereby given shall not prejudice the right of such loyal citizen from taking possession of or otherwise recovering possession of such property, or any part thereof; or if such possession should be obtained, the right of such loyal citizen to the benefit of such liability imposed by this act shall not be prejudiced thereby; and the right to obtain, or when obtained to enforce such judgment, shall not be impaired by reason of the recovery of the possession of the property so sold.

3. A lien is hereby created and declared to exist on the real and personal estate of the persons against whom such liability may exist, from the passage of this act. *Lien created*

4. No record proof shall be required of the election or appointment of the pretended officers herein referred to; but acting in such offices, and otherwise recognizing such usurped government, shall be deemed sufficient. *Record proof not required*

5. For such sales made before the passage of this act, the persons who would be liable under its provisions may, within sixty days from the passage of this act, restore the property sold, or pay to the person injured the full value of such property, and become thereby discharged of the liability under this act; otherwise, upon their failure to do so, the liability shall exist. *Property, how restored*

6. This act shall be in force from its passage. *Commencement*

CHAP. 84.—An ACT to prevent the unnecessary Consumption of Grain by Distillers and other Manufacturers of Spirituous and Malt Liquors.

Passed March 12, 1862.

1. Be it enacted by the general assembly, that it shall not be lawful for any person hereafter to make or cause to be made any whisky, or other spirituous or malt liquors, out of any corn, wheat, rye or other grain; and any person so offending shall be deemed guilty of a misdemeanor, and upon conviction thereof shall be fined for every offence not less than one hundred dollars nor more than five thousand dollars, and be subject to imprisonment in the county jail not exceeding twelve months, at the discretion of the court. *Distillation prohibited* *Penalties*

2. Be it further enacted, that every day which any distillery, or any other machine, implement or structure for the manufacture of spirits shall, in violation of the foregoing section, be in operation, shall be taken and held to be a separate offence within the meaning of this act. *What constitute separate offence*

3. Be it further enacted, that in addition to the penalty prescribed by the first section of this act for a violation of its provisions, the distillery or other machine and implements used therewith for the purpose of making liquor, in violation of this act, shall be forfeited to the commonwealth; and it shall be the duty of the court, in pronouncing judgment upon any conviction under this act, to add the judgment of forfeiture, and to order the sheriff to make sale of such distillery or other machine and implements, by such execution as issues for the commonwealth in other cases. And it shall be the *Distillery and implements, how forfeited*

duty of the sheriff to pay the proceeds of such sale into the treasury of the commonwealth, after deducting to himself five per cent. commission.

4. Be it further enacted, that as soon as any person may be presented or indicted for any violation of the provisions of this act, the court of any county or corporation in which said proceeding is had, shall immediately issue an order to the sergeant or sheriff of such county or corporation, directing him, unless within ten days thereafter the defendant shall enter into bond with sufficient security, in the penalty of one thousand dollars, conditioned to answer the judgment of the court, and also to have forthcoming, when required by law, any property alleged to be forfeited under this act, then at once to seize and take possession of the spirituous and malt liquors, grain, distilling machine and other implements used or employed in making liquor in violation of this act, and the grain, the distilling of which is hereby prohibited, and hold the same subject to the judgment of said court as herein provided.

Bond, how given

When liquor, &c. to be seized

5. Be it further enacted, that all corn, wheat or other grain purchased or obtained for the manufacture of liquor, in violation of the provisions of the first section of this act, shall be forfeited to the commonwealth. And it shall be the duty of all sheriffs, constables, commissioners of the revenue and other officers of the commonwealth, to make diligent enquiry into all violations of this act, and report the same promptly to the attorney for the commonwealth or any justice of the peace of the county in which the offence may be committed. If any officer shall fail to perform the duties required of him by this act, he shall be fined at the discretion of a jury for each neglect or failure, not less than ten nor more than five hundred dollars.

When grain to be forfeited

Penalty on officer

6. And be it further enacted, after such presentment shall have been made, if the defendant should continue to operate his distillery, it shall be the duty of the sheriff or sergeant to seize and take possession of the grain, distillery and liquors, unless he shall enter into bond in the penalty of one thousand dollars, with the clerk of the court in which said presentment is depending, conditioned that he will cease the distillation of corn, wheat, rye or other grain.

7. All prosecutions under this act shall be tried at the first term of the court in which they may be instituted, unless good cause be shown for a continuance.

Prosecutions, when tried

8. This act shall be in force within ten days from and after its passage, and continue in operation during the present war.

Commencement

MISCELLANEOUS.

CHAP. 85.—An ACT to amend and re-enact the act entitled an act providing for the employment of Negro Convicts on the Public Works, passed April 7th, 1858.

Passed December 6, 1861.

Be it enacted, that the act entitled an act providing for the employment of negro convicts on the public works, passed April seventh, eighteen hundred and fifty-eight, be so amended as to read as follows: *Act of 1858 amended*

1. Be it enacted by the general assembly, that the governor of this commonwealth shall at his discretion employ upon the public works owned wholly or in part by the commonwealth, all or any free negroes heretofore or who may hereafter be sentenced to confinement in the penitentiary, during the whole or any portion of the term for which they may be so sentenced, or cause the same to be hired to the proprietor of any iron works engaged in making iron to be used in manufacturing cannon or other munitions of war for the use of the commonwealth of Virginia or of the confederate government, or any salt works or any other company engaged in the manufacture of iron, or any internal improvement company. *When free negroes to be employed on public works*

2. That the governor of the commonwealth shall, at his discretion, likewise employ upon the said public works, all or any slaves who have been heretofore sentenced by the court, to sale and transportation beyond the limits of the United States, or who may hereafter be sentenced by the court to sale and transportation beyond the limits of the Confederate States, or who have been or may hereafter be convicted of an offence, the punishment of which has been or may be commuted by the governor to sale and transportation; or cause the same to be hired to the proprietor of any iron works engaged in making iron to be used in manufacturing cannon or other munitions of war, for the use of the commonwealth of Virginia or of the confederate government; or any salt works, or any other company engaged in the manufacture of iron, or any internal improvement company. *Slaves sentenced, when to be employed* *Iron works*

3. That the said convicts shall be employed upon the said works and in said iron works or other works, upon such terms and under such rules and regulations as the governor may prescribe, in order to promote the efficient direction of their labor to insure their safe keeping: provided, that in every case they shall be so employed, without any expense to the commonwealth for transporting them to and from work, or for maintenance, supervising and guarding them, except that when employed on a work owned wholly by the commonwealth, such expenses may be paid out of any funds applicable to the construction or repair of such work. *Rules to be prescribed by the governor*

4. This act shall be in force from its passage. *Commencement*

CHAP. 86.—An ACT to prevent the Escape of Slaves in Tide Water Counties.

Passed March 31, 1862.

Powers of county courts

1. Be it enacted by the general assembly, that the county courts of all the tide water counties shall have power, upon the application of any three freeholders of their respective counties, to adopt such measures as in their opinion may be necessary to prevent the escape of slaves in boats to the public enemy: and for this purpose may direct all boats to be removed from the water and secured in some safe place; and when necessary may order the said boats to be destroyed, after having them valued by three discreet and disinterested citizens. The value of said boats, upon proper proof exhibited, shall be paid to the owners thereof, out of the county levy: provided, that before any proceedings by the county courts under this act, all the justices of the peace of said counties respectively shall be duly summoned for that purpose, and a majority shall be present.

Boats, how destroyed

Justices to be summoned

Commencement

2. This act shall be in force from its passage.

CHAP. 87.—An ACT providing for Annual Sessions of the General Assembly.

Passed March 27, 1862.

Preamble

Whereas annual instead of biennial sessions of the legislature are ordained by the amended constitution of Virginia, proposed by the late convention, and ratification of said constitution at the late election may be ascertained and proclaimed by the governor, whereby legislation may become necessary: Therefore,

Act of 1853 amended

1. Be it enacted by the general assembly, that the first section of the act passed the fifth of April eighteen hundred and fifty-three, entitled an act to amend the first section of chapter fifteen of the Code of Virginia, fixing the time and place for the meeting of the general assembly, be so amended and re-enacted as to read as follows:

When general assembly to meet

"The general assembly shall meet on the first Monday in December in the year eighteen hundred and sixty-two, and every year thereafter. It shall sit at the capitol in the city of Richmond, but may, during a session, or at the end thereof, adjourn to meet at any other place."

Commencement

2. When the governor, in pursuance of the schedule to the amended constitution and form of government for this commonwealth, proposed and submitted by the late convention of Virginia

to the voters for ratification or rejection, shall ascertain the result of the votes to be a majority in favor of ratification, and shall proclaim said amended constitution as ratified and adopted, and not till then, this act shall be in force.

CHAP. 88.—An ACT to authorize Vacancies to be filled pro tempore in certain Offices, after the Ratification of the Amended Constitution.

Passed March 27, 1862.

1. Be it enacted by the general assembly, that in the event of the ratification of the constitution proposed by the late convention of Virginia, and the proclamation of the result by the governor, if any vacancy exist or occur in the office of constable, surveyor, commissioner of the revenue or overseer of the poor, in any county or corporation, it shall be lawful for the court of the county or corporation to fill such vacancy, pro tempore, by the appointment of a suitable person. Such person shall give bond and surety, and qualify for his office according to existing laws, and shall thereupon be entitled to all the rights and be subject to all the duties and liabilities incident to the office. The person appointed under this act may be superseded in office by appointment under such laws as the general assembly may hereafter enact. *Vacancies in offices of constable, &c. how filled*

2. Be it further enacted, that in the event specified in the foregoing section, if any vacancy exist or occur in the office of clerk, or attorney for the commonwealth, it shall be lawful for the court of the county or corporation, if the vacancy be of an office of the county or corporation court; and for the circuit court, or the judge thereof in vacation, if the vacancy be of an office of the circuit court, within the terms of the said amended constitution, to fill such vacancy, pro tempore, by the appointment of a suitable person, who shall be removable and be superseded in office by appointment under such laws as the general assembly may hereafter enact. Such person appointed under this act, shall give bond and surety, and qualify for his office according to existing laws, and shall thereupon be entitled to all the rights and be subject to all the duties and liabilities incident to the office. *Clerk and attorney for commonwealth*

3. This act shall be in force from and after the proclamation of the governor announcing the ratification or adoption of the amended constitution, and not till then. *Commencement*

CHAP. 89.—An ACT to Abolish the Office of Superintendent of Weights and Measures, and transfer the duties of that office to the Register of the Land Office.

Passed March 31, 1862.

Office of superintendent of weights and measures abolished

1. Be it enacted by the general assembly, that the office of superintendent of weights and measures be and the same is hereby abolished; and that the duties required of the superintendent shall be transferred to and performed by the register of the land office for the time being, without additional compensation.

Commencement

2. This act shall take effect from the first day of April one thousand eight hundred and sixty-two.

CHAP. 90.—An ACT authorizing the erection of a Gallery in the Hall now occupied by the Confederate States Congress.

Passed March 31, 1862.

Commissioners appointed

Gallery

1. Be it enacted by the general assembly, that James Lyons, Wyndham Robertson, John O. Steger and Thomas H. Wynne, or a majority of them, be and they are hereby appointed commissioners to contract for the erection of a gallery in the hall now occupied by the house of representatives of the Confederate States, and to cut a door in the wall at the foot of the steps now leading from the clerk's office of that house, so that persons can ascend into said gallery from the hall in which the statue of Washington is, or to cut a door elsewhere, if they should deem proper.

Cost, how paid

2. When the said work shall be completed, the said commissioners shall certify the cost of the same to the auditor of public accounts, who shall thereupon draw his warrant upon the treasury for the same, out of any money in the treasury not otherwise appropriated.

Commencement

3. This act shall be in force from its passage.

CHAP. 91.—An ACT changing the Lines of Pulaski and Wythe Counties.

Passed March 10, 1862.

County lines changed

1. Be it enacted by the general assembly, that so much of the line that divides the county of Pulaski from the county of Wythe, where the said line intersects with the second corner of Joshua A. Holmes' land, described as two white oaks on a ridge, shall be and

the same is hereby changed, so that the dwelling house and plantation of the said Joshua A. Holmes shall be included within the county of Pulaski.

2. This act shall be in force from its passage. Commencement

CHAP. 92.—An ACT requiring the Penitentiary Storekeeper to make Quarterly Reports to the Board of Directors.

Passed March 10, 1862.

1. Be it enacted by the general assembly, that the penitentiary storekeeper shall be and he is hereby required to render to the board of directors of the penitentiary quarterly statements of the transactions of the entire subjects over which he has control, the first quarter commencing on the first day of April eighteen hundred and sixty-two; and in case of his failure to do so for ten days after the end of each quarter, he shall forfeit his entire commissions for each quarter in which he shall fail to make such statement. Quarterly statements, how made

2. This act shall be in force from its passage. Commencement

PRIVATE OR LOCAL ACTS.

CHAP. 93.—An ACT to amend an act entitled an act amending the Charter of the Town of Danville, passed March 4th, 1854, and incorporating into one the subsequent acts amendatory thereof.

Passed March 7, 1862.

1. Be it enacted by the general assembly, that the territory com- *Charter amended* prehended and included in the following boundaries, viz: Beginning *Corporate limits* at a point on Dan river, directly opposite a spring called Lynn's spring, on the canal; thence, by said spring, in a direct line, to the northwest corner of the public burying ground; thence, along the western line of said burying ground, to the southwest corner of the same; thence, in a direct line, to the southwest corner of William T. Sutherlin's lot, including the same, and following the line of the said lot until it reaches the southeast corner thereof; thence, in a direct line, to the junction of the road leading by Nathaniel T. Green's with Calhoun street, leading by the house lately owned by R. L. Downes, and now by Thomas Grasty; thence, along the southwest side of said street, to the southwest corner of the said Grasty's lot, in the line of the said Nathaniel T. Green; thence, along the said Grasty's southern line, to the rear of his lot; thence, with the back line of said lot, until it reaches the northeast corner of the same; thence, in a direct line, to the southern bank of Dan river, to a point where once stood a large poplar tree, which marked the northeast corner of the town; thence, up the southern bank of the said river, as it meanders, to the beginning—shall continue to be the town of Danville: and the white inhabitants within said boundaries, and their successors, shall be a corporation, under the name and style of The Town of Danville; and the fifty-fourth and fifty-sixth chapters of the Code of Virginia, so far as they are consistent with this act, shall be applicable to said corporation and to the council of said town.

2. There shall continue to be for the said corporation a court of *Municipal authority* record, which shall be called "the court of hustings for the town of Danville;" and the same shall be held by the mayor and aldermen of said town, or any three or more of them, except where it shall be otherwise provided. The monthly terms of said court shall be held *Time of holding courts* on the Thursday before the third Monday in each month, and the quarterly terms thereof shall be in the months of March, June, August and November.

TOWNS.

Jurisdiction

3. The jurisdiction of said court, except as to matters of police, which shall belong to the council, shall correspond with that of the county courts as established by law; and the said court shall continue to have jurisdiction, and the said mayor and aldermen shall continue each to have the powers of a justice of the peace, not only within the said corporate limits, but also for the space of one mile without and around the limits of said town, in all matters arising within the said town or the said space of one mile, according to the laws of the commonwealth and the ordinances of the town, and shall execute the same in like manner and under like responsibilities, and receive the like compensation for services rendered by them in court, as the justices of the peace of the county courts within this commonwealth receive; to be paid by said corporation: provided, however, that not more than three aldermen shall receive compensation for any one day of such services in court, unless such court be a court of oyer and terminer. And the said aldermen shall classify themselves for services in court, in like manner as justices of the peace in counties are classified by law; and any presentment in said court by a grand jury for an offence against the said laws, committed within the jurisdiction of said court, may be presented in said court in like manner, and like proceedings be had thereon as in the county court of Pittsylvania; and the said court of hustings shall bear the same relation to the circuit court for the town of Danville as the county court of said county bears to the circuit court thereof; and appeals may be taken, and writs of error, supersedeas, certiorari, and any other judicial writ may be sued out and prosecuted in like manner as is done in the county courts of the commonwealth.

Compensation

Delegated powers

4. The court of hustings shall have the sole power to settle tavern rates, and to license, in the manner prescribed by law, tavern keepers and retailers of wine, ardent spirits, or a mixture of either, within the limits of said town.

Corporate powers, where vested

5. There shall be a board, called "the council of the town of Danville;" which shall be composed of eight members, any five of whom shall constitute a quorum for the transaction of business.

6. There shall be held annually an election on the third Thursday in May, or in case of a failure from any cause to hold the election on that day, on such day thereafter as the council shall appoint, to elect a mayor, nine aldermen, eight councilmen, a sergeant, treasurer and a commissioner of the revenue for the corporation.

Election of clerk

7. A clerk for the court of hustings shall be elected every sixth year, and an attorney for the commonwealth in the same court, every fourth year, on the day on which the election shall be held for the officers provided for in the section immediately preceding this.

8. In all elections for officers of the corporation, every free white male citizen of the commonwealth, twenty-one years of age, who

shall have resided in the said town for the space of twelve months next immediately preceding such election, and paid the corporation tax of the preceding year, if he shall have been assessed with any, shall have the right to vote, and be eligible as a member of the council or of the court of hustings; and in all other elections, those who are qualified to vote for members of the general assembly shall be permitted to vote.

9. The said elections shall be held at the courthouse of said town, or at such other place in the corporation as the council shall appoint. The council shall in all cases cause to be published due notice of the time and place for holding such elections, for at least two weeks in one or more newspapers published in the said town, if any such newspaper be then in course of publication in said town.

10. For superintending said elections, the council shall, previous thereto, appoint three commissioners, any two of whom may act; and said commissioners shall have such powers and perform such duties as are prescribed by the sixth section of chapter seven of the Code of Virginia, and shall take the oath required in the seventh section of said chapter, a certificate of which shall be returned to the clerk of the council, to be preserved in his office. The second section of said chapter shall apply to the poll at such election.

11. It shall be the duty of the sergeant, either by himself or deputy, under the superintendence and control of said commissioners (after having taken the oath prescribed by the tenth section of the said chapter, a certificate of which shall be returned to the clerk of the council), to conduct the said election. He shall cause the polls to be publicly opened; proclaim and see recorded the votes admitted by the commissioners; preserve order and remove force. He shall employ writers, at such rate of compensation as the council may direct; and such writers shall respectively take an oath, to be administered by the sergeant or deputy, to record the votes faithfully and impartially. He shall deliver to each writer a poll book for those officers as to whom such writer is to record the votes, and each writer shall enter the name of each voter in a column to be headed "Names of voters;" and on a line with such name he shall enter the initial letters of the name of such voter, or a cross mark, if the commissioner so direct, under the name of each person for whom he votes for any of said offices. The said votes shall be given as prescribed by the fourth section of the third article of the constitution; but at the time the vote is given the officer shall receive from each voter a paper or ticket (with his name written on it), which shall specify the names of the persons for whom he votes, and for what offices.

12. After the names of all persons qualified, who have offered to vote within the time prescribed by law, have been entered, the poll shall be concluded, and as soon thereafter as practicable the commis-

sioners and officers conducting the election shall examine the polls, strike therefrom the votes, above one, of any person who has voted more than once, attach to the poll a list of the votes stricken therefrom, with the reasons therefor, and certify the correctness of the poll so taken.

13. The certificate of said officer, with the poll books, of the election of the clerk of the court of hustings and attorney for the commonwealth, shall be delivered by them to the clerk of the hustings court, to be preserved in his office; and their certificates and the poll books of all other elections shall be delivered to the clerk of the council, to be laid before that body, and preserved in his office.

14. In all elections for clerk of the hustings court and attorney for the commonwealth, in case two or more persons shall have the highest and an equal number of votes, the officer conducting the elections shall decide forthwith by lot to whom the certificate shall be given; and he shall forthwith set up at the front door of the courthouse a notice of the result of said election.

15. The council may decide between two or more persons having the highest and an equal number of votes for the same municipal office, which of them is elected; prescribe the manner of determining contested elections for such offices in cases not provided for in this act; and in regard to any other question in respect to which it directs a poll to be taken, it may make such rules and regulations as it may deem proper.

16. The mayor, aldermen and members of the council, who may be in office at the time their successors are elected, shall continue in office until such successors, or a legal quorum thereof, are qualified; and all other persons holding office mentioned in the sixth and seventh sections of this act, shall continue in office until their successors shall qualify.

Vacancies, how filled

17. All vacancies in any of said offices, occasioned by death, resignation or otherwise, shall be filled by a new election for the unexpired term thereof. To fill a vacancy in the office of the clerk of the court of hustings and attorney for the commonwealth, the writ shall be issued by the said court, directed to the sergeant of the corporation, who shall hold the election under the superintendence of commissioners to be appointed by the court, any two of whom may act. In all other cases, the writ for a new election shall be issued by the council, and the election shall be held by the sergeant, under the superintendence of commissioners in like manner appointed by them.

Form of election

The said elections shall be held and conducted, and the returns made and contests conducted and decided in the same manner as in general elections of said officers. In case of a vacancy in the office of clerk of the court of hustings, the court may appoint a clerk pro tempore.

18. The mayor, aldermen and members of the council, within one week after their election, or as soon thereafter as convenient, shall make oath or affirmation before the mayor, or an alderman for the time being, faithfully and impartially to discharge the duties of their respective offices, and shall take the other oaths of office prescribed by the Code of Virginia.

19. The council shall, immediately after qualifying, or as soon thereafter as may be, convene, and elect a president and a clerk. The president shall be one of their own body, and shall preside at all times when present, and in his absence the council may elect a president pro tempore. The clerk shall keep a faithful record of the proceedings of the council, and in another book, to be kept for the purpose, a fair copy of every ordinance, by-law and regulation which may be made and adopted by the same. All ordinances, by-laws, rules and regulations of the council shall be signed by the president and attested by the clerk.

20. The mayor shall be the chief executive officer of the corporation; preside in the hustings court when present; exercise control and superintendence over the police officers, and administer the police regulations of the town. And should a vacancy in the office of mayor occur from any cause, its duties shall devolve on the senior alderman until, by a new election, such vacancy shall be filled; and to determine who is the senior alderman, it is hereby declared that he who received the highest number of votes at the general election shall be so regarded; and should two or more have received the highest and an equal number of votes, then it shall be decided by lot who is the senior.

21. The council shall have power to purchase, receive, lease and hold lands, tenements, goods and chattels, either in fee simple or any less estate therein, either for the use of the said town, or in trust for the benefit of any persons or associations therein; and the same to let, sell, or grant or assign again; to purchase a quantity of land, not exceeding fifty acres, outside of said town, for the purpose of a cemetery, with jurisdiction over the same, for its proper use and preservation; to erect a town hall and market house, and regulate the same; a work house, jail and other buildings deemed necessary and convenient for the said town; to establish and organize fire companies, and purchase engines; to regulate and graduate the streets and alleys of said town, and pave the same; to have the footways or sidewalks of the streets paved at the expense of the owners or occupiers of the lots or parts of lots: and in case they or any of them shall neglect or refuse to pave the same when required, it shall be lawful for the council to have the same paved, and recover the expense thereof, for the use of the town, before the mayor or any alderman of the corporation: and in all cases where a tenant shall be re-

quired to pave in front of the property in his or her occupation, the expense of pavement shall be a good offset against so much of the rent as he shall have paid towards such pavement. The council shall have power to open and establish new streets and alleys in the said town, whenever it shall think the public convenience requires it; grant or refuse licenses to auctioneers, hawkers and peddlers, keepers of bowling alleys, or for theatrical performances, or for any other public show or performance to be used or exhibited in said town, or in one mile thereof; to impose a tax on any such license, in addition to any tax paid to the state; and to adopt in all such cases such rules and regulations as it may deem proper; to prevent the practice of running horses and firing guns in said town; to levy a fine on those who create a nuisance, public or private; to lay and collect taxes on the real estate in said town, in proportion to its value, such value to be ascertained in such manner as the council may prescribe: provided, that the same does not exceed one-half of one per centum on each hundred dollars value; to tax slaves in said town above the age of twelve years, and such other property therein as it may deem proper; to tax dogs in such manner as they may prescribe; to tax the occupiers of houses and all free male persons in the town above the age of sixteen years: and in order the better to determine what persons are liable to taxation in said town, it is hereby declared that all tithable persons resident in said town on the first day of February shall be subject to taxation the then current year. The council shall also have power to appoint all officers necessary for conducting the affairs of the corporation, not otherwise provided for in this act; to take from the treasurer, and the sergeant as collector of the corporation taxes, bonds with security in such penalties and with such conditions as to the council may seem fit, payable to the town of Danville; and to make such by-laws, rules and regulations for the government of said town, as shall not be contrary to the constitution and laws of the Confederate States or of this state; and to enforce the observance of all such by-laws, rules and regulations, by reasonable fines and penalties, not exceeding for any one offence the sum of twenty dollars, to be recovered with costs, before the mayor or any alderman of said town; such fines to be paid into the treasury of the town; and by corporal punishment when other than white persons are offenders.

Delegated powers

22. The council may, in the name and for the use and benefit of said corporation, subscribe to the stock of any company incorporated for the purpose of constructing any improved or artificial road to the said town: provided the question of subscription shall have been first submitted to the qualified voters of said town, and two-thirds of the persons voting upon the said question shall have approved the same. It may also contract loans and issue certificates of debt, and provide a sinking fund for the payment of the same; but no loan contracted shall be irredeemable for a longer period than thirty-four

years, nor shall the outstanding debt of the said corporation at any one time exceed the sum of seventy-five thousand dollars.

23. The council may grant compensation, out of the funds of the town, to the mayor; which shall be fixed by law, and which shall not be increased or diminished during the term for which he is elected; to commissioners of the revenue, treasurer, and to any other officers appointed by their own body. They shall also make provision for the payment of such salary to the attorney for the commonwealth, and such compensation for ex-officio services, to the clerk of the hustings court and the sergeant of the corporation, as the said hustings court shall deem reasonable, the same having been certified to them by the direction of the said court. *Compensation*

24. The mayor and aldermen of the said town, when elected and qualified, shall be conservators of the peace within the jurisdiction prescribed by the third section of this act, and as such, exercise all the powers given to a conservator of the peace by chapter two hundred and one of the Code of Virginia. *Delegated powers*

25. The collector of the taxes of said town may distrain and sell therefor in like manner as a sheriff may distrain and sell for state taxes, and shall have in other respects like power to enforce the collection of the same; and there shall be a lien on real estate in said town for the taxes assessed thereon, from the first day of February in each year for which it was assessed. The council may require real estate in the said town, delinquent for the non-payment of taxes, to be sold for the same, with interest thereon, and such per centum as it may prescribe for charges, and it may regulate and prescribe the terms on which real estate so delinquent may be redeemed. *Delegated powers*

26. The sergeant of said corporation may appoint as many deputies as he may think the business and duties of his office require, to be approved by the court of hustings. He shall execute and return all process lawfully directed to him, and shall moreover be the collector of the state revenue in said town; and as such, shall have all the powers, and shall be subject to all the duties and liabilities of a sheriff, and be entitled to like compensation for his services therein as are prescribed by the Code of Virginia. And should the said sergeant, as the collector of the taxes of the said corporation, fail to collect and pay over the same at the time prescribed by the council of said town, he and his securities in the bond which he shall have given for that purpose, his and their executors and administrators, shall be subject to such proceedings, by motion or otherwise, before the court of hustings of said town, for enforcing the payment over of such taxes at the suit of said town, as are prescribed by the Code of Virginia in proceedings against sheriffs. *Delegated powers*

27. No person shall be capable of holding at the same time more *Proviso*

than one of the offices enumerated or mentioned in the sixth section of this act.

28. The corporation of the town of Danville shall have all the estates, rights, titles and privileges, all the funds, revenues and claims, and all the powers, capacities and immunities which were vested in, or conferred upon, or belonged or appertained to the corporation of the town of Danville, or to the mayor and commonalty of the town of Danville, by or under any acts of the general assembly heretofore passed, and not in conflict with this act.

Delegated powers

29. All the estates, rights, titles and privileges, and all the funds, revenues and claims of the town shall be under the care, management, control and disposition of the council, and all the corporate capacities, franchises and immunities of the town shall be exercised by the same, or under its authority, unless where it is otherwise expressly provided.

30. All acts and parts of acts coming within the purview of this act, are hereby repealed; but all rights accrued, proceedings had, and all claims and contracts under existing laws and ordinances now in force, shall not be affected thereby, but continue and remain as if this act had not been passed.

Commencement

31. This act shall be in force from its passage.

CHAP. 94.—An ACT to amend and re-enact the 1st section of the act entitled an act to extend the jurisdiction and enlarge the powers of the Corporation of the Borough of Norfolk, passed February 4th, 1818.

Passed March 29, 1862.

First section of act 1818 amended

1. Be it enacted by the general assembly, that the first section of the act entitled an act to extend the jurisdiction and enlarge the powers of the borough of Norfolk, passed February fourth, eighteen hundred and eighteen, be so amended and re-enacted as to read:

Jurisdiction extended

"§ 1. That the jurisdiction of the corporation of the city of Norfolk, of the mayor, recorder and aldermen thereof, as justices of the peace, and of the court of hustings, in all cases, civil and criminal, shall extend to all vessels, persons and things in the port or harbor, or on the Elizabeth river, and its intersecting water, from the southern limits of the navy yard on the southern, and for one mile from the city limits on the eastern branch of said river, to and in Hampton Roads, as far as Old Point Comfort, and for the space of one mile without and around any part of the eastern, northern and western boundaries of said city; and any presentment made by a grand jury in the said hustings court of said city, for an offence against the

Form of presentment

laws of the commonwealth, committed within the jurisdiction of said hustings court, may be prosecuted in said court, and the like proceedings be had therein as in the county courts of the commonwealth: provided, however, that nothing contained in this section shall be so construed as to infringe or impair the rights of the justices and the courts of Norfolk county and the city of Portsmouth, as by law established."

Proviso

2. This act shall be in force from its passage.

Commencement

CHAP. 95.—An ACT amending the Charter of the Town of Fredericksburg.

Passed January 8, 1862.

1. Be it enacted by the general assembly, that the police officers of the town of Fredericksburg shall be conservators of the peace in the said town, and in all criminal cases shall have the same powers, perform the same duties, be entitled to the same fees, and be subject to the same penalties that are prescribed by law to constables.

Delegated powers

Fees

2. This act shall be in force from its passage.

Commencement

CHAP. 96.—An ACT amending an act passed the 29th day of March 1861, entitled an act amending the Charter of the Town of Union in the County of Monroe.

Passed March 29, 1862.

Be it enacted by the general assembly, that the first, second and third sections of the act passed on the twenty-ninth day of March eighteen hundred and sixty-one, entitled an act amending the charter of the town of Union in the county of Monroe, be amended and re-enacted so as to read as follows:

Certain sections of act 1861 amended

1. Be it enacted by the general assembly, that the board of trustees of the town of Union in the county of Monroe shall annually appoint a sergeant of said town, whose duty it shall be to collect all the town taxes, levies and fines. He shall give bond and security, to be approved by the board, in the penalty of three thousand dollars, payable to the commonwealth, conditioned for the faithful performance of his duties as such sergeant, and shall take the several oaths prescribed by law for officers, to be administered by or in the presence of said board, a minute whereof shall be recorded by the board. And thereupon the said sergeant shall have all the powers in said town, and be liable to all the liabilities of a constable of a county; and may act in all civil and criminal cases within the said town of Union, to the same extent as a constable of a county; and

Delegated powers

Bond to be given

Delegated powers Liabilities

TOWNS.—PRIVILEGES, ETC.

Record preserved

his bond, when approved of as aforesaid, shall be recorded by the board, and filed in the clerk's office of the county court of Monroe county for safe keeping, and may be put in suit from time to time, in the same manner as constables' bonds are put in suit. Upon a failure to collect the taxes or fines of said town, and pay the same over according to law, or to collect and pay over all claims placed in his hands for collection as a constable, the board of trustees, or other person aggrieved, shall have power and authority to proceed upon said bond, in the circuit or county courts of the county of Monroe, by

Liable to taxation

motion or otherwise. All persons and property resident or situated in town on the first day of February, shall be liable to taxation for the current year.

Oath of office

2. That each member of said board shall be a conservator of the peace in said town, and for one mile around the same. The president of the board shall be mayor of the town, and as such, shall take the oath of office, and the oaths prescribed by law for other officers, before or in the presence of said board, of which a minute shall

Delegated powers

be made in the proceedings of the board. The mayor shall have all the jurisdiction of a justice of the peace in both civil and criminal cases, within the limits of the said town of Union, reserving to the parties the same right of appeal from his judgment that they have

Fees

from the judgment of a justice. He shall also be entitled to the same fees for taking depositions, the acknowledgment of deeds, and so forth, which are allowed to justices, and may be allowed a sum for his services by the board, not exceeding fifty dollars per annum.

Delegated powers

3. The board of trustees, instead of the county court, shall have power to appoint patrols in and for said town, and for one mile around the same.

Commencement

4. This act shall be in force from its passage.

CHAP. 97.—An ACT for the relief of John S. Currell, James W. Gresham, administrator of George W. Flowers, and William N. Kirk.

Passed January 23, 1862.

Amount appropriated

1. Be it enacted by the general assembly, that the auditor of public accounts be and he is hereby directed to pay, out of any money in the treasury not otherwise appropriated, the sum of six hundred dollars to John S. Currell, the assessed value of a negro slave named Randall, convicted of felony by the county court of Lancaster county; to James W. Gresham, administrator of George W. Flowers, the sum of eight hundred dollars, the assessed value of a negro slave named Hiram; and to William N. Kirk, the sum of

six hundred dollars, the assessed value of a negro slave named Spencer; the said two last mentioned slaves being also convicted of felony by the said county court of Lancaster.

2. This act shall be in force from its passage.

CHAP. 98.—An ACT to authorize the County Court of Powhatan County to correct the assessment of the Lands of A. S. Wooldridge's estate.

Passed March 20, 1862.

1. Be it enacted by the general assembly, that the county court of Powhatan county is hereby authorized to correct the assessment of the tract of land in said county, called the "Huguenot springs tract," containing about one hundred and fifty acres, which stands on the commissioner's books as part of the estate of A. S. Wooldridge deceased: provided, however, that the court shall summon the late assessor of the said county to appear, and such other evidence as in the opinion of the court may be necessary in the case, the attorney for the commonwealth being present.

2. This act shall be in force from its passage.

CHAP. 99.—An ACT authorizing a reassessment of a House and Lot in Lynchburg, owned by Barney McKinney and James Casey, and for the repayment to them of certain Taxes.

Passed March 1, 1862.

1. Be it enacted by the general assembly, that it shall be lawful for Barney McKinney and James Casey, of the city of Lynchburg, assessed with a house and lot number four hundred and sixty-four in said city, to apply to the court of hustings of said city, within six months from the passage of this act, to have the assessment of said house and lot corrected: provided, that before making such application, they give notice to the assessor and the attorney of the commonwealth for said city, and that they shall be subject to all the restrictions, and be governed by all the provisions of the act passed the tenth of March eighteen hundred and fifty-six, except so far as the same may be inconsistent with the provisions of this act, and shall also incur and pay all legal costs attending such application or correction: and provided also, that the action of said court, in considering the subject or granting any relief herein provided for, shall be based upon and governed by what, in the opinion of the court, was the true value of the land at the time the assessment of such land was made.

Amount appropriated

2. When the provisions of the foregoing section shall have been fully complied with, and a return thereof made to the auditor of public accounts, he the said auditor is hereby authorized and required to refund to Barney McKinney and James Casey, out of any money in the treasury not otherwise appropriated, the taxes, if any, improperly paid by them, by reason of the erroneous assessment of eighteen hundred and fifty-six.

Record, how preserved

3. The correction of the assessment made under the provisions of this act shall be entered on the book of town lots of said city by the commissioner of the revenue of the same for the year eighteen hundred and sixty-two; and such assessment, so made, shall be certified by the clerk of the hustings court of said city to the auditor of public accounts, and such certificate shall serve as a voucher for the sheriff of said county in his settlement with the auditor.

Commencement

4. This act shall be in force from its passage.

CHAP. 100.—An ACT to authorise the Auditor of Public Accounts to settle the Claim of the Commonwealth against the Sureties of John A. M. Lusk, late Sheriff of Rockbridge County.

Passed March 29, 1862.

Auditor to settle claim

1. Be it enacted by the general assembly, that the auditor of public accounts be and he is hereby authorized to settle the claim of the commonwealth against the sureties of John A. M. Lusk, late sheriff of Rockbridge, on account of a collateral inheritance tax collected of Hopkins and Campbell, by receiving from said sureties the amount refunded by the state to said Hopkins and Campbell, with interest at six per centum from the time it was so refunded, and the costs incurred in the proceedings against them: provided, however, that this act shall not be in force, unless said sureties shall so settle said claim against them within thirty days from the passage of this act.

Proviso

Commencement

2. This act shall be in force from its passage.

CHAP. 101.—An ACT refunding to the Securities of Thomas K. Davis, late Sheriff of Prince William County, Damages paid by them as such.

Passed March 4, 1862.

Amount appropriated

1. Be it enacted by the general assembly, that the auditor of public accounts is hereby authorized and directed to issue his warrant on the treasury of the commonwealth, to be paid out of any money in the treasury not otherwise appropriated, in favor of the securities of

Thomas K. Davis, late sheriff of Prince William county, for the damages by them paid into the treasury of the commonwealth as such securities, after deducting the actual expenses of collection. But the said securities shall not have the benefit of this act, unless within sixty days after the passage hereof, they pay into the treasury all that remains of the principal unpaid, interest, damages, costs and other dues to the commonwealth, for which the said securities may be liable: provided, however, that nothing herein contained shall be so construed as to release the said Thomas K. Davis from the payment of said damages. *Conditions*

2. This act shall be in force from its passage. *Commencement*

CHAP. 102.—An ACT for the relief of William T. Fitchett, Commonwealth's Attorney for the County of Northampton.

Passed March 15, 1862.

1. Be it enacted by the general assembly, that the auditor of public accounts be required to issue his warrant on the treasury, payable out of any money therein not otherwise appropriated, in favor of William T. Fitchett, or his legal representative, for the sum of fifty dollars, for services rendered by the said William T. Fitchett as commonwealth's attorney for the county of Northampton during the year eighteen hundred and sixty-one. *Amount appropriated*

2. This act shall be in force from its passage. *Commencement*

CHAP. 103.—An ACT for the relief of John W. Vaughan and others.

Passed March 12, 1862.

1. Be it enacted by the general assembly, that the auditor of public accounts be and he is hereby authorized and required to issue his warrant upon the treasury, payable out of the special fund deposited therein by J. J. Simpkins, late collector at the port of Norfolk, under the federal government, by order of the governor of this commonwealth, in favor of John W. Vaughan, for the sum of one hundred and fifty-five dollars and fourteen cents; in favor of James M. Vaughan, for the sum of one hundred and twelve dollars; in favor of R. B. Chisman, for the sum of sixty-seven dollars and twenty cents; in favor of A. Thomson, for the like sum of sixty-seven dollars and twenty cents; in favor of William Clinton, for the like sum of sixty-seven dollars and twenty cents; and in favor of James McFarlane, for the like sum of sixty-seven dollars and twenty cents— these being the several sums of money claimed to be due to the per- *Amount appropriated*

sons herein mentioned, for services rendered as keeper, mate and seamen aboard of the light vessel at Willoughby Spit, from the first day of January to the twenty-second day of April eighteen hundred and sixty-one; also in favor of Thomas L. Kendal, for the sum of one hundred and twenty-five dollars, and in favor of John U. Wrenn, for the sum of seventy-five dollars—these being the several sums of money claimed to be due to the last named persons as keeper and assistant keeper of the light-house at Point of Shoals, from the first day of January to the thirty-first day of March eighteen hundred and sixty-one: also in favor of George W. Harrison, for the sum of one hundred dollars, that being the sum due the said Harrison as keeper of Jordan's Point light-house from the first of January to the thirty-first of March eighteen hundred and sixty-one.

Proviso

2. Before payments shall be made under this act to the persons entitled thereto, satisfactory evidence shall be produced to the auditor of public accounts of the justice and amount of their claims, and of their loyalty to the state and to the confederate government.

Commencement

3. This act shall be in force from and after its passage.

CHAP. 104.—An ACT authorizing the Judge of the Court of Hustings of the City of Richmond to grant a new Trial in the case of the Commonwealth against Edward Kersey and Hammett A. Pearce.

Passed February 1, 1862.

Judgment to be set aside

1. Be it enacted by the general assembly, that the judge of the court of hustings for the city of Richmond be and he is hereby authorized to set aside a judgment heretofore rendered by him on a forfeited recognizance against Edward Kersey and Hammett A. Pearce, for the sum of three hundred and twenty-five dollars and

Case reinstated

one cent, in favor of the commonwealth of Virginia, and to reinstate the case in which the said judgment was rendered upon the docket, for a new trial thereof.

Commencement

2. This act shall be in force from its passage.

CHAP. 105.—An ACT for the relief of E. A. W. Hore, late Sheriff of Stafford County.

Passed March 29, 1862.

Auditor to restate settlement

1. Be it enacted by the general assembly, that the auditor of public accounts be authorized to restate his settlement with E. A.

W. Hore, late sheriff of Stafford county, and remit and refund any damages, interest and costs which may appear to have been improperly recovered and paid by said sheriff.

2. This act shall be in force from its passage. *Commencement*

CHAP. 106.—An ACT to pay to John Kelley, surviving partner of Kelley & Larguey, the amount of a judgment of the Circuit Court of the City of Richmond against the Board of Public Works.

Passed March 27, 1862.

1. Be it enacted by the general assembly, that the auditor of public accounts be directed to issue his warrant on the treasury, payable out of any money therein not otherwise appropriated, in favor of John Kelley, surviving partner of Kelley & Larguey, for the sum of seventeen thousand three hundred and sixty-four dollars and seventy-one cents, with interest from the nineteenth day of February eighteen hundred and sixty-one, that being the sum recovered by judgment in his favor against the board of public works, in the circuit court of the city of Richmond, on the fifth day of June eighteen hundred and sixty, on account of a contract between Kelley & Larguey and the board of public works, for the construction of the Blue Ridge tunnel on the Blue Ridge rail road. *Amount appropriated*

2. This act shall be in force from its passage. *Commencement*

CHAP. 107.—An ACT for the relief of the Securities of Robert O. Doss, late Sheriff of the County of Campbell.

Passed March 10, 1862.

Whereas the act of twenty-ninth March eighteen hundred and sixty-one is not deemed sufficient to afford to the securities of Robert O. Doss, late sheriff of the county of Campbell, the relief thereby intended: *Preamble*

1. Be it enacted by the general assembly, that the auditor of public accounts is hereby authorized and directed to issue his warrant on the treasury, payable out of any money therein not otherwise appropriated, in favor of said securities, for the sum of four hundred and eighty-one dollars and thirty-five cents; that being the amount standing to the credit of said securities, upon the release of the damages authorized to be released by said act. *Amount appropriated*

2. This act shall be in force from its passage. *Commencement*

CHAP. 108.—An ACT for the relief of Joel D. Ashberry, Wescon Lewis and others, being the Officers and Crew of the York Spit Light Vessel.

Passed March 15, 1862.

1. Be it enacted by the general assembly, that the board created by an ordinance of the convention of Virginia to audit and settle the army and navy expenses, he and they are hereby authorized and required to allow to Joel D. Ashberry, Wescon Lewis, Augustine Sadler, Joel Shackleford, Robert Owens, William Owens and George White, their claims, for services rendered on board the York Spit light vessel from the first of January to sixteenth of April eighteen hundred and sixty-one, or for any portion of said time, upon the presentation before said board of the proper evidence of said service. *Appropriation limited* But the amounts to be paid to the aforesaid persons shall not exceed the rate of compensation to which said parties were severally entitled from the United States.

How appropriated 2. That when said claims, or either of them, are established by proper evidence as aforesaid, the same, or such as shall be so established, shall be paid by the auditor's warrants upon the treasury, to be paid out of the fund of six thousand and eighteen dollars and seventy cents, deposited in the treasury by Dr. J. J. Simpkins, late superintendent of lights, and collector of customs of the United States, in pursuance of an order of the executive of thirtieth of August eighteen hundred and sixty-one.

Commencement 3. This act shall be in force from its passage.

CHAP. 109.—An ACT allowing further time to the Owners of Lots in the Town of Columbia in the County of Fluvanna to build on and improve the same.

Passed March 14, 1862.

Extension of time 1. Be it enacted by the general assembly, that the further time of ten years (to be computed from the expiration of the time heretofore prescribed by law) shall be and is hereby allowed to the owners of lots in the town of Columbia in the county of Fluvanna, to build on *Forfeitures and penalties remitted* and improve the same, hereby remitting all forfeitures and penalties which may have accrued under the act of assembly establishing the said town, or under any amended act in relation to the same.

Commencement 2. This act shall be in force from its passage.

PRIVILEGES, ETC. 125

CHAP. 110.—An ACT for the relief of Archibald M. Drew.

Passed March 28, 1862.

Amount appropriated

1. Be it enacted by the general assembly, that the auditor of public accounts be and he is hereby authorized and required to issue his warrant on the treasury, payable out of any money therein not otherwise appropriated, in favor of Archibald M. Drew of the county of Prince George, for the sum of eighty dollars; being the amount paid into the treasury for license tax improperly paid.

2. This act shall be in force from its passage. *Commencement*

CHAP. 111.—An ACT compensating David W. Frobel, for services connected with the Militia of Nicholas and Greenbrier Counties.

Passed March 28, 1862.

Amount appropriated

1. Be it enacted by the general assembly, that the auditor of public accounts be and he is hereby directed to issue his warrant upon the treasury in favor of David W. Frobel, for fifty dollars, for services connected with the militia of Nicholas and Greenbrier counties, under the orders of the colonels of the regiments of said militia.

2. This act shall be in force from its passage. *Commencement*

CHAP. 112.—An ACT for the relief of Robertson Cooke.

Passed March 28, 1862.

Preamble

Whereas it is represented to the general assembly of Virginia, that on account of the disturbed condition of our national affairs, no term of the county court of the county of Wyoming has been held since the July term eighteen hundred and sixty-one: Therefore,

Amount appropriated

1. Be it enacted by the general assembly, that the auditor of public accounts be and he is hereby authorized and directed to issue his warrant on the treasury, payable out of any money therein not otherwise appropriated, in favor of Robertson Cooke, or his legal representatives, for the sum of two hundred and eleven dollars, for the maintenance and clothing furnished to Charlotte Meddows, a lunatic of Wyoming county, from December twenty-first, eighteen hundred and sixty, to December eighteenth, eighteen hundred and sixty-one; payment of a similar claim by the auditor of public accounts, on the order of the county court of the county of Wyoming, being heretofore made.

2. This act shall be in force from its passage. *Commencement*

CHAP. 113.—An ACT to pay to George Cooper a certain sum of money for services as Clerk of the 115th Regiment of Militia.

Passed March 20, 1862.

Amount appropriated

1. Be it enacted by the general assembly, that the sum of sixty-five dollars be and the same is hereby appropriated, out of any moneys in the public treasury not otherwise appropriated, to be applied to the payment of George Cooper of Elizabeth City county, for his services as clerk of the court of enquiry for the one hundred and fifteenth regiment Virginia militia, it being impossible to call a court of enquiry to authorize the payment of the same, in consequence of the invasion of the country by the enemy.

Commencement

2. This act shall be in force from its passage.

CHAP. 114.—An ACT to authorize the issue of registered Certificates of State Stock to Dr. Peter F. Brown, in lieu of two lost Bonds.

Passed March 5, 1862.

Preamble

Whereas it has been satisfactorily shown to the general assembly, that two coupon bonds of the state of Virginia, the property of Doctor Peter F. Brown of Accomack county (numbered, respectively, three thousand nine hundred and fifty-three, and seven thousand two hundred and fifty-six, and each for the sum of one thousand dollars), were taken by, and are now in the possession of the enemy; and the said Doctor Peter F. Brown having advertised the loss, and given notice thereof to the proper authorities of the state: Therefore,

Stock, how issued

1. Be it enacted by the general assembly, that the second auditor be and he is hereby directed to issue two registered certificates of state stock for the sum of one thousand dollars each, in lieu of the coupon bonds thus lost, conformably to the laws in relation to the issue of registered certificates of state stock; and the said coupon bonds are declared to be null and void, and the second auditor is directed to make proclamation thereof: provided, however, that before the same shall be issued, the said Doctor Peter F. Brown shall file, in the office of the second auditor, a bond, payable to the commonwealth, in the penalty of five thousand dollars, with one or more sufficient securities, to be approved by the governor of the commonwealth, conditioned to indemnify the commonwealth and all persons against loss in consequence of the issuing of said certificates, or either of them, in place of the said lost bonds: and provided further, that before the same shall be issued, that said Doctor Peter F. Brown shall, in accordance with an ordinance of the convention, passed June twenty-sixth, eighteen hundred and sixty-one, satisfy the commissioners of the sinking fund that the said lost coupon

Bond filed

PRIVILEGES, ETC.   127

bonds do not come within the provisions of the said ordinance of June twenty-sixth, eighteen hundred and sixty-one, nor within the provisions of an ordinance of the convention, passed on the first day of July eighteen hundred and sixty-one.

2. Be it further enacted, that the commissioners of the sinking fund be and they are hereby directed to pay to the said Dr. Peter F. Brown, or his legal assignee or agent, the interest on said lost bonds, due and remaining unpaid on the first day of January eighteen hundred and sixty-two. *Amount appropriated from sinking fund*

3. This act shall be in force from its passage. *Commencement*

CHAP. 115.—An ACT for the relief of the Sureties of John C. Harrison, Sheriff of Tazewell County.

Passed March 24, 1862.

1. Be it enacted by the general assembly, that the sureties of John C. Harrison, sheriff of Tazewell county, are hereby released from the payment of the damages on judgments in favor of the commonwealth against them as sureties, rendered by the circuit court of the city of Richmond. But the sureties shall not have the benefit of this act, unless they pay into the treasury, on or before the first day of July eighteen hundred and sixty-two, or sooner, if required by the auditor of public accounts, all that remains unpaid of the principal, interest, cost and actual expenses of collection of said judgments: provided, that this act shall not be construed as in any way releasing the said John C. Harrison, sheriff as aforesaid, from the payment of any damages adjudged against him. *Sureties released* *Proviso*

2. This act shall be in force from its passage. *Commencement*

CHAP. 116.—An ACT for the relief of John H. Haskins, Sheriff of Amelia, and his Sureties.

Passed March 27, 1862.

1. Be it enacted by the general assembly, that the auditor of public accounts be and he is hereby authorized to issue his warrant upon the treasury in favor of John H. Haskins, sheriff of Amelia county, and his sureties, for the damages obtained in the judgment against them for the May eighteen hundred and sixty-one license taxes of said county, less the costs and expenses in collecting said judgment. *What appropriated*

2. This act shall be in force from its passage. *Commencement*

CHAP. 117.—An ACT to authorise Hughes Dillard to erect a Dam half across Smith's River in the county of Henry, in a manner not inconsistent with the rights of the Smith's River Navigation Company.

Passed January 15, 1862.

Improvements 1. Be it enacted by the general assembly, that Hughes Dillard is hereby authorized and empowered to erect a mill dam half across Smith's river in the county of Henry, at or on his plantation lying on the north side of said river, and known as "River field," and to divert from the said river so much of the water thereof as may be necessary to propel the mills and other machinery which the said *Proviso* Dillard proposes to erect thereon : provided, that the said Dillard, and all other persons claiming under him, shall, whenever required by the Smith's river navigation company, or any other company that may be hereafter incorporated for the purpose of navigating said river, provide suitable sluices and locks to permit the free navigation of said river: and provided furthermore, that the rights of individuals whose property may be injured by the erection of said dam, shall *Damages* not be affected thereby ; but they shall be entitled for such injury to such damages as a jury may assess, in the manner now prescribed by law in such cases.

Commencement 2. This act shall be in force from its passage.

CHAP. 118.—An ACT to relieve the Sureties of Robert Chambers, late Sheriff of Boone County.

Passed March 25, 1862.

Sureties released 1. Be it enacted by the general assembly, that the sureties of Robert Chambers, late sheriff of Boone county, are hereby released from the payment of the damages imposed upon them by two judgments of the circuit court of Richmond city, less the actual costs of the collection of said judgments. But this act shall not take effect unless the principal, interest and costs of collection are paid into the treasury within sixty days : provided, however, that this act shall not be construed to release the said sheriff from any part of said judgments.

Commencement 2. This act shall be in force from its passage.

CHAP. 119.—An ACT for the relief of the Personal Representative of A. J. Whitehead deceased, late Sheriff of Pittsylvania County.

Passed March 13, 1862.

Amount appropriated 1. Be it enacted by the general assembly, that the auditor of public accounts be and he is hereby authorized and directed to issue his warrant on the treasury, payable out of any money therein not otherwise appropriated, in favor of the personal representative of A. J. Whitehead deceased, late sheriff of Pittsylvania county, for the sum of fifty-three dollars and thirty-three cents; being the amount of insolvent lists for the year eighteen hundred and fifty-seven, heretofore disallowed by the said auditor.

2. This act shall be in force from its passage. *Commencement*

CHAP. 120.—An ACT for the relief of Coalman D. Bennett, Executor of Howard Craft deceased, of Pittsylvania County.

Passed March 13, 1862.

1. Be it enacted by the general assembly, that the second auditor be and he is hereby authorized and directed to issue his warrant on the treasury, payable out of the literary fund, in favor of Coalman D. Bennett, executor of Howard Craft deceased, of Pittsylvania county, for the sum of ninety-seven dollars; the same being the amount of three fines paid by said Craft in his lifetime, under a judgment of the county court of said county; which judgment was afterwards reversed by the circuit court of said county. *Amount appropriated from literary fund*

2. This act shall be in force from its passage. *Commencement*

CHAP. 121.—An ACT compensating Norman C. Smoot and James Caudy, Commissioners of the Revenue for the County of Hampshire, for services performed.

Passed February 12, 1862.

1. Be it enacted by the general assembly, that the auditor of public accounts be and he is hereby authorized to ascertain what would be an equitable allowance to Norman C. Smoot and James Caudy, commissioners of the revenue for the county of Hampshire, for assessments in the year eighteen hundred and sixty-one. In case of the failure of either or both of the aforesaid commissioners to return to the office of the auditor of public accounts the books containing the assessments of eighteen hundred and sixty-one, the said auditor shall assume, as a basis of said allowance, the assessments of eighteen hundred and sixty; and he is hereby authorized to issue his warrant on the treasury, payable out of any money therein not otherwise appropriated, in favor of said commissioners respectively, or their legal representatives, for the sum so ascertained. *What appropriated*

2. This act shall be in force from its passage. *Commencement*

130   PRIVILEGES, ETC.

CHAP. 122.—An ACT to compensate William H. Dulany, Attorney for the Commonwealth for the Circuit Court of Fairfax, for his services for the Spring Term 1861.

Passed February 19, 1862.

Amount appropriated

1. Be it enacted by the general assembly, that the auditor of public accounts be authorized to issue his warrant on the treasury in favor of William H. Dulany, attorney for the commonwealth for the circuit court of Fairfax county, for the sum of fifty dollars; the same being for his services as such attorney for the spring term of said court in the year eighteen hundred and sixty-one.

Commencement

2. This act shall be in force from its passage.

CHAP. 123.—An ACT for the relief of John R. Cunningham, administrator of Newton Cunningham, late Sheriff of Prince Edward County.

Passed February 20, 1862.

Amount appropriated

1. Be it enacted by the general assembly, that the auditor of public accounts shall issue his warrant on the treasury, payable out of any money therein not otherwise appropriated, to John R. Cunningham, administrator of Newton Cunningham, late sheriff of Prince Edward, for ninety dollars and eighty-six cents; being the amount of money improperly paid into the treasury by the said Newton Cunningham.

Commencement

2. This act shall be in force from its passage.

CHAP. 124.—An ACT releasing the Securities of Thomas K. Davis, late Sheriff of Prince William County, from the payment of Damages.

Passed February 17, 1862.

What appropriated

1. Be it enacted by the general assembly, that the securities of Thomas K. Davis, late sheriff of the county of Prince William, are hereby released from the payment of the damages on a judgment in favor of the commonwealth against them as such securities, rendered by the circuit court of the city of Richmond. But the said securities shall not have the benefit of this act, unless they pay into the treasury, within sixty days from the passage hereof, all that remains unpaid of the principal, interest, costs and actual expenses of collection of said judgment, and all other dues to the commonwealth for which said securities may be liable: provided, that this act shall not be construed as releasing the said Thomas K. Davis, late sheriff of Prince William county, from the payment of any damages adjudged against him.

Commencement

2. This act shall be in force from its passage.

PRIVILEGES, ETC.   131

Chap. 125.—An ACT refunding to the County of Amherst a License Tax paid by George L. Shrader, advanced to him by the County Court of said County.

Passed February 11, 1862.

1. Be it enacted by the general assembly, that the auditor of public accounts be and he is authorized to issue his warrant on the treasury, payable out of any money therein not otherwise appropriated, in favor of the treasurer of Amherst county, for the sum of sixty-three dollars, the amount of a license tax paid by George L. Shrader; which license was never used by him, because he immediately voluntarily enlisted in the military service of the state, and the county court of said county advanced the said amount to enable him to enter said service.

Amount appropriated

2. This act shall be in force from its passage.

Commencement

Chap. 126.—An ACT to refund to Edmund W. Bayley a sum of money erroneously paid by him into the treasury.

Passed February 7, 1862.

Whereas it appears that Edmund W. Bayley, a commissary in the confederate service, did, on the eleventh day of November eighteen hundred and sixty-one, pay into the treasury of the state the sum of five thousand dollars to the credit of the sheriff of Accomack county, and that the said sum has since been paid into the treasury by the said sheriff, without the knowledge that it had previously been paid by the said Bayley for him; and it thus appearing that the said amount has been twice paid: And whereas it further appears that the object of the said Bayley in making the said payment, was to save the risk to the Confederate States and to the state of Virginia, of conveying the said sum across the Chesapeake bay, and that the said payment by him was made under a mistake of facts: Therefore,

Preamble

1. Be it enacted by the general assembly, that the auditor of public accounts be and he is hereby directed to issue his warrant on the treasury, payable out of any money not otherwise appropriated, in favor of Edmund W. Bayley, or his legal representatives, for the sum of five thousand dollars; the same being the amount so erroneously paid by him.

Amount appropriated

2. The said sheriff shall not be entitled to a credit on his account for said sum of five thousand dollars; and the auditor of public accounts is directed to correct the books in his office, and to disregard the said sum so erroneously credited to him.

3. This act shall be in force from its passage.

Commencement

CHAP. 127.—An ACT authorizing the Commissioner of the Revenue for the Southern District of Halifax County to issue a License to David Apt as a Hawker and Peddler in said County.

Passed January 30, 1862.

Amount appropriated

1. Be it enacted by the general assembly, that the commissioner of the revenue for the southern district of the county of Halifax is authorized and required to issue to David Apt a license as a hawker and peddler in the said county of Halifax, from the time of issuing said license to the thirtieth day of April eighteen hundred and sixty-three; and upon the production of the same to the sheriff of said county, and the payment to him of a tax of fifty dollars by the said Apt in the manner in which the tax is paid upon other licenses, he the said Apt shall have power and authority to sell, by retail, goods, wares and merchandise as a hawker and peddler, within the limits of the said county of Halifax, until the said thirtieth day of April eighteen hundred and sixty-three.

2. The said commissioner shall make report to the auditor of public accounts of said license, in his general report of licenses of his said district.

Commencement

3. This act shall be in force from its passage.

CHAP. 128.—An ACT making compensation to A. F. Haymond, Attorney for the Commonwealth.

Passed January 16, 1862.

Amount appropriated

1. Be it enacted by the general assembly, that the auditor of public accounts be authorized and directed to issue his warrant for the sum of fifty dollars, payable to A. F. Haymond, or his representative, out of any money in the treasury not otherwise appropriated; the same being allowed him for his services as attorney for the commonwealth in the circuit court of Marion county, for the half year closing with the June term eighteen hundred and sixty-one of that court.

Commencement

2. This act shall be in force from its passage.

CHAP. 129.—An ACT compensating George Duffey, late Commissioner of the Revenue for the City and County of Alexandria, for services performed.

Passed January 22, 1862.

Amount appropriated

1. Be it enacted by the general assembly, that the auditor of public accounts be and he is hereby authorized to ascertain what would be

an equitable allowance to George Duffey, late commissioner of the revenue for the city and county of Alexandria, for assessments in the year eighteen hundred and sixty-one, assuming as a basis the assessment for the year eighteen hundred and sixty, and to issue his warrant on the treasury, payable out of any money therein not otherwise appropriated, in favor of said Duffey, or his legal representatives, for the sum so ascertained.

2. This act shall be in force from its passage.

CHAP. 130.—An ACT authorizing and directing the sale and delivery by the Governor of a Convicted Slave, named Richard, to John Washington of Caroline County.

Passed January 22, 1862.

1. Be it enacted by the general assembly, that the governor of the commonwealth be and he is hereby authorized and directed to sell and deliver to John Washington of Caroline county, a slave named Richard, formerly belonging to said Washington, who has been lately convicted of grand larceny, in the hustings court of Richmond city, and condemned to be transported without the limits of the United States: provided the said Washington shall first pay all the costs of the prosecution of said slave, and relinquish all claim against the commonwealth for his value, and shall also enter into a proper bond, conditioned immediately to sell said slave beyond the limits of this commonwealth.

2. This act shall be in force from its passage.

CHAP. 131.—An ACT to compensate E. J. Buckwalter and W. H. Pate, Jailors of Bedford County, for keeping certain Negro Convicts confined in the Jail of said County in the year 1861.

Passed January 15, 1862.

1. Be it enacted by the general assembly, that the auditor of public accounts be and he is hereby directed to issue his warrant on the treasury, to be paid out of any money not otherwise appropriated, in favor of E. J. Buckwalter of Bedford, for the sum of one hundred and eighty-six dollars and thirty cents; and also to issue his warrant upon the treasury, to be paid in like manner, in favor of William H. Pate of said county, for the sum of sixteen dollars and ninety-five cents; they being the amounts due them, respectively, for imprisoning and keeping certain negro convicts hired to Rosser & Co. on the public works, who escaped from service, were apprehended as runaways, and confined in the jail of Bedford county.

2. This act shall be in force from its passage.

CHAP. 132.—An ACT to amend and re-enact an act entitled an act refunding to Moses G. Booth Damages paid by him as surety of Samuel S. Turner, late Sheriff of Franklin County, passed March 19, 1861.

Passed January 16, 1862.

Preamble

Whereas an act was passed by the general assembly on the nineteenth of March eighteen hundred and sixty-one, entitled an act refunding to Moses G. Booth damages paid by him, as surety of Samuel S. Turner, late sheriff of Franklin county, and it appearing that further legislation is necessary to afford the relief thereby intended:

1. Be it therefore enacted by the general assembly, that the first section of said act be amended and re-enacted so as to read as follows:

Amount to be paid out.

"§ 1. The auditor of public accounts is hereby authorized and directed to issue his warrant on the treasury of the commonwealth, to be paid out of any money therein not otherwise appropriated, in favor of Moses G. Booth, for the sum of three hundred and fourteen dollars and three cents, being the amount of damages, over and above the principal, interest, costs and actual expenses of collection, of a judgment rendered in the circuit court of the city of Richmond, against the said Samuel S. Turner and his securities, which was paid into the treasury of the commonwealth by the said Booth, as surety of said Turner: provided, however, that nothing herein contained shall be construed as releasing said Turner from the payment of said damages."

Commencement.

2. This act shall be in force from its passage.

CHAP. 133.—An ACT imposing a Tax on Dogs in the Counties of Alleghany and Botetourt.

Passed March 14, 1862.

Power delegated to county courts.

1. Be it enacted by the general assembly, that it shall be lawful for the county courts of Alleghany and Botetourt, when they assemble for the purpose of laying their county levies, to impose a tax of not less than one dollar nor more than three dollars upon every dog kept in said counties; exempting, however, from said tax one dog in every family and on every plantation. The money to be derived from said tax to be applied by the county courts for county purposes.

Time of action.

2. It shall be the duty of the county courts of Alleghany and Botetourt, at their first terms after the passage of this act, to cause all the justices of said counties to be summoned to their next succeeding terms, for the purpose of deciding whether the tax authorized by this

act shall be laid; and if the courts shall authorize such tax, it shall *Duty of commissioners of revenue* be the duty of the commissioners of the revenue of said counties to make out and return to the said county courts, with their lists of taxable property, a list of the dogs in said counties, and by whom owned or kept: and the said courts shall levy a tax, as prescribed by the first section of this act; to be collected and accounted for as other county levies, and to be applied to the county expenses of said counties.

3. This act shall be in force from its passage. *Commencement*

CHAP. 134.—An ACT authorizing the County Court of Brunswick County to impose a Tax on Dogs.

Passed March 29, 1862.

1. Be it enacted by the general assembly, that it shall be lawful *Power delegated to county courts* for the county court of Brunswick, when it assembles for the purpose of laying the county levy, to impose a tax of one dollar upon every dog kept in said county; exempting, however, from said tax two dogs in every family and on every plantation: the money derived from said tax to be applied by the county court for county purposes.

2. It shall be the duty of the county court of Brunswick, at its *Time of action* first term after the passage of this act, to cause all the justices of said county to be summoned to the then next succeeding term, for the purpose of deciding whether the tax authorized by this act shall be laid; and if two-thirds of all the justices shall be in favor thereof, the court shall authorize such tax: and it shall be the duty of the *Duty of commissioner of revenue* commissioner of the revenue of said county to make out and return to the said county court, with his list of taxable property, a list of the dogs in said county, and by whom owned or kept: and the said court shall levy a tax, as prescribed by the first section of this act; to be collected and accounted for as other county levies, and to be applied to the county expenses of said county.

3. This act shall be in force from its passage. *Commencement*

CHAP. 135.—An ACT to amend the first section of an act passed March 29, 1858, entitled an act concerning Ferries in the Counties of Russell and Wise.

Passed March 31, 1862.

1. Be it enacted by the general assembly, that the first section of *Amending 1st section of act March 29, 1858* the act passed March twenty-ninth, eighteen hundred and fifty-eight, entitled an act concerning ferries in the counties of Russell and Wise, be amended and re-enacted so as to read as follows:

Delegated authority

"§1. That the several county courts of the counties of Russell, Wise, Washington, Scott and Lee may have and exercise the power and authority to establish and control the ferries within their respective counties, without having the justices previously summoned for that purpose."

Commencement

2. This act shall be in force from its passage.

CHAP. 136.—An ACT constituting part of New River a lawful Fence.

Passed December 20, 1861.

New river a lawful fence to the mouth of Gauley river

1. Be it enacted by the general assembly of Virginia, that New river, from the falls thereof in Raleigh county, down the same to the mouth of Gauley river in the county of Fayette, be and the same is hereby constituted a lawful fence.

Commencement

2. This act shall be in force from its passage.

CHAP. 137.—An ACT declaring a portion of New River a lawful Fence.

Passed March 15, 1862.

New river a lawful fence to the county lines of Montgomery and Pulaski

1. Be it enacted by the general assembly of Virginia, that New river, from the mouth of Little Stony creek in the county of Giles, to the county lines of Montgomery and Pulaski, be and the same is hereby constituted a lawful fence.

Commencement

2. This act shall be in force from its passage.

CHAP. 138.—An ACT constituting a part of New River a lawful Fence.

Passed January 17, 1862.

New river a lawful fence to the mouth of Greenbrier

1. Be it enacted by the general assembly, that New river, from the mouth of Indian creek to the mouth of Greenbrier river in the county of Monroe, be declared a lawful fence.

Commencement

2. This act shall be in force from its passage, subject to repeal, alteration or amendment, at the pleasure of the general assembly.

CHAP. 139.—An ACT to incorporate the Bellevue Hospital in the vicinity of the City of Richmond.

Passed March 17, 1862.

Whereas James Beale, Francis H. Deane, Frederick Marx, Robert H. Cabell, F. W. Roddey and James Bolton, practitioners of medicine in the city of Richmond, have purchased real estate, with buildings thereon, which they have fitted up for a hospital in the vicinity of said city of Richmond, and said hospital has been used for several years for the accommodation of the citizens of the commonwealth of Virginia, and more recently for the care and treatment of the sick and wounded soldiers of the Southern Confederacy, and said hospital has been used as a school of practical instruction in medicine and surgery: Therefore, *Preamble*

1. Be it enacted by the general assembly of Virginia, that the said James Beale and others, and their lawful successors, be and are hereby made a body politic and corporate, under the name and title of Bellevue Hospital, for the purpose of receiving the sick and wounded, and of employing suitable means for their cure and relief, and for the purpose of imparting practical instruction in the science of medicine and surgery, and their collateral sciences: and the said corporation is hereby invested with all the rights, powers and privileges conferred by the Code upon corporations, and subject to all the rules, regulations, restrictions and provisions of the Code, in regard to corporations, so far as the same are applicable to such corporation as that hereby created. *Company incorporated* *Powers of company*

2. It shall be lawful for said corporation to enact such laws, rules and regulations as they may deem necessary and proper for carrying out successfully the design of their institution, as may be consistent with the laws of the Confederate States and of the commonwealth of Virginia.

3. It shall be lawful for said corporation to hold the real estate now held by them in joint ownership, at the northern angle of the intersection of Broad and Twenty-second streets, in the county of Henrico, and also to add thereto, by purchase or otherwise, such additional real estate adjoining thereto, and erect thereon such additional buildings as may be deemed requisite for enlarging the accommodations of their institution: provided, that the amount invested in such real estate, buildings, furniture, &c. shall not exceed the sum of thirty thousand dollars. *Proviso* *Limitation*

4. This act shall be in force from the passage thereof. *Commencement*

BENEVOLENT INSTITUTIONS.

CHAP. 140.—An ACT to incorporate Marengo Lodge No. 109, I. O. O. F. at Martinsburg in the County of Berkeley.

Passed March 27, 1862.

Lodge incorporated

1. Be it enacted by the general assembly, that Israel Robinson, E. G. Alburtis, Joseph C. Rawlins, Joseph Schoppert and Philip Showers, and such other persons as may be hereafter regularly associated with them, be and they are hereby incorporated and made a body politic and corporate, under the name and style of Marengo Lodge number one hundred and nine, I. O. O. F. in the county of Berkeley; and by that name, shall have perpetual succession and a common seal; and may sue and be sued, plead and be impleaded;

Property to be held

and may purchase and hold, to them and their successors, any lands and tenements, chattels and goods of what kind soever, as may be conducive of the objects of such association: provided, that the whole amount of property, personal and real, of said association shall at no time exceed in amount or value the sum of five thousand dollars.

Delegated powers

2. Be it further enacted, that it shall be lawful for each and every person composing the association heretofore known by the name of Marengo Lodge number one hundred and nine, the society proposed to be incorporated, to transfer, by writing, under his hand, to the body politic and corporate hereby created, all his right, title and interest of, in or to the property, real or personal, in possession or in action, belonging to the said association, as such; and thereupon the said body politic and corporate shall be vested with all the right, title and interest so designed to be transferred, of all and every person and persons executing such transfer in writing; and shall have power and authority to sue for the same in its own name, in any court of law or equity, in like manner as each person or all the persons executing such transfer or transfers might have sued.

Commencement

3. This act shall be in force from its passage.

CHAP. 141.—An ACT to amend the second section of the act incorporating the Thorn Rose Cemetery at Staunton.

Passed March 27, 1862.

Amending 2d section of act passed Feb. 24, 1849

1. Be it enacted by the general assembly, that the second section of the act passed February twenty-fourth, eighteen hundred and forty-nine, entitled an act incorporating the Thorn rose cemetery company at the town of Staunton, be amended and re-enacted so as to read as follows:

Power delegated

"§ 2. That said company shall have the right to purchase and hold, in or near the town of Staunton, not exceeding in quantity thirty acres of land, for the purposes of said cemetery; and shall have power to lay out and ornament the same; to erect such buildings thereon as it may deem necessary and proper; to arrange burial lots; and to make and enforce, by reasonable fines and penalties, such by-laws, rules and regulations for the government of the establishment, as it shall judge best: provided the same be not contrary to the constitution and laws of the Confederate States or of this state." *Power to enforce fines*

2. This act shall be in force from its passage. *Commencement*

CHAP. 142.—An ACT authorizing the Trustees of Oak Grove Church in the County of Pocahontas to sell and convey Property.

Passed March 20, 1862.

1. Be it enacted by the general assembly, that the trustees of Oak grove church in the county of Pocahontas be and they are hereby authorized and empowered to sell and convey the following portion of the parsonage property belonging to said church, and to apply the proceeds thereof to the use of said church, to wit: That part thereof beginning at a white oak tree at the side of the road; thence south forty degrees, west four poles and five links; thence, north fifty degrees, west thirty-seven links, to a stake; thence, north forty degrees, east four poles and five links, to a stake in the road; thence south fifty degrees, east thirty-seven links, to the beginning. *Power delegated to trustees*

2. This act shall be in force from its passage. *Commencement*

CHAP. 143.—An ACT to authorize the establishment of a Military School as a part of the Instruction of Randolph Macon College.

Passed January 22, 1862.

1. Be it enacted by the general assembly of Virginia, that the trustees of Randolph Macon college shall be authorized to establish a military school as the part of the course of instruction in said institution. *Institution incorporated*

2. The board of trustees may make by-laws and regulations, not inconsistent with the laws of the state, for the government and management of this department, as they now do for the academic department of the institution; and may, for the purpose of transacting such business as in its opinion can be transacted by a less number than the majority, authorize not less than four members to constitute a quorum in matters connected either with this or the academic department, to be called "the executive committee." *How managed*

Delegated authority

3. They shall have authority to build an arsenal, or to convert any building they now have, or any portion of said buildings, into an arsenal, for the purpose of preserving the arms and other property, which shall be guarded or preserved.

4. They shall appoint such professors to give instructions in military science as they may deem proper, and may remove them for good cause, as already provided for in their charter; but no order to remove a professor shall be made without the concurrence therein of a majority of the whole number of trustees.

5. They shall prescribe the terms upon which all students may be admitted to the course of their instruction, and the nature of their service; and whilst they shall subject every student to military discipline and drill, they shall not require any student to pursue the studies of the military school proper, without his consent, if he be twenty-one years of age, or the consent of his parent or guardian, if he be a junior.

Proviso

6. The students so admitted shall constitute a military corps of cadets, under the command of such officer or officers as the board of trustees may direct, and shall constitute the guard of the institution.

Duty of officers

7. The said officer or officers shall from time to time inspect the arms in the arsenal; cause the same to be kept safe and clean; give receipts for such arms as may be brought there to be deposited; and obey such orders for the delivery of arms therefrom as he or they may receive from the governor, as directed by the twenty-seventh chapter of the Code of Virginia.

Board of visitors

8. The governor of the state shall appoint two, and the board of trustees two persons, who shall constitute a board of visitors, whose duty it shall be to attend the annual examinations both in the academic and military departments; inspect the arms and other property; audit accounts; and make a report to the board of trustees

Form of returns

of the condition of the institution; and shall, by the first day of October of each year, make a return to the adjutant general, to be by him laid before the governor, showing the names and number of the officers and cadets in both academic and military departments of instruction; distinguishing those between the ages of eighteen and forty-five, and showing also the public arms, ordnance, equipments and accoutrements at the arsenal, and under charge of said corps; and shall accompany each report with such suggestions affecting the interest of the institution, as they may deem proper: and this board of visitors shall be ex-officio members of the board of trustees.

Delegated privilege

9. The governor may furnish arms, ordnance, equipments and accoutrements in such manner and upon such conditions as they are now furnished to the Virginia military institute; and the corps of

SCHOOLS AND COLLEGES. 141

cadets shall be subject to his order in case of invasion or insurrection, or any other cause by him deemed sufficient, as entirely as the armed-volunteer companies of the state.

10. The governor of the state and the board of trustees and faculty of the institution may confer the degree of graduate upon any cadet who may have passed an approved examination on the studies of the military ticket. Authority to confer degrees

11. Commissions shall be issued to the commanding officer of the corps, professors, assistant professor or assistant professors of tactics, corresponding with those of colonel, major and captain of militia; but such commissions shall confer no rank in the militia, nor entitle any person holding the same to any pay or emolument by reason thereof, unless ordered into the service of the state. Commissions

12. This act shall be in force from its passage. Commencement

---

CHAP. 144.—An ACT to Incorporate the Hillsville Military Academy in the County of Carroll.

Passed March 28, 1862.

1. Be it enacted by the general assembly of Virginia, that Leonidas E. Reid, James B. Johnson, Fielden L. Hall, James Early, Ira B. Coltrain, Thomas M. Dobyns, John Wilkinson, John Early, James S. Tipton, James B. Davidson, Samuel Staples and William C. Thornton, and their associates and successors, be and they are hereby constituted a body politic and corporate, under the name and style of The Trustees of the Hillsville Military Academy, in the town of Hillsville in the county of Carroll; and by that name, shall have perpetual succession and a common seal; and may sue and be sued, plead and be impleaded, in any court of law or equity. The said trustees shall be capable in law to receive, hold and dispose of personal property and real estate not exceeding ten or less than two acres, in order to carry out the purposes of their corporation: provided, that a majority of said trustees and their successors may at any time hereafter increase the number of trustees to twenty: and provided further, that a majority of said trustees shall be stockholders in said academy. Company incorporated

Delegated authority

2. The said Hillsville military academy shall be under the control and management of said trustees, and their associates and successors, who shall appoint a principal, professors and a treasurer, and such other officers as they may deem proper, and make and establish from time to time such by-laws, rules and regulations for the government of said academy as to them may seem fit, not contrary to the laws How managed

of this state or the Confederate States. A majority of the trustees shall constitute a quorum for the transaction of business; and any vacancy or vacancies in said board of trustees, occasioned by death, resignation or otherwise, shall be supplied by appointment of the remaining trustees; and they may remove any member of their body; two-thirds of the whole number. being present and concurring.

Treasurer's duty

Bond to be executed

3. The treasurer shall receive all moneys accruing to the said academy, and property delivered to his care, and shall pay and deliver the same to the order of the board of trustees. Before entering upon the discharge of his duties, he shall give bond, with such security in such penalty as the board may direct, made payable to the trustees for the time being, and their successors, and conditioned for the faithful performance of the duties of his office, under such rules and regulations as the board may adopt.

Mode of subscription

4. The said trustees shall have power, by themselves or their agents, to take and receive subscriptions for said academy; in case any person shall fail to pay his or her subscription, to enforce the collection of the same. They may in their discretion sell scholarships in said academy, upon such terms as may by the board be deemed advisable.

5. The stock of said academy shall be deemed personal estate, and may pass or descend and be disposed of by the holder as any other personal estate.

Commencement

6. This act shall be in force from its passage, subject to alteration or repeal, at the pleasure of the general assembly.

RESOLUTIONS.

No. 1.—Joint Resolutions in relation to the Re-enlistment of the Volunteer Forces of the State.

Adopted January 17, 1862.

Whereas the war, in defence of our liberty and independence, has heretofore been successfully conducted by the brave and generous volunteers, who, without hesitation, came forward, at the first call of their country, to conquer or die in its defence; and the general assembly has an abiding confidence in the fortitude, courage and patriotism of the Virginia volunteers now in the field, and does not doubt their readiness to continue in the service, when assured that this further sacrifice is earnestly desired, to aid in repulsing our insolent enemies, and securing the sacred soil of our country from the tread of the invader: *Preamble*

1. Resolved, therefore, by the general assembly, that we earnestly appeal to our volunteer forces to re-enlist, with the assurance that Virginia will ever hold in grateful remembrance their patriotic and disinterested services; and the general assembly will take care that all their reasonable wants shall be supplied, and their grievances, if any, redressed. *Appeal to re-enlist*

2. Resolved, that the commandants be requested to return the cordial thanks of the general assembly to the forces under their respective commands, for their generous, brave and patriotic conduct during this war, and cause it to be made known in the several companies, that in the opinion of the general assembly, it is of the highest importance to the success of our cause that they should at once re-enlist, and that the general assembly be promptly informed of the date and number of such re-enlistments.

3. Resolved, that a copy of the foregoing resolutions be immediately furnished by the clerk of the house of delegates to each commandant of the Virginia forces now in service, with the request that such commandant cause the same to be forthwith published to the forces under his command.

No. 2.—Joint Resolutions declaring the intent and meaning of an act providing for raising Virginia's Quota of the Confederate Army.

Adopted March 3, 1862.

1. Resolved by the general assembly, that the true intent and meaning of the act passed on the tenth day of February eighteen hundred and sixty-two, providing for raising Virginia's quota of the confederate army, makes it the duty of the governor to fill up companies now in service, to a minimum of one hundred men, to be supplied by voluntary enlistment or draft: that until the companies now in service have been so filled, the organization of new companies is in contravention of the policy adopted by the general assembly in the act aforesaid.

Delegated authority

2. That the governor therefore be and he is hereby requested not to accept any new companies until those already in service have been filled up as the law directs, unless hereafter specially authorized so to do.

No. 3.—Joint Resolutions authorizing the Governor to receive Volunteer Companies from any County or Corporation which may have furnished its quota to the Confederate Army.

Adopted March 14, 1862.

Delegated powers

1. Resolved by the general assembly, that the governor be and he is hereby authorized to commission the officers of a cavalry company in the county of Norfolk, consisting of one hundred men, recently organized by Messrs. James G. Martin, jr. and John Cooper, and to accept and muster said company into the service for three years, or for the war, as soon as he shall ascertain that the county of Norfolk has contributed her quota of troops required to be furnished by the act of tenth of February eighteen hundred and sixty-two.

Quota

Governor to commission officers

How received

2. And be it further resolved, that the governor is hereby required to receive into the service of the state for three years, or for the war, and commission the officers, of any company with the complement of men, from any county in which drafts cannot be made, by reason of the presence of the public enemy; or from any county, city or town that has furnished its full quota of troops, for three years, or for the war, for the confederate service, under existing laws.

No. 4.—Joint Resolution authorizing the Governor to accept a Light Infantry Company from Middlesex County.

Adopted March 6, 1862.

Delegated authority for governor to

Resolved by the general assembly, that the governor of this commonwealth be and he is hereby authorized to receive a light infantry company, recently organized in the county of Middlesex, into the service of the state for three years, or the war, and to commission the officers of the same: but the governor shall not accept said company or commission its officers until he has ascertained that the county of Middlesex has already furnished the full quota of volunteers required to be furnished by said county for the confederate service, under existing laws.

receive a light infantry company

No. 5.—Resolution authorizing the Governor to receive a Light Infantry Company organized in the County of Halifax.

Adopted March 13, 1862.

Resolved by the general assembly, that the governor of this commonwealth be and he is hereby authorized to receive a light infantry company recently organized in the county of Halifax by the election of John C. Gregory captain, into the service of the state for three years, or for the war, and to commission the officers of the same: but the governor shall not accept said company or commission its officers until he has ascertained that the county of Halifax has already furnished the full quota of volunteers required to be furnished by said county for the confederate service, under existing laws.

Governor authorized to receive company organized in county of Halifax

---

No. 6.—Joint Resolution requesting the Governor to Commission Captain C. N. Lawson and other Officers of his Company.

Adopted March 11, 1862.

Resolved by the general assembly of Virginia, that the governor be requested to commission Captain C. N. Lawson and other officers of his company, receive the same, and turn them over to the confederate government, as a portion of Virginia's quota, and to the credit of Lancaster county.

Governor to commission Capt. C. N. Lawson and others

No. 7.—Resolution of request to the Secretary of War, in relation to the acceptance of New Companies, &c.

Adopted March 5, 1862.

Resolved by the general assembly, that the secretary of war of the Confederate States be respectfully requested to decline to receive any additional volunteers from the state of Virginia, either by regiments, battalions or companies, until the quota of Virginia to the confederate army, called for by the president of the Confederate States, shall be fully raised and mustered into service.

Proviso

146 RESOLUTIONS.

No. 8.—Resolution concerning a Volunteer Company in the City of Petersburg.

Adopted March 15, 1862.

Company from Petersburg organized

Resolved by the general assembly, that permission be and is hereby granted to raise a company of riflemen, not less than one hundred strong, from the city of Petersburg: provided said company furnish itself with rifles. And the governor is hereby authorized to receive the said company into service for the war, as a part of Virginia's quota: provided said company is tendered to the governor, satisfactorily armed, on or before the twenty-fifth of March eighteen hundred and sixty-two.

No. 9.—Joint Resolution authorizing Free Negroes to be carried out of the State, to be engaged in the Manufacture of Salt Petre and other Munitions of War.

Adopted January 7, 1862.

Preamble

Whereas the manufacture of salt petre and other munitions of war is of prime necessity to the Confederate States: And whereas the general assembly are anxious to afford every facility in their power to enterprising and patriotic citizens engaged in such manufacture: And whereas it has been represented to the general assembly, that the free negro population of the state may be used advantageously in said manufacture, outside of the limits of Virginia, by voluntary agreements on their part: Therefore,

Delegated powers

1. Resolved by the general assembly, that J. Marshall McCue, or any other citizen of the commonwealth engaged in the manufacture of salt petre or other munitions of war, be authorized to carry out of the state of Virginia to any other state of the Confederacy, any number of free negroes for the purpose of manufacturing salt petre or other munitions of war.

Term of expiration

2. Be it further resolved, that at the expiration of the term for which said negroes may agree to hire themselves, liberty is reserved to them to return to the commonwealth of Virginia.

No. 10.—Resolution in relation to the Pay of Non-commissioned Officers and Privates.

Adopted January 1, 1862.

Increase of pay of non-commissioned officers, &c.

Resolved by the general assembly, that the senators from Virginia in the congress of the Confederate States be instructed, and the members of the house of representatives be requested to use their influence to procure the passage of a law to increase the pay of the non-commissioned officers and privates in the confederate army four dollars per month during the existing war.

RESOLUTIONS.   147

No. 11.—Joint Resolution for the appointment of temporary Clerks in the Adjutant General's Office.

Adopted March 6, 1862.

Resolved by the general assembly, that the adjutant general be authorized to employ any number of clerks temporarily, as may be necessary to prepare the returns of the enrollment of the militia, and the reports from the camps of the volunteers in service, to provide for a draft of the militia at the earliest possible day.

Temporary clerks

No. 12.—Resolution authorising the Governor to send Special Messengers to obtain Enrollments.

Adopted March 4, 1862.

Resolved, that the governor be authorized and requested to send a proper number of messengers at once to procure the enrollment of the military forces provided for by the act of eighth February eighteen hundred and sixty-two, and that he pay said messengers such compensation as he may deem expedient, out of the military contingent fund.

Enrollment of military forces

No. 13.—Joint Resolution concerning the Discharge of such portion of the Virginia Militia as is not necessarily required by the public service.

Adopted February 12, 1862.

Resolved by the general assembly, that the governor of the commonwealth be requested to confer with the president of the Confederate States, and endeavor to procure the discharge of such portion of the Virginia militia as is not necessarily required by the public service.

Virginia militia

No. 14.—Joint Resolution in relation to Discharges of Militia mustered into service of the Confederate States.

Adopted March 15, 1862.

Resolved by the general assembly, that the secretary of war be and he is hereby requested to discharge from service such of the militia of any county as have been mustered into the service of the Confederate States prior to and since the proclamation of the governor of this commonwealth, dated March tenth, eighteen hundred and sixty-two, whenever he is satisfied, upon the production of the same evidence as required by the board provided for in the act of the general assembly, passed February eighteenth, eighteen hundred and sixty-

Militia, how discharged

two, that they belong to the classes which are, by joint resolutions of the general assembly providing who shall be exempt from militia duty, under the call of the governor, by the proclamation aforementioned, declared to be exempt. But such discharge shall not be construed to exempt such persons from the operation of the act of the general assembly, passed February tenth, eighteen hundred and sixty-two.

Not exempted from draft

No. 15.—Joint Resolution to ascertain the amounts with which the several Corporations of the State would be assessed under the act of Congress to provide a War Tax, &c.

Adopted February 26, 1862.

Resolved by the general assembly, that the auditor of public accounts shall, as early as practicable, ascertain the amounts which would be payable by the several corporations of the state, under the act of the confederate congress to authorize the issue of treasury notes, and to provide a war tax for their redemption, and the amounts which may be payable into the treasury by the said corporations, under the laws of the state; and that he also ascertain the amount of taxes assessed and payable under said act of congress, by the several corporations of the state, exempt from state taxation; and that he report the same to the general assembly.

Auditor to furnish statements

No. 16.—Preamble and Resolution relative to Col. William J. Willey's case.

Adopted March 13, 1862.

Whereas Colonel William J. Willey, while in command of the thirty-first regiment of Virginia volunteers, was taken prisoner by the enemy, and during the time he was in their hands, another person was appointed colonel, and assigned to the command of said regiment by the governor; and a question has arisen whether Colonel Willey is entitled to pay while such prisoner: Therefore,

Preamble

Resolved by the general assembly, that in its opinion Colonel William J. Willey did not lose his right to pay, or to be restored to his command when released, by reason of his having been taken prisoner; but such pay is due from the confederate government; and there is no obligation on the state to pay either of said colonels.

Pay due

No. 17.—Resolution in relation to the Claims of Colonel William J. Willey.

Adopted March 17, 1862.

Be it resolved by the general assembly of Virginia, that the auditing board of Virginia be authorized, and they are hereby directed

Appropriation to Col. W. J. Willey

to allow and direct the payment of such claims as Colonel William J. Willey now or hereafter may be entitled to as a colonel in the military service of the state of Virginia; and the said auditing board are hereby required to make a special report of the circumstances of this case to the confederate government, when they shall make report of the expenditures of money incurred by Virginia prior to the union under the provisional government, with a view to the demand of the payment thereof by the commonwealth of Virginia from the said government.

No. 18.—Resolutions concerning Exempts, under the Proclamation of the Governor of the 10th March 1862.

Adopted March 14, 1862.

1. Resolved by the general assembly, that it shall be the duty of the boards of exemptions, acting under the act of February eighteenth, eighteen hundred and sixty-two, and any acts amendatory thereof, to take cognizance of all cases of exemption arising under these resolutions; and that the governor shall cause one or more boards, with similar powers, to be organized at the several places of rendezvous indicated by his proclamation of the tenth instant, by the commanding officer thereof, to be composed of such persons as such commanding officer may designate. *Duty of boards of exemption*

2. That the following persons shall be exempt under the said proclamation, to wit: All officers and employees of any rail road, canal, steam boat or telegraph company, whose services the president and superintendent of such company, or either of them, shall certify on honor to be indispensable for conducting the operations thereof; also such clerks as the quartermaster general and paymaster general of Virginia shall certify, on honor, to be necessary to conduct the business of their respective departments; and all superintendents and operatives in the paper mills of this commonwealth; also all persons whose services may be deemed by the board of exemptions to be indispensable in mining or manufacturing lead, iron, coal, salt, oakum, saltpetre, gunpowder, firearms, or other implements or munitions of war; also, all employees in woolen and cotton mills and incorporated shoe factories, the proprietors of which are under contracts to do work for the state or confederate government; and all tanners and shoemakers having contracts to do work for the state or Confederate States government, as long as necessary to complete such contracts; also, such officers of the several banks of circulation in this commonwealth, and their branches, as the respective presidents or cashiers may certify on honor to be indispensable to the proper management of the business of the banks, and may be so deemed by the said board of exemptions; also, such millers, blacksmiths and tanners, and overseers of committees of insane persons, *Who exempt*

as the said boards shall deem indispensable to the comfort of the community in which they may live, or who shall be in the employment of the state or confederate government; also, one editor of each newspaper now being published, and such employees as the editor or proprietor may certify on honor to be indispensable for conducting the publication of his newspaper, so long as the same is regularly published at least once a week; also, the jailor of every city, and such guard as the hustings court thereof may certify to be indispensable to the safe custody of prisoners; and the jailor of Henrico county, and such guard as the county court thereof may certify to be indispensable to the safe custody of prisoners.

Further exemptions

3. In each apothecary store now established and doing business, one apothecary, in good standing, who is a practical druggist, shall be exempt; also, the public printer, and the printer for the state senate, and such employees as each may certify on honor to be indispensable to the efficient performance of the public printing; also, one deputy sheriff for every twelve thousand inhabitants of every county; provided, however, that every county having less than twelve thousand inhabitants, shall have one deputy sheriff; and one deputy of every clerk of a court who may be deemed by the board incompetent, by reason of physical or mental disability, to discharge the duties of his office, or who may be absent therefrom in the public service.

When overseers exempt

4. It shall be competent for the board of exemptions, whenever in their judgment it may be indispensable for the police and convenience of the community, to exempt from the performance of military duty, under the proclamation aforesaid, overseers on the farms of widows and orphans, who have heretofore contracted for that service for the present year.

Professors exempt

5. That the professors of the university of Virginia and other incorporated colleges are hereby declared to be exempt, under the said proclamation.

Certificate

6. Whenever by these resolutions any class of employees or operatives are entitled to exemption on the certificate of other persons, it shall not be necessary for the applicants to appear in person before the board, but the exemption shall be ordered by the board, on the production of the certificate alone.

7. That persons claiming exemption under these resolutions, shall be entitled thereto so long only as the militia called out by the proclamation aforesaid may remain in service, and while such exempts remain in the employment by reason of which such exemption was allowed.

Draft not to be delayed

8. Nothing in these resolutions shall be construed to apply to, in-

terfere with, hinder or delay the draft under the act of February tenth, eighteen hundred and sixty-two, to raise the quota of Virginia to the confederate army, or to impair the effect of the act of February eighteenth, eighteen hundred and sixty-two, or any acts amendatory thereof, in relation to exempts.

No. 19.—Joint Resolution in relation to Exemptions.

Adopted March 13, 1862.

Resolved by the general assembly of Virginia, that the governor be authorized and required to exempt from the operation of his proclamation of the eleventh instant, all persons who may be certified to him by the war or navy department to be necessary to the work of the government of the Confederate States: provided, however, that no such person shall thereby be exempt from draft under the act of February tenth, eighteen hundred and sixty-two, or any other draft to fill up any future requisition. or shall thereby lose his privilege to volunteer in the state or Confederate States service.

Delegated authority

Proviso

No. 20.—Resolution in relation to Exemptions.

Adopted March 12, 1862.

Resolved, that a joint committee of five of the house and three of the senate, be appointed to enquire and report such legislation in regard to exemption from militia duty as may be necessary, by reason of the recent proclamation of the governor calling out the entire militia.

Exemption from militia duty

No. 21.—Joint Resolution exempting Clerks of District Courts.

Adopted March 17, 1862.

Resolved by the general assembly, that the clerks of the district courts of Virginia be and they are hereby declared to be severally exempt from military duty, under the proclamation of the governor of the tenth March eighteen hundred and sixty-two; and in case the said clerks are drafted under any law to supply the quota of the state to the confederate government, or either of them, authority and directions are hereby given that such clerk, in such case, shall deposit the papers and records of his office, for safe keeping, with the clerk of some other court of record, where such district court is required by law to be held.

Clerks of district courts exempt

No. 22.—Joint Resolution in relation to the Exemption of Deputy Sheriffs, &c.

Adopted March 11, 1862.

Code, chap. 22, § 2, amended

Resolved by the general assembly, that the act entitled an act amending and re-enacting the second section of chapter twenty-two of the Code of Virginia, respecting persons exempt from all military duties, and providing the mode of exemption, passed eighteenth of February eighteen hundred and sixty-two, was not intended and does not exempt from such duty any deputy of a sheriff of any county, or of a sergeant of any corporation, or of the clerk of any court, or the deputy of any other officer.

No. 23.—Joint Resolution exempting an additional Deputy Sheriff of the County of Franklin.

Adopted March 20, 1862.

Whereas it appears that the sheriff elected for the county of Franklin has farmed his office, and is himself now in the military service of the Confederate States:

Deputy exempted

Be it therefore resolved by the general assembly, that the governor of the commonwealth, if in his opinion the interest of the state will thereby be promoted, may exempt from militia duty in said county, one deputy sheriff, in addition to the one already authorized by law to be exempted.

No. 24.—Joint Resolution in relation to the appointment of a Joint Committee to enquire into the Treatment of Prisoners from this State now confined in Camp Chase, near Columbus, Ohio.

Adopted January 11, 1862.

Joint committee appointed

Resolved, that a joint committee, composed of three members on the part of the house of delegates, and two on the part of the senate, be appointed to ascertain and report how the prisoners from this state, confined in the federal prison at Camp Chase, near Columbus in the state of Ohio, are treated, and what steps should be taken by the authorities of this state to render them more comfortable.

No. 25.—Joint Resolution concerning Prisoners held at Wheeling.

Adopted February 1, 1862.

Treatment of prisoners

Resolved by the general assembly, that the joint committee appointed to enquire into the treatment, &c. of prisoners now held by the enemy at Camp Chase, Ohio, be instructed to enquire likewise in regard to prisoners held in Wheeling.

No. 26.—Joint Resolution in relation to Impressments.

Adopted February 5, 1862.

1. Resolved by the general assembly of Virginia, that our representatives in the congress of the Confederate States be requested to use their utmost efforts to procure the passage by congress of a law authorizing and limiting impressments for the military service of the Confederate States, and providing for the payment to the owner of land and personal property, such losses and damages as his property may have sustained while in the possession and use of the Confederate States of America. *Losses for damages sustained, how paid*

2. Resolved, that the clerk of this house forward, without delay, a copy of the foregoing resolution to each of our representatives in the confederate congress.

No. 27.—Resolutions approving the declarations of sentiment and purpose contained in certain Joint Resolutions of the Legislature of Georgia, and affirming and adopting the same.

Adopted January 8, 1862.

1. Resolved by the senate and house of delegates, that the declarations of sentiment and purpose contained in the joint resolutions of the legislature of Georgia, communicated this day, the sixth of January eighteen hundred and sixty-two, to the general assembly, by the governor of Virginia, are eminently just and patriotic; should be cordially and approvingly responded to by every state in the Southern Confederacy; and in the name and in behalf of this commonwealth, we do hereby affirm and adopt the same. *Approving action of legislature of Georgia*

2. Resolved, that the action of this general assembly be forthwith communicated to the executives of each of the other states of the Confederacy, together with a copy of the message of Governor Letcher, accompanying the resolutions of the state of Georgia, to be by them laid before their respective legislatures.

No. 28.—Joint Resolutions relative to the Jurisdiction of Virginia.

Adopted January 17, 1862.

Whereas the public enemy, invited by domestic foes, being in power within some of the counties in Virginia, where they are confiscating the property of loyal citizens, and otherwise oppressing them in a cruel manner: And whereas the traitors there, contemplating a division of this time-honored commonwealth, with the aid *Preamble* of this public enemy, have set up a pretended government over the same, which, under the force of circumstances, could not be prevented by the timely sending of an adequate military force: And whereas the legislature desires to reassure all loyal citizens throughout the commonwealth of their desire and intention to protect them: Therefore,

Jurisdiction of state

1. Resolved, by the senate and house of delegates, that in no event will the state of Virginia submit to, or consent to the loss of a foot of her soil: That it is the firm determination of the state, and known to be that of the confederate government, to assert and maintain the jurisdiction and sovereignty of the state of Virginia, to the uttermost limits of her ancient boundaries, at any and every cost.

Resolutions to be communicated

2. That the governor be requested to present a copy of these resolutions, properly certified, to the provisional congress now in session, and to the permanent congress, to convene on the twenty-second of February, for their approval.

No. 29.—Resolution for Joint Committee to confer with Confederate Authorities, and devise measures for Defence in Western Virginia against the Invasion of the Enemy.

Adopted January 8, 1862.

Resolved by the general assembly, that a joint committee of five members of the senate and seven of the house of delegates, be appointed to confer with the confederate authorities, and devise co-operative movements on the part of the state with the confederate government, for prompt protection to the persons and property of citizens, and the general defence in western Virginia against the invasion of the enemy.

No. 30.—Joint Resolution requiring R. M. Nimmo to execute a new Official Bond, and in the event of his failure to do so, providing for his Removal from Office.

Adopted March 26, 1862.

Bond to be given

1. Resolved by the general assembly, that Robert M. Nimmo, as the general agent and storekeeper of the penitentiary, is hereby required to execute a new official bond, with sufficient security, before the thirty-first day of March, eighteen hundred and sixty-two;

When to be removed

and if the said Nimmo fail to execute such bond before the said day, the general assembly will, by a joint vote of both houses, proceed on that day to remove him from office. But the execution of such new bond shall not operate to discharge the said Nimmo, or any of his sureties, from liability on account of any breach of the condition of his official bond as general agent and storekeeper of the penitentiary, bearing date on the thirtieth day of December eighteen hundred and sixty.

2. Resolved further, that the keeper of the rolls cause a copy of this resolution to be forthwith delivered to the said Robert M. Nimmo. *Copy to be sent*

No. 31.—Joint Resolution in relation to Judge E. P. Pitts of the Fifth Circuit.

Adopted February 21, 1862.

Whereas E. P. Pitts, judge of the fifth circuit of the state of Virginia, has been charged before this house with disloyalty against the state of Virginia and against the Confederate States of America, in adhering to and giving aid and comfort and counsel to the enemies of the said state and of the Confederate States, and it is proper for the general assembly to take such charges into consideration, and if sustained by sufficient evidence, to remove said E. P. Pitts from his office aforesaid: Therefore, *Preamble*

1. Be it resolved, with the concurrence of the senate, that on the twenty-fifth day of March eighteen hundred and sixty-two both houses of the general assembly will proceed to consider and decide upon the aforesaid charges against said E. P. Pitts, judge as aforesaid, and if such charges be sustained, to remove him from his said office.

2. Resolved further, that notice be given to said E. P. Pitts, Judge as aforesaid, of the proceedings proposed to be had against him, and of the causes alleged for his removal, by a publication of this preamble and resolutions in one of the newspapers printed in Richmond and in one of the newspapers printed in Norfolk, for four successive weeks prior to the said twenty-fifth day of March eighteen hundred and sixty-two. *Notice to be given*

No. 32.—Joint Resolution relative to the Publication of the Constitution of the Confederate States.

Adopted December 12, 1861.

Resolved by the general assembly, that the public printer be and he is hereby required to publish, with the Acts of the present session of the general assembly, the permanent constitution of the Confederate States. *Constitution to be published*

RESOLUTIONS.

No. 33.—Joint Resolution requiring the Auditor and other State Officers and Corporations, in the event of the Ratification of the Amended Constitution, to make Annual Reports.

Adopted March 27, 1862.

Resolved by the general assembly of Virginia, that in the event of a ratification of the amended constitution proposed by the late convention of Virginia, and the governor's proclamation announcing that result, it shall be the duty of the auditor of public accounts, the treasurer, the second auditor, and all other officers and corporations, instead of biennial reports, as now required by law, to make annual official reports to the same person, at the same period of the year, and of the same character as required by such laws, except so far as a substitution of annual for biennial reports requires modification.

No. 34.—Joint Resolution rescinding the Resolutions providing for the Publication of the Sketches of the Acts and Resolutions of the General Assembly.

Adopted March 26, 1862.

Resolved by the general assembly, that the joint resolutions providing for the publication of the sketches of the acts and resolutions of the general assembly, adopted March twenty-second, eighteen hundred and fifty-one, be and the same are hereby rescinded.

No. 35.—Resolution to authorize the Joint Committee appointed to confer with the Lessees of the Washington and Smyth County Salt Works, to send a deputation to said works.

Adopted December 20, 1861.

The joint committee who were charged with the duty of conferring with the lessees of the Washington and Smyth county salt works in reference to the supply of salt, respectfully report, that they have had the subject under consideration, and have opened a correspondence with them, asking a personal interview on the subject, and have received a reply, herewith filed, indicating a willingness to meet the committee in this city at any time they may designate. The committee have obtained much valuable and interesting information on the subject of the capacity of those works; which will be embodied in a subsequent report.

In view of the early recess of the general assembly, they recommend the adoption of the following resolution:

That the joint committee be authorized to send a deputation of their body to make a personal examination of the works, ascertain as far as practicable their capacity, the prospect for an increase in the supply of salt, and if deemed advisable, make a provisional contract therefor, subject to the approval and ratification of the general assembly.

No. 36.—Resolutions ratifying and confirming the Provisional Contract made for the Purchase of Salt to be furnished by Stuart, Buchanan & Co. of the Washington and Smyth Salt Works.

Adopted March 8, 1862.

1. Resolved by the general assembly, that the provisional contract made by the joint committee of the senate and house of delegates, for the purchase on behalf of the state of four hundred thousand bushels of salt, to be furnished by Stuart, Buchanan & Co., be approved, and the same is hereby ratified and confirmed. *Contract confirmed*

2. Resolved, that the committee be instructed to report a bill to carry into effect the provisions of said contract, and a proper distribution of said salt. *Bill to be reported*

No. 37.—Resolution for the appointment of a Joint Committee to make Arrangements for the proper Accommodation of the Senate and House of Representatives of the Confederate States.

Adopted December 21, 1861.

Resolved by the general assembly, that the governor of Virginia be and he is hereby authorized to provide suitable accommodations within the capitol, for the sessions of the congress of the Confederate States: provided, that the same shall not materially interfere with the sessions of the general assembly, and until the congress shall have time to procure more convenient accommodations. *Providing accommodation*

No. 38.—Joint Resolution in relation to the Expenditures of the Civil and Military Departments.

Adopted January 15, 1862.

Whereas the due equipment, subsistence and comfort of our brave men who, far from their homes, are daily periling health and life in defending our hearths and firesides against northern outlaws and barbarians, are objects of indispensable justice and necessity, enjoining a guarded economy upon all entrusted with the direction of the public expenditures, more especially of expenditures for civil services: *Preamble*

158 RESOLUTIONS.

Joint committee appointed

Resolved, that a committee of five be appointed, to act jointly with a committee of the house of delegates, with instructions diligently to examine the expenditures of the several departments, civil and military, and report whether any, and if any, what deductions may be justly made therein without detriment to the public interest.

No. 39.—Joint Resolution in relation to changing the Office of the Southern Protection Insurance Company, and also its place of meeting.

Adopted January 11, 1862.

Preamble

Whereas, by the act passed January thirtieth, eighteen hundred and fifty-four, incorporating the Southern protection insurance company, the said company was located at Alexandria, and the general office of the said company required to be held at that place, and it appears that it is impossible to hold any meetings of either the directors or stockholders of said company at Alexandria, by reason of its occupation by the enemy: Therefore,

Permission to change office of S. P. Insurance company

Be it resolved by the general assembly, that it shall be lawful for a majority of the directors of the Southern protection insurance company to change the office of said company from Alexandria to any other point within the state they may select, and to hold the meetings of the directors and stockholders of such company at such times and place as a majority of said directors may appoint.

No. 40.—Joint Resolution in relation to certain Coupon Bonds held by C. W. Purcell & Co. and R. H. Maury & Co.

Adopted March 31, 1862.

Preamble

Whereas C. W. Purcell & Co. and R. H. Maury & Co., prior to the twenty-sixth of June eighteen hundred and sixty-one, in pursuance of their licensed privilege as brokers, were in the habit of purchasing the coupon bonds of the state held in the city of New York, causing the said bonds to be canceled, and in that condition, to avoid risk, transmitting the same to the city of Richmond, where, in pursuance of an arrangement with the second auditor, a new bond would be issued in lieu of the one so canceled and delivered to the said second auditor: And whereas it is represented that the said C. W. Purcell & Co. and R. H. Maury & Co., about the twenty-sixth of June eighteen hundred and sixty-one, made several purchases of bonds in New York, which were canceled as aforesaid, but before they were delivered and converted into new stock, the convention of Virginia passed an ordinance suspending the payment of interest on all bonds held by residents of the United States prior to the twenty-sixth of June eighteen hundred and sixty-one, which was construed to prohibit the conversion of certain bonds purchased and held by said C. W. Purcell & Co. and R. H. Maury & Co., which remain in their hands and subject to waste and destruction: And whereas the said C. W. Purcell & Co. and R. H. Maury & Co., without at this time seeking to obtain the interest due on said bonds, but merely to have the evidence of the arrangement perpetuated:

It is resolved by the general assembly, that the second auditor be and he is hereby authorized to convert all such bonds so held by C. W. Purcell & Co. and R. H. Maury & Co. into the registered debt of the state, specifying on the records of his office on what occasion the same are converted, and that the payment of the interest thereon be suspended during the war, unless otherwise ordered by the general assembly, and endorse the same on the bonds: provided, that said conversion to said Purcell & Co. shall not exceed the amount of canceled bonds contained in a list thereof filed in the office of the second auditor, and endorsed as such by John Brannon, as chairman of the committee of finance of the senate, and the conversion for said R. H. Maury & Co. not to exceed three thousand dollars.

Auditor autho-rized to convert

SEPARATE ELECTION PRECINCTS.

Accomack—Court-house; Chingoteague; New Church; Corbin and Fletcher's; Mapp's; Guilford; Newstown; Onancock; Pungoteague.

Albemarle—Court-house; Lindsay's Turnout; Everettsville; Stony Point; Earleysville; Blackwell's; Free Union; Whitehall; Woodville; Batesville; Hillsborough; Crossroads; Covesville; Porter's; Warren; Wingfield's; Milton; Scottsville; Monticello House; Howardsville.

Alexandria—Five districts—Identical with magisterial districts.

Alleghany—Court-house; Robert Skeen's Hotel; John O. Taylor's; George Stull's; Clifton Forge; Jabez Johnston's; Griffith's Mill; Fork Run.

Amelia—At the same place as magisterial elections.

Amherst—New Glasgow; New Hope; Orozoco; Chestnut Grove; Folly; Temperance; Pedlar Mills; Elon; Court-house; Buffalo Springs.

Appomattox—Court-house; Union Academy; Wesley Chapel; Hamner's; Spout Spring; Oakville.

Augusta—Court-house; Waynesborough; Middlebrook; Spring Hill; Mt. Meridian; Greenesville; District No. 2, Staunton; Mt. Sidney; Stuart's Draft; Fishersville; Churchville; New Hope; Craigsville; Deerfield; Mt. Solon; Swoop's Mill; Midway; Newport.

Barbour—Court-house; Burner's; Nutter's; Bartlett's; Mitchell's; Yeager's; Glady Creek; Holtsberry's; Coal Precinct.

Bath—Court-house; Cedar Creek; Hamilton's; Cleek's Mill; Williamsville; Milton; Green Valley.

Berkeley—Court-house; Billingre's Hotel; Mill Creek; Hedgesville; Falling Waters; Robinson's Mill; Gerrardstown; Oak Grove; Glen Spring; Crossroads.

Boone—Court-house; Adkins' on Mud river; Adkins' on Big Coal; Lawrence's; Curtiss'; Daniel Laurel's; Thompson's Mill; Miller's.

Botetourt—Court-house; Mountain Union; Carver's; Buchanan; Rocky Point Mills; Jackson; Junction Store; Dibrell's Spring; Amsterdam.

Braxton—Court-house; Triplett's; Rilney's; Cool's; John Crite's former Residence; Christian Moda's former Residence; Haymond's Mill; Cunningham's; Saulsberry; Stonestreet; Jacob P. Conrad's.

Brooke—At same places as magisterial elections; Goodwill School-house.

Brunswick—Court-house; Benton Precinct; Trotty's Store; Oak Grove; Lucy's Store; Smoky Ordinary; Nicholson's Precinct.

Buckingham—Court-house; Stanton's Shop; New Store; Wright's; Curdsville; Allen's.

Cabell—Court-house; Guyandotte; Laidley's Store; Spurlock's; Doolittle's Mill; Barrett's Precinct; McComas'; Falls of Guyandotte; Killgore's Precinct; Peter Buffington's

Campbell—Places the same as for magisterial elections.

Caroline—Court-house; Reedy Church; Oakley's; Needwood; Sparta; Pitts'; Port Royal; Sycamore; Golansville; Madison's.

Carroll—Court-house; Polly Quesenberry's; Thomas Quesenberry's; Laurel Fork; Kinzey's; Easter's; Newman's; Sulphur Springs; Richard Haynes'; Nathaniel Haynes'.

Charles City—Court-house; Delarue's; Ladd's; Waddell's; Apperson's; Vaiden's.

Charlotte—Court-house; Keysville; Smith's Tavern; Clement's; Wyliesburg; Roby's Shop; Hawrey's Store; Matthews & Smith's Store.

Chesterfield—Court-house; Britton's Shop; Shell's Tavern; Manchester; Robinson's Store; Clover Hill.

Clarke—Court-house; Russell's Tavern; White Post; Millwood; Royston's Tavern; Collier's Toll-gate.

Craig—Court-house; Carper's Tavern; Walker's Store; Scott's Tavern; Martin Huffman's; George Sarver's.

Culpeper—Court-house; Rixyville; Colvin's; Stevensburg; Pottsville; Gathright's; Wellsborough; Griffinsburg.

Cumberland—Court-house; Tavern Precinct; Oak Forest; Irwin's.

Dinwiddie—Court-house; Billups'; Goodwynsville; Williams' Shop; Darvill's; Williams'; Sutherland's.

Doddridge—Court-house; Allen's; Bond's; Kay's; Davis'.

Elizabeth City—Court-house; Liveley's Ordinary; Fox Hill.

Essex—Court-house; Occupacion; Lloyd's; Miller's; Bestland; Centre Cross.

Fairfax—Court-house; Crossroads; Arundel's; Sangster; Ross'; Dranesville; Anandale; West End; Accotink; Centreville; Falls Church; Fars; Bayless; Pulman's.

Fauquier—Court-house; Plains; Salem; White Ridge; Farrowsville; Orleans; Liberty; Morrisville; Paris; New Baltimore; Rectortown; Weaversville; Upperville.

Fayette—Court-house; Blake's; Gauley Bridge; Fleshman's; Lewis'; Keeney's; Terry's; Coleman's.

Fluvanna—Court-house; Howard's Store; Columbia; Morris' Store; Kent's Store; Haden's Store; Bashan and Snead's; Bledsoe's; Union Grove.

Franklin—Court-house; Allen's; Union Hall; Booth's Store; McVey's Tanyard; Helm's; Dickerson's; Kinsey's; Richland Grove; Bush's Store; Sydnorsville; Snow Creek; Aldridge's Store.

Frederick—Court-house; Engine-house; Gwinn's Tavern; Hoover's Tavern; Newtown; Middletown; Russell's; Anderson's; Brucetown; Swhier's; Cole's School-house; Pughtown.

Giles—At the same places as magisterial elections; Howe's Hotel.

Gilmer—Court-house; Jerkland; Burke's; Widow Stumps; De Kalb's; Peregrine Hays'; Knott's; Hewett's; Troy.

SEPARATE ELECTION PRECINCTS.   163

Goochland—Court-house; Little Store; Perkinsville; Smith's Shop; Mills'; Holland's; Poor's; Jennings'.

Gloucester—Places the same as for magisterial elections.

Greenbrier—Court-house; Blue Sulphur Springs; Lick Creek; Anthony's Creek; Spring Creek; Southside; Lewisburg; White Sulphur; Miller's; Irish Corner; Williamsburg; Frankfort.

Greene—Court-house; Ruckersville; Terrill Shifflett's; McMullansville.

Greenesville—Court-house; Ryland's Depot; Blunt's Mill; Poplar Mount.

Halifax—Court-house; Meadesville; Mount Carmel; Halifax Springs; High Hill; Hudson's; Garrett's Store; Whiteville; Republican Grove; Brooklyn.

Hampshire—Court-house; John Liller's; Miers'; Burlington; Taylor's; Doyles'; Thompson's; Lupton's; Kisner's; Lovett's; Mrs. Offutt's; Stump's; Fority; Sherrard's School-house; Hash's; Blair's; Arnold's; Piedmont.

Hancock—Court-house; Holliday's Cove; New Manchester; Aton's School-house.

Hanover—Court-house; Hughes'; Jones' Crossroads; Negrofoot; Dentonsville; Cold Harbor; Ashland.

Harrison—Court-house; Shinnston; Union Meeting-house; West Milford; Lumberport; Bridgeport; Davis'; Lynch's; Sardis; Swisher's Mills.

Henrico—Court-house; Kidd's; Sweeney's; Alley's; Lovingsteine's; Dickman's; Hughes'; Walkerton; Hungary.

Henry—Court-house; Rough and Ready; Irisburg; Oak Level; Leatherwood; Ridgway; Horse Pasture.

Highland—Monterey; Ruckmansville; Wiley's; Crab Bottom; Doe Hill; McDowell; Pullins' School-house; Gwin's.

Jackson—Ripley; Click's; Jones'; Range's; California; Depue's; Three forks of Reedy; Trumansville; Ravenswood; Squire Slaven's; Murrayville; Moor's Mill; McGrew's Mill.

James City—Court-house; Burnt Ordinary; York River.

Jefferson—Eight districts—Places the same as for magisterial elections.

Kanawha—Court-house; Fleetwood's; Richards'; Bradley Low's; Atkinson's Mill; Alts's; Conts' Month; Dog Creek; Givens'; Malden; Fork Coal; Harper's; Gatewood's; Month Sandy; Brooks' Store.

King George—Court-house; Hampstead; Clifton; Shiloh.

King & Queen—Court-house; Clark's Store; Stevensville; Newtown; Centreville.

King William—Court-house; Plain Dealing; Aylett's; Lanesville.

Lancaster—Court-house; Litwalton; Kilmanock; White Stone.

Lewis—Court-house; McLaughlin's Store; Jane Lew; Freeman's Creek; Skin Creek; Hall's Store; Leading Creek; Collins' Settlement.

Logan—Same places as for magisterial elections.

Loudoun—Court-house; Waterford; Lovetsville; Hillsborough; Waters'; Purcell's Store; Snickersville; Union; Middleburg; Mt. Gilead; Gum Spring; Whaley's; Goresville.

Louisa—Court-house; Free Union; Hopkins' Mill; Trevilian's; Bell's Crossroads; Walton's Tavern; Terrell's Store; Parrish's Store; Frederickshall; Bumpass' Turnout; Thompson's Crossroads; Isbell's Store; Hope's Tavern; Gentry's Store; Coshy's Tavern.

Lunenburg—Court-house; Brown's Store; Pleasant Grove; Knight and Oliver's Mill; Lochlomond; Bagley's Store; Jordan's Store.

Madison—Court-house; Stony Hill; Criglersville; Huffman's Mill; Graves' Mill; Rapidan Meeting-house; Fleshman's Shop; Locust Dale.

Marion—Places the same as those for magisterial elections, and at Glover's Gap.

Marshall—Court-house; Pleasant Hill; Jones' Hotel; Bleak's School-house; Parsons' Precinct; Mouth of Fish Creek; Sand Hill; Crossroads; Smart's School-house; Burley's; Terrill's School-house; Big Run; Fair View; Linn Camp.

Mason—Court-house; Berriage Precinct; Love Precinct; Barnett Precinct; West Columbia; Neaso Precinct; Eighteen Mile Precinct; Grigg's; Sixteen Mile Precinct; Thirteen Mile Precinct.

Matthews—Same places as for magisterial elections.

Mecklenburg—Court-house; Jones'; Edmundson's; Clarkesville; Reeke's; Overhy's; Wright's; Harwell's; Christiansville; Gillespie's.

Middlesex—Jamaica; Saludo; Sandy Bottom.

Monongalia—Court-house; Guseman's; Jones'; Osburn's Ross'; Lofter's; Cassville; Christman's; Laurel Point; Cox's; Moore's River; Tenant's; Dowall's; Warren.

Monroe—Court-house; Dickson's; Miller's Store; Rollinsburg; Mrs. Peck's; Red Sulphur; Haynes'; Centreville.

Montgomery—Court-house; Guerrant's; Peterman's; Price's Forks; Keister's; Crumpacker's; Lafayette; Kent and McConkey's; Rough and Ready; Lovely Mount.

Morgan—Court-house; Lowe's; Baker's; Unger's; Hume's; Swann's; Miller's.

Nansemond—Court-house; Hargrove's Tavern; Harrison's Shop; Holyneck; Chuckatuck; Somerton; Darden's Store; Cypress Chapel.

Nelson—Fortune's; New Market; Faber's Mill; Greenfield; Massie's Mill; Roberts'.

New Kent—Court-house; Barhamsville; Chandler's Store; Ratcliff's Tavern.

Nicholas—Court-house; Taylor's; Brown's; Neil's; Dunhar's; Nutter's; Sawyer's; Pierson's.

Norfolk City—Four Wards.

Norfolk County—Court-house; Glebe School-house; Sycamore's; Deep Creek; School-house District No. 2; School-house in Providence; Pleasant Grove School-house; Butts' Road School-house.

Northampton—Court-house; Bay View; Franktown; Johnsontown; Capeville.

Northumberland—Court-house; Lottshurg; Burgess' Store; Wicomico.

Nottoway—Court-house; Jennings' Ordinary; Wilson and Jones'; Blackfare.

Orange—Court-house; Barboursville; Thomas Smith's; Thomas Rhoade's; Locust Grove.

Page—Court house; Honeyville; Oakham; George Price's Mill; Springfield; Mohler's Mill; Rileysville; Pranty's Mill.

SEPARATE ELECTION PRECINCTS. 165

Patrick—Court-house; Robertson's; Aldridge's and Lee's; Penn's Store; Carter's Store; Hancock's; Elamsville; Slusher's; Connor's; Shilor's; Gates'; Mankin's.

Pendleton—Franklin; Harper's; Kiser's; Vint's; Cowyer's Mill; Mallow's; Seneca; Circleville.

Petersburg—Centre Ward; East Ward; South Ward; West Ward.

Pittsylvania—Court-house; Danville; Spring Garden; Whitmell; Cascade; Smith's; Beaver's; Riceville; Rorer's; Strail's Store; White's; Laurel Grove; Chalk Level; Mooman's.

Pleasants—Court-house; Spring Run; Sugar Creek; Pine Grove; Hale's Mill.

Pocahontas—Four districts—Places of election the same as for magistrates.

Powhatan—Court-house; Clarke's Mill; Macon; Sublett's.

Preston—Brandonville; Miller's; Burnel's; Feather's; Summit School-house; Germany; Graham's; Huddlesin's; Kingwood; Martin's; Independence; Evansville; Nine's; Funk's.

Princess Anne—Court-house; Kempsville; London Bridge; Capp's Shop; Creed's Bridge; Blackwater.

Prince Edward—Court-house; Marble Hill; Spring Creek; Prospect; Farmville; Sandy River.

Prince George—Court-house; City Point; Lilley's School-house; Tuttle's Precinct; Harrison's Store; Templeton.

Prince William—Dumfries; Colo's; Occoquan; Roevn's; Brentsville; Kinchelon's; Haymarket; Ludley.

Pulaski—Court-house; Brown's; Galbreath's; Ruper's; Thorn Spring Camp.

Putnam—Court-house; Bailey's; Pocatalico; Alexander's; Red House; Jones'; Hurricane Bridge; Wheeler's; Buffalo; Eighteen Mile Precinct.

Raleigh—Same places as magisterial elections.

Randolph—Court-house; Pennington's; Minear's; Taylor's; Kemp's; Lee.

Rappahannock—Washington; Sperryville; Yates'; Amissville; Catherine Deatheridge.

Richmond City—Jefferson Ward; Madison Ward; Monroe Ward.

Richmond County—Court-house; Stony Hill; Tavern-House; Farnham Church; Lyell's Store.

Ritchie—Harrisville; Skelton's; Leedan's; Ireland's; Deems'; Rawson's; Tebbs'; Murphy's.

Roanoke—Court-house; Big Lick; Cave Spring; Barnett's.

Rockbridge—Court-house; Brownsburg; Fairfield; Natural Bridge; Collierstown; Kerr's Creek; Trevey's; Hamilton's School-house; Paxton's School-house; Wilson's Shop; Broad Creek; Goshen.

Rockingham—Harrisonburg; Keezletown; McGaheysville; Conrad's Store; Spartapolis; Henton's Mills; Gordon's Store; Bowman's Mill; Timberville; Menonite School-house; Bridgewater; Ottobine; Wittig's Store; Sprinkle's Store; Taliaferro's Store; Port Republic; Mount Crawford; Samuel Coots'.

Russell—Court house; Grisle's; Pound; Holly Creek; Guest's Mountain; Castlewood's; Fugate's; Hanson's; Aston's Store; Cook's Mills; Dorton's; Baylor's Store; Gibson's; Hendrick's Store.

Scott—Court-house; Winegar's; Hart's; Smith's; Pullieng's; Nickelsville; Alley's; Osborne's Ford; Stony Creek; Peters'; Rye Cove; Carter's; Neil's; Roller's.

Shenandoah—Court-house; Strasburg; Crossroads Meeting-house; Conner's Church; Town Hall; Keller's School-house; Edinburg; Columbia Furnace; Mount Jackson; Crossroads School-house; New Market; Ferrestville.

Smyth—Court-house; Broad Ford; Hays'; Sanders'; St. Clair's Bottom; Burton's Store; Ashlin's; Atkins'.

Spotsylvania—Court-house; Fredericksburg; Mount Pleasant; Andrews'; Chancellor's.

Stafford—Court-house; White Oak; Master's; Tackett's Mill; Falmouth; Coakley's; Harwood's; Acquia.

Southampton—Court-house; Drewrysville; Crosskeys; Joyner's; Murfee's; Black Creek Church; Berlin; Falson's Store.

Surry—Four districts—At the same places as for election of magistrates.

Sussex—Court-house; Comann's Mill; Henry; Stony Creek; Newville; Owen's Store.

Taylor—Court-house; Mahaney; Reed's; Claysville; Knottsville; Haymond's; Fetterman; Grafton.

Tazewell—Court-house; Repass; Tiffany's; Mouth of Slate; Gibson's; Crabtree's; Litzeville; Liberty Hill; Tugg.

Tyler—Court-house; Centreville; David John's; Hammond's; Underwood's; Dancer's; Sistersville; Pleasant Mills.

Upshur—Court-house; Reedy Mills; Simpson's Mill; Posty; Marples; Marshall's; Chesney's.

Warren—Court-house; Boyd's Mill; Bentonville; Leary's School-house; Cedarville; Howellsville.

Warwick—Three precincts—The same as for election of magistrates.

Washington—Court-house; Clark's; Davis'; Waterman's; Merchaut's; Gobble's; Mills'; Worley's; Williams'; Morell's; Fullen's School-house; Clark's; Kelly's School-house; Delusko Mills; Oss'; Miller's; Good Hope; Green Spring.

Wayne—William Cram's. (No other returned.)

Westmoreland—Court-house; Hague; Warrensville; Oak Grove.

Wetzel—Court-house; Forks of Proctor; Knob Fork; Church's; Cohorn's; Ice's; Willey's School-house.

Williamsburg—Court-house.

Wirt—Court-house; Foster's; Petty's.

Wood—Precincts at the same places as election for magistrates.

Wyoming—Court-house; Gad's; Rhinehcart's; McKinney's; Bailey's; Lester's.

Wythe—Eight districts—Precincts at same places as for election of magistrates.

York—Three districts—Precincts at the same places as for election of magistrates.

TABLE

Showing the Times for the Commencement of the Regular Terms of each Circuit, County and Corporation Court.

Counties and corporations.	Circuit courts. When terms commence.	County and corporation courts. Monthly terms.	County and corporation courts. Quarterly terms.
	Circuits.		
Accomack,	5. 1st Monday in May and 1st day of November,	Last Monday,	March, May, August, Novem.
Albemarle,	10. 2d Monday in May and Oct.	First Monday,	Do. June, do. do.
Alexandria,	9. 3d Monday in May and 2d Monday in November,	Fourth Monday,	Feb'y, May, do. do.
Alleghany,	14. 9th of April and September,	Third Monday,	March, June, do. do.
Amelia,	2. 25th April and 20th Oct'r,	Fourth Thursday,	Do. May, do. do.
Amherst,	10. 22d of March and August,	Third Monday,	Do. June, do. do.
Appomattox,	3. 21st April and September,	Thursday after 1st Monday,	Do. May, do. do.
Augusta,	11. 1st June and 1st November,	Fourth Monday,	Do. do. do. Octo'r.
Barbour,	21. 6th May and October,	First Monday,	Do. June, do. Novem.
Bath,	11. 15th May and October,	Second Monday,	Do. do. do. do.
Bedford,	4. 25th April and September,	Fourth Monday,	Feb'y, May, July, do.
Berkeley,	13. 24th April and September,	Second Monday,	March, June, August, do.
Boone,	15. 2d Monday after 4th Monday in April and September,	Wednesday after 2d Monday,	Do. do. do. do.
Botetourt,	14. 26th May and October,	Second Monday,	Do. do. do. do.
Braxton,	19. 27th April and September,	First Tuesday,	Do. do. do. do.
Brooke,	20. 18th March and August,	Last Monday,	Feb'y, May, July, do.
Brunswick,	2. 27th March and 2d of Oct.	Fourth Monday,	March, do. August, do.
Buckingham,	3. 5th April and September,	Second Monday,	Do. do. do. do.
Cabell,	18. 27th March and August,	Fourth Monday,	Do. June, do. do.
Calhoun,	19. 12th April and September,	First Tuesday after 4th Monday,	Do. do. do. do.
Campbell,	3. 18th May and October,	Second Monday,	Do. do. do. do.
Caroline,	6. 1st March and 18th Sept.	Second Monday,	Feb'y, May, do. do. (To take effect June 1, 1861.)
Carroll,	16. Monday before last Monday in March and August,	First Monday,	March, June, August, Novem.
Charles City,	4. 18th May and November,	Third Thursday,	Do. May, do. do.
Charlotte,	3. 25th March and August,	First Monday,	Do. June, do. do.
Chesterfield,	2. 7th May and 12th Nov'r,	Second Monday,	Do. do. do. do.
Clarke,	12. 12th May and October,	Second Monday in June and 4th in other months,	Feb'y, May, July, Octo'r.
Clay,	15. 1st April and September,	Second Monday,	March, June, August, Novem.
Craig,	14. Tuesday after 1st Monday in March and August,	Fourth Monday,	Do. do. do. do.
Culpeper,	10. 1st Monday June and Nov.	Third Monday,	Do. May, do. do.
Cumberland,	3. 5th March and August,	Fourth Monday,	Feb'y, do. July, Octo'r.
Danville,	3. 22d March and August,	Thursday after 2d Monday,	March, June, August, Novem.
Dinwiddie,	2. 20th March and 25th Sept.	Third Monday,	Do. May, do. do.
Doddridge,	19. 22d May and October,	Fourth Monday,	Do. June, do. do.
Elizabeth City,	6. 15th March and September,	Fourth Thursday,	Do. May, do. do.
Essex,	8. 25th April and 12th Nov.	Third Monday,	Do. do. do. do.
Fairfax,	9. 1st Monday June and Nov.	Third Monday,	Do. June, do. do.
Fauquier,	9. Tuesday after 1st Monday in April and September,	Fourth Monday,	Do. May, do. do.
Fayette,	15. 7th June and November,	Thursday after 2d Tuesday,	Do. June, do. do.
Floyd,	16. 1st Monday April and Sept.	Thursday after 3d Monday,	Do. do. do. do.
Fluvanna,	10. 10th April and September,	Fourth Monday,	Do. May, do. do.
Franklin,	4. 15th May and October,	First Monday,	Do. June, do. do.
Frederick,	12. 10th June and November,	Monday before 1st Tuesday,	Do. do. do. do.
Fredericksburg,	— — —	Second Thursday,	Do. do. Octo'r, Decem.
Giles,	15. 20th May and October,	Second Monday,	Do. do. August, Novem.
Gilmer,	19. 19th April and September,	Tuesday after 3d Monday,	Feb'y, do. do. do.
Gloucester,	6. 13th April and October,	First Monday,	March, May, do. do.
Goochland,	10. 1st April and September,	Third Monday,	Do. do. do. do.
Grayson,	16. 4th Monday April and Sept.	Fourth Monday,	Feb'y, do. July, do.
Greenbrier,	14. 8th May and October,	Fourth Monday,	March, June, August, Novem.
Greene,	10. 3d Monday June and Nov.	Wednesday after 2d Monday,	Do. do. do. do.

Counties and corporations	Circuit courts. When terms commence.	County and corporation courts. Monthly terms.	County and corporation courts. Quarterly terms.
	Circuits.		
Greenesville,	1. 28th April and 2d Nov'r,	First Monday,	March, May, Aug't, October.
Halifax,	3. 1st day of May and Oct.	Fourth Monday,	Do. June, do. Novem.
Hampshire,	13. 1st April and September,	Fourth Monday,	Do. do. do. do.
Hancock,	20. 10th March and August,	Tuesday after 2d Monday,	
Hanover,	8. 10th March and 26th Sept.	Fourth Tuesday,	Jan'y, April, June, October.
Harrison,	21. 15th April and September,	First Monday,	Feb'y, April, July, November.
Hardy,	12. 20th April and September,	Monday before 1st Tuesday,	March, June, Aug't, do.
Henrico,	6. 23d April and October,	First Monday,	Do. do. do. do.
Henry,	4. 1st April and September,	Second Monday,	Do. May, do. do.
Highland,	12. 2d May and October,	Thursday after 3d Monday,	Do. June, do. do.
Isle of Wight,	1. 16th May and 18th October,	First Monday,	Do. May, do. October.
Jackson,	16. 2d May and October,	Second Monday,	Do. June, do. Novem.
James City and Williamsburg,	6. 25th May and November,	Second Monday,	Feb'y, do. do. do.
Jefferson,	13. 20th May and October,	Second Monday in June and October, 3d in other months,	March, do. do. October.
Kanawha,	16. 27th May and October,	Third Monday,	Do. do. do. do.
King George,	6. 23d March and 19th Sept.	First Thursday,	Feb'y. do. do. Novem.
King & Queen,	8. 2d May and 19th Nov'r,	First Thursday,	March, do. do. do.
King William,	6. 13th May and 25th Nov'r,	Fourth Monday,	Do. May, do. do.
Lancaster,	8. 15th April and 2d Nov'r,	Third Monday,	Do. do. do. do.
Lee,	17. 2d Monday after 4th Monday in April and Sept.	—	Do. June, do. do.
Lewis,	19. 8th May and October,	Second Monday,	April, do. do. Septem.
Logan,	15. 1st Monday after 4th Monday in April and Sept.	Third Monday,	March, do. do. Novem.
Loudoun,	9. 4th Monday in April and 3d Monday in October,	Second Monday,	Do. do. do. do.
Louisa,	10. 20th April and September,	Second Monday,	Do. do. do. do.
Lunenburg,	2. 13th April and 6th October,	Second Monday,	Do. May, do. do.
Lynchburg,	3. 3d of June and 3d Nov'r,	First Monday,	Do. June, do. October.
Madison,	10. 1st Monday Mar. and Aug.	Fourth Thursday,	Feb'y. do. do. do.
Marion,	21. 10th June and November,	First Monday,	March, do. do. Novem.
Marshall,	20. 1st May and 1st October,	Third Monday,	Do. do. do. do.
Matthews,	6. 6th April and September,	Second Monday,	Do. May, do. do.
Mason,	18. 19th April and 16th Sept.	First Monday,	Feb'y, June, do. do.
Mecklenburg,	2. 2d of April and 15th Sept.	Third Monday,	Do. May, do. do.
Mercer,	15. 27th May and October,	Thursday after 2d Monday,	March, June, do. do.
McDowell,	17. 1st Monday Mar. and Aug.	Second Monday,	Do. do. do. do.
Middlesex,	6. 1st April and October,	Fourth Wednesday,	Do. May, do. do.
Monongalia,	20. 1st April and September,	Fourth Monday,	Do. June, do. do.
Monroe,	14. 25th April and September,	Third Monday,	Do. do. do. do.
Montgomery,	16. 2d Monday in Ap'l and Sept.	First Monday,	Do. do. do. do.
Morgan,	13. 6th May and October,	Fourth Monday,	Do. do. Sept. do.
Nansemond,	15. 16th April and 19th Oct'r,	Second Monday,	Do. do. Aug. do.
Nelson,	10. 27th day of April and Sept.	Fourth Monday,	Feb'y, May, July, do.
New Kent,	8. 10th May and November,	Second Tuesday,	March, do. Aug. do.
Nicholas,	15. 6th April and September,	Monday before 2d Tuesday,	Do. June, do. do.
Norfolk city,	1. 1st June and 15th Nov'r,	Fourth Monday,	Feb'y, April, July, October.
Norfolk county,	1. 1st April and 20th Sept.	Third Monday,	March, June, Aug't, Novem.
Northampton,	5. 3d Monday in April and Sep.	Second Monday,	Do. do. Sept. do.
Northumberland,	8. 9th April and 29th Oct'r,	Second Monday,	Do. May, Aug. do.
Nottoway,	2. 20th April and 15th Oct'r,	First Thursday,	Do. do. do. do.
Ohio,	20. 10th May and October,	First Monday,	Feb'y, July, Sept'r, Decem.
Orange,	10. 1st May and October,	Fourth Monday,	March, May, Aug't, Novem.
Page,	12. 11th April and September,	Fourth Monday,	Feb'y, do. July, do.
Patrick,	4. 12th April and September,	Fourth Monday,	Do. do. do. do.
Pendleton,	13. 27th April and September,	Thursday after 1st Tuesday,	March, June, Sept. do.
Petersburg,	2. 22d May, 16th November,	Third Thursday,	Do. do. do. Decem.
Pittsylvania,	4. 28th May and October,	Third Monday,	Do. do. Aug. Novem.
Pleasants,	19. 30th May and October,	Thursday after 2d Monday,	Feb'y, May, July, October.
Pocahontas,	14. 16th April and September,	First Tuesday,	March, June, Aug't, Novem.
Powhatan,	2. 2d May and 27th October,	First Wednesday,	Do. do. do. October.
Preston,	21. 19th March and August,	Second Monday,	Feb'y, May, July, Novem.
Princess Anne,	1. 25th May and 22d Sept'r,	First Monday,	March, June, Aug. do.
Prince Edward,	3. 15th March and August,	Third Monday,	Feb'y, May, July, do.
Prince George,	2. 17th May and 19th Nov'r,	Second Thursday,	March, do. Aug. do.
Prince William,	9. 2d Monday in May and Oct.	First Monday,	Do. June, do. do.
Pulaski,	16. 3d Monday April and Sept.	Thursday after 1st Monday,	Do. do. do. do.
Putnam,	18. 8th April and September,	Fourth Monday,	Do. do. do. do.
Raleigh,	15. 3d Monday April and Sept.	First Monday,	Do. do. do. do.
Randolph,	21. 26th May and October,	Fourth Monday,	Do. do. do. do.

TIMES AND PLACES OF COURTS.

Counties and corporations.	Circuit courts. When terms commence.	County and corporation courts. Monthly terms.	County and corporation courts. Quarterly terms.
	Circuits.		
Rappahannock,	9. 3d Monday in March and 1st Monday in October,	Second Monday,	March, May, August, Novem.
Richmond city,	7. 1st of Nov. and 1st May,	Second Monday,	Jan'y, Ap'l, July, Octo'r.
Richmond co.	8. 3d April and 23d October,	First Monday,	March, May, August, Novem.
Ritchie,	19. 15th April and September,	Tuesday after 1st Monday,	Feb'y, June, do. do.
Roane,	18. 17th May and October,	First Monday,	Jan'y, Ap'l, July, Sept'r.
Roanoke,	14. Wednesday after 4th Monday in March and Aug't,	Third Monday,	March, June, August, Novem.
Rockbridge,	11. 12th April and September,	Monday before 1st Tuesday,	Do. do. do. do.
Rockingham,	12. 11th May and October,	Third Monday,	Feb'y, May, do. do.
Russell,	17. 4th Monday April and Sept.	Tuesday after 1st Monday,	March, June, do. do.
Scott,	17. 3d Monday after 4th Monday April and September,	Tuesday after 3d Monday,	Do. do. do. do.
Shenandoah,	12. 30th March and August,	Monday before 2d Tuesday,	Do. do. do. do.
Smyth,	17. 1st Monday April and Sept.	Tuesday after 1st Monday,	Do. do. do. do.
Southampton,	1. 2d May and 7th October,	Third Monday,	Do. do. do. do.
Spotsylvania,	8. 20th May and 6th October,	First Monday,	Do. do. do. do.
Stafford,	9. 4th Monday Mar. and Sept.	Third Wednesday,	Do. do. do. do.
Staunton,	— — —	Wednesday after 1st Monday,	Feb'y, May, July, Octo'r.
Surry,	1. 10th May and 25th October.	Fourth Monday,	March, do. August, Novem.
Sussex,	1. 24th April and 29th October.	First Thursday,	Do. do. do. Octo'r.
Taylor,	21. 4th March and August,	Fourth Monday,	Do. June, do. Novem.
Tazewell,	17. Last Monday Mar. and Aug.	Wednesday after 1st Monday,	Feb'y, May, July, Octo'r.
Tucker,	21. 22d May and October,	Third Monday,	March, June, August, Novem.
Tyler,	20. 22d April and September,	Second Monday,	Do. do. do. do.
Upshur,	21. 4th April and September,	Third Monday,	Do. do. do. do.
Warren,	12. 25th March and August,	Third Monday,	Do. May, do. do.
Warwick,	6. 21st March and September,	Second Monday,	Do. June, do. Decem.
Washington,	17. 3d Monday April and Sept.	Fourth Monday,	Do. do. do. Novem.
Wayne,	18. 20th March and August,	Tuesday after 1st Monday,	Do. do. do. do.
Webster,	15. 14th April and September,	Fourth Tuesday,	Do. do. do. do.
Westmoreland,	8. 28th March and 18th Oct.	Fourth Monday,	April, May, do. do.
Wetzel,	20. 12th April and September,	Tuesday after 1st Monday,	Feb'y, do. July, Octo'r.
Williamsburg,	6. 25th May and November,	Fourth Monday,	March, June, August, Novem.
Winchester,	— — —	First Saturday,	Do. May, do. do.
Wirt,	19. 3d April and September,	Tuesday after 4th Monday,	Feb'y, June, do. do.
Wise,	17. 1st Monday after 4th Monday in April and Sept.	Fourth Monday,	March, do. do. do.
Wood,	19. 5th June and November,	Third Monday,	Feb'y, do. do. do.
Wyoming,	15. 4th Monday April and Sept.	Friday after 3d Monday,	March, do. do. do.
Wythe,	16. 1st Monday May and Oct.	Second Monday,	Do. do. do. do.
York,	6. 25th March and September,	Third Monday,	Do. May, do. Octo'r.

RECEIPTS AND DIS

1860.
Oct'o. 1, To balance, per last annual report, — — — 139,305 18
31, To receipts in October 1860, — — — 69,367 35
Nov. 30, To do. in November 1860, — — — 114,266 04
Dec. 31, To do. in December 1860, — — — 1,616,084 00

$ 1,939,022 57

1861.
Jan'y 1, To balance brought down, — — 252,842 57
31, To receipts in January 1861, — — 382,915 39
Feb'y 28, To do. in February 1861, — — — 138,562 97
March 30, To do. in March 1861, — — — 308,808 41

$ 1,083,129 44

April 1, To balance brought down, — — — 307,932 72
30, To receipts in April 1861, — — — 259,984 92
May 31, To do. in May 1861, — — — 1,278,619 78
June 29, To do. in June 1861, — — — 1,126,455 33

$ 2,972,992 75

July 1, To balance brought down, — — — 172,355 16
31, To receipts in July 1861, — — — 4,199,120 40
Aug. 31, To do. in August 1861, — — — 2,496,468 21
Sept'r 30, To do. in September 1861, — — — 1,175,391 89

$ 8,043,335 66

Oct'o. 1, To balance this day against the treasurer, exclusive of the funds under the direction of the second auditor, — $ 138,214 84

BURSEMENTS—1860-61.

By amount of warrants paid in October 1860,	· ·	157,812 93
By do. do. November 1860,	· ·	113,833 90
By do. do. December 1860,	· ·	1,414,533 07
Balance 31st December 1860,	· ·	252,842 67
		$ 1,939,022 57
By amount of warrants paid in January 1861,	· ·	581,849 08
By do. do. February 1861,	· ·	66,211 47
By do. do. March 1861,	· ·	127,136 17
Balance 30th March 1861, ·	· ·	307,932 72
		$ 1,083,129 44
By amount of warrants paid in April 1861,	· ·	210,241 02
By do. do. May 1861,	· ·	1,598,533 69
By do. do. June 1861,	· ·	991,862 88
Balance 29th June 1861,	· ·	172,355 16
		$ 2,972,992 75
By amount of warrants paid in July 1861,	· ·	4,333,811 56
By do. do. August 1861,	· ·	2,366,093 54
By do. do. September 1861,	· ·	1,205,215 72
Balance 30th September 1861,	· ·	138,214 84
		$ 8,043,335 66

Total amount of warrants issued by the auditor from the 1st October 1860 to the 30th September 1861, inclusive, - · ·   13,166,732 98
Add warrants issued by the auditor prior to the 1st October 1860, and paid after that day,   ·   ·   ·   ·   505 11

                                                                                                                                                                     13,167,238 09

Deduct warrants No. 4174, $ 5 64
                        6194,   1 50
                        6450,   6 78   Issued prior to the 1st Oct. 1861,
                        8092,   9 14   and unpaid on that day,   -   103 06
                        8827,   55 00
                        11472,   25 00

                               Paid by the treasurer in the fiscal year 1860-61,   *$ 13,167,135 03

Auditor's Office, 14th Nov. 1861.

* This large amount of disbursements is caused by the redemption of temporary loans contracted, and treasury notes issued within the fiscal year, amounting to $4,397,424 37.

INDEX.

ACTS AND RESOLUTIONS OF THE GENERAL ASSEMBLY.
Resolution abolishing sketches, 156

ADJUTANT.
Ordinance concerning office, amended, 59
How appointed, 59
Rank and pay, 59

ADJUTANT GENERAL.
Pay of, 60
To appoint a clerk, 60
Where to reside, 60

ADJUTANT GENERAL'S OFFICE.
Resolution in regard to the appointment of a temporary clerk in, 147

ADMINISTRATIONS.
See Taxes.

ALLEGHANY AND BOTETOURT COUNTIES.
Tax on dogs authorized, 134
Power to county courts, 134
Time when exercised, 134
Duty of commissioner of revenue, 134

AMENDED CONSTITUTION.
Resolution as to, 156

AMHERST COUNTY.
Refunding to, a license tax paid by Geo. L. Shrader, 131
Amount appropriated, 131

APPROPRIATIONS.
What appropriated, 26
General assembly, 27
Representation, 27
State convention, 27
Electors, 27
Officers of government, 27
Criminal charges, 27
Slave convicts, 27
Support of convicts, 27
Penitentiary, 27
Courts, 27
Records, 27
Adjutant general, 27
Military contingent fund, 27
Military institute, 27
Public guard, 27
Water rent, 27
Armory, 27
Repair of arms, 27
Commissioners of revenue, 27
Lunatic asylum at Staunton, 27
Lunatic asylum at Williamsburg, 28
Lunatics, 28
Deaf, dumb and blind, 28
Pensioners, 28
Civil contingent fund, 28
Civil prosecutions, 28
Governor's house, 28
Capitol, 28
Messenger, 28
Grattan's Reports, 28
Leigh's Reports, 28
Guaranteed bonds of James river and Kanawha company, 28
Registration, 28
Commissions, 28
Temporary loans, 28
Chesapeake and Ohio canal, 28
Pages, 28
Porter to senate, 28
Services in capitol, 29
Public debt, 29
Secretary of commissioners of sinking fund, 29
Public printing, 29
General fund, 29
Disposal of general fund, 29
When payments made, 29

APT, DAVID.
Authorising the commissioner of the revenue for the southern district of Halifax county to issue a license to, as a hawker and peddler, 132
Amount of license, 132

BANKS.
Authority to change place of business, 87
Ordinance of convention amended, 87
Provisos, 87
Savings banks and insurance companies, 87
Authorized to issue small notes, 85-6
State stock banks, 86
Repealing clause, 86

BANK DIRECTORS.
Provisions as to, 88
Proviso, 88

BANK OF PITTSYLVANIA.
Preamble, 93
Acts of directors legalised, 93

BAYLEY, E. W.
Refunding a sum of money to, 131
Amount appropriated, 131

BELLEVUE HOSPITAL.
Act Incorporating, 137
Company incorporated, 137
Powers of company, 137
By-laws, 137
Real estate, 137
Proviso, 138

BENNETT, COALMAN D.
Amount appropriated from literary fund to, 129

BOARDS OF EXEMPTION.
Powers of, 49
Act of Feb. 18, 1862, construed, 49
Discharge, how granted, 49
Punishment of, 50
Substitutes, 50
Act of Feb. 18, 1862, amended, 50
Claim for exemption filed with clerk, 50
How tried, 50
See Exemptions.

BOOTH, MOSES G.
Act for relief of, 134
Amount, 134

BROWN, Dr. PETER F.
Registered certificates of state stock to be issued to, 126
Preamble, 126
Stock, how issued, 126
Bond filed, 126
Amount appropriated, 127

BRUNSWICK COUNTY.
County court authorized to impose a tax on dogs, 135
Time of action, 135
Duty of commissioners, 135

BUCKWALTER, E. J. ET. AL.
Compensation for keeping certain negro convicts, 133
Amount appropriated, 133

CHAMBERS, ROBERT.
Sureties of, released, 126

CHESAPEAKE AND OHIO CANAL.
See Guaranteed bonds.

CHURCH PROPERTY.
Code amended, 82
Number of acres to be held, 82

CIVIL CONTINGENT FUND.
Amount appropriated to, 31, 32

CIVIL RIGHTS AND REMEDIES.
Exercise of, extended in certain cases, 99
What period to be excluded, 99

CIRCULATION OF SMALL NOTES.
Act of March 1854 amended, 88
How amended, 88

CLERKS OF DISTRICT COURTS.
Resolution exempting them, 151

COLLECTION OF ARMS.
Of state and Confederate States, 55
Arms, how collected, 55
To be returned to adjutant general, 55
Compensation for collecting, 55
Notice, how given, 55
Arms, how transmitted, 55
Penalty, 55
How penalty recovered, 56

COLUMBIA.
Act allowing time to build on lots in, 124

COMMISSIONERS IN CHANCERY.
Code amended, 80
Temporary, how appointed, 80
Special commissioners, 81

CONSTITUTION OF THE CONFEDERATE STATES.
Resolution in relation to publication of, 155

CONFEDERATE STATES TREASURY NOTES.
Receivable in payment of taxes, 32

CONFEDERATE STATES WAR TAX.
Treasury notes, how issued, 32
Banks authorised to lend, 32
Auditor to issue warrants, 32-3
To whom payable, 33
How approved, 33
Faith of commonwealth, 33
Interest, 33
Whom auditor to consult during session, 33
In recess, 33
Obligations, when canceled, 33

CONGRESS OF CONFEDERATE STATES.
Joint resolution in relation to the accommodation of, 157

COOKE, ROBERTSON.
An act for the relief of, 125

COOPER, GEORGE.
An act to pay for his services as clerk of the 115th regiment of militia, 126

CORPORATIONS OF THE STATE.
Joint resolution in relation to the assessment of a war tax, under act of congress, on, 148

COUNTY COURTS.
Jurisdiction of, extended, 99
Ordinance amended, 99

COUNTY ROADS.
Code amended, 81
Who to work road, 81
Fines, 81
How recoverable, 81

COUPON BONDS.
Resolution in relation to bonds held by C. W. Purcell et al. 158

INDEX.

CULPEPER MINUTE MEN AND RIFLES.
Reorganization of, 56
How reorganized, 56
To report to adjutant general, 56
When to be reorganized, 57

CUNNINGHAM, J. E.
Act for relief of, 130
Amount appropriated, 130

CURRENCY—SMALL NOTES.
See Illegal currency.

CURRILL, JOHN S.
An act for the relief of, 118
Amount appropriated, 118

DANVILLE.
Charter of, amended, 109
Corporate limits, 109
Municipal authority, 109
Time of holding courts, 109
Jurisdiction, 110
Compensation, 110
Delegated powers, 110
Corporate powers, where vested, 110
Election, 110
Election of clerk, 110
Voters, 110
Where elections held, 111
Commissioners, 111
How elections held, 111–12
Vacancies, how filled, 112
Form of election, 112
Oath of office, 112
Council, 112
Mayor, 113
Powers of council, 113–14
Power to subscribe to stock, 114
Compensation to mayor, 115
Conservators of the peace, 115
Delegated powers, 115
Sergeant, 115
Repealing clause, 115

DAVIS, THOMAS K.
Damages refunded to securities of, 120
Damages released to, 130

DECEDENTS, ESTATES OF.
See Taxes.

DEEDS.
See Taxes.

DEFAULTING DISLOYAL OFFICERS.
Act concerning, 38
Preamble, 38
Remedies, 38
Account, where filed, 38
Judgment, how entered, 39
Interest, 39
Time of computation, 39
Basis of account, 39
Lien of judgment, 39
Limitation for reversal, 39
Proviso, 40

DEPUTY SHERIFFS.
Resolution in relation to their exemption, 152
Resolution exempting additional deputy sheriff of Franklin, 152

DESERTERS.
Code amended, 81
Who treated as, 81

DILLARD, HUGHES.
An act authorizing him to erect a dam half across Smith's river, 128
Proviso, 128
Damages, 129

DISTILLATION.
See Grain.

DISTRESS FOR RENT.
Code amended, 77
Legal proceedings against persons in military service, 77
Exception, 77

DIVIDENDS.
See Taxes.

DOSS, R. O.
Securities of, released, 123
Preamble, 123
Amount appropriated, 123

DREW, A. M.
Act for the relief of, 125

DUFFEY, GEORGE.
Act compensating, 132
Amount appropriated, 132

DULANY, W. H.
Act compensating, 130
Amount appropriated, 130

ENROLLMENT OF ACTS, ETC.
Code amended, 79
Keeper of rolls, 79
Rolls, how made, 79
Copies, how made, 79
Publication of acts, 79

ENROLLMENT OF MILITARY FORCES.
Rolls, how obtained, 40
Requirements, 40
Who enrolled, 40
Exempts, 40
Powers of governor, 40
Punishment for failure to enroll, 41
Penalties on officers, 41
Compensation to officers, 41

EXCHANGE BANK AT WESTON.
Act concerning money stolen from, 89
Preamble, 89
How recovered, 89
General provisions, 89–90
Who liable for money, 90
Who may sit as juror, 90
Officer, when liable, 90

INDEX.

EXEMPTIONS FROM MILITARY DUTY.

Who exempted,	47
Who not exempted,	47
Officers of city, &c., how exempted,	48
When exempt remanded to service,	48
How places of exempts to be filled,	48
Boards of, how constituted,	48
Their powers,	48
Discharges, how granted,	49
Claims for exemption, how tried,	49
Penalties on boards of,	49
Repealing clause,	49
Certain parties exempt on religious grounds,	50
Who exempt,	50
Terms of exemption,	51
Proviso,	51
To surrender all arms,	51
Duty of sheriffs and collectors,	51
Duty of board,	51
Proviso,	51
Joint resolution in relation to exemptions,	151
Resolutions in relation to exempts under proclamation of the governor,	149
Who exempt,	149
Further exemptions,	150
When overseers exempted,	150
Professors exempted,	150
Certificate,	150
Draft not to be delayed,	150

EXPENDITURES.

Of the civil and military departments,	157
Resolution in relation thereto,	157

FERRIES.

Act amending act concerning, in the counties of Russell and Wise,	135

FITCHETT, W. T.

Act for the relief of,	121

FOREIGN INSURANCE COMPANIES.

See Taxes.

FORFEITED AND DELINQUENT LANDS.

Act to enforce penalties as to,	36
Preamble,	36
Failure of commissioner,	36
Motion,	36
Amount, how ascertained,	37
Reservation to commissioner,	37
Notice, how given,	37
Judgment, for what amount,	37
Act of 1861 repealed,	37

FREE NEGROES.

To be engaged in the manufacture of saltpetre and other munitions of war,	146
Joint resolution in relation thereto,	146
Preamble,	146
Authorized to carry, out of state,	146
Term of service; liberty to return,	146
Enrollment and employment of,	61
Ordinance to provide for, amended,	61
How enrolled,	61
Requisition, how made,	62
Penalty on officers,	62
To be received in public service,	62
Penalty for refusing to obey requisition,	62
Subject to articles of war,	62
Volunteers, how accepted,	63
Clerk of house to furnish copy,	63

FREDERICKSBURG.

Act amending charter of,	117

FROBELL, DAVID W.

Act compensating him for services connected with the militia of Nicholas and Greenbrier,	125

GALLERY.

To be erected in congress hall,	106
Commissioners to superintend erection of,	106
Costs, how paid,	106

GRAIN.

Unnecessary consumption of, prevented,	101
Distillation prohibited,	101
Penalties,	101
What constitutes separate offence,	101
Distillery and implements, how forfeited,	101
Bond, how given,	102
When liquor to be seized,	102
When grain to be forfeited,	102
Penalty on officer,	102
Prosecutions, when tried,	102

GRAZIERS BANK OF VIRGINIA.

Preamble,	90
Bank incorporated,	90
Name of bank,	90
Assets,	90
Liabilities,	91
Proviso,	91
Limitations,	91
Proviso,	91
Redemption of notes,	91
Reservation of power by general assembly,	92
Special deposit,	92
Powers delegated,	92
Location,	92
Capital stock,	92
General provisions,	93

GEORGIA.

Resolution approving resolutions from,	153

GENERAL ASSEMBLY.

Annual sessions of, provided for,	104
Act of 1853 amended,	104
When to meet,	104

GENERAL ASSEMBLY, MEMBERS OF.

Code amended,	80
Oaths, how taken by,	81

GRESHAM, G. W.

See Carrill, John S.

GUARANTEED BONDS.

Interest on,	34
How paid,	34

INDEX. 177

Corporations, how proceeded against, 34
Proviso, 34

HARRISON, J. C.
Act for the relief of the sureties of, 127

HASKINS, J. H.
Act for the relief of, and his securities, 127

HAYMOND, A. F.
Act for relief of, 132
Amount appropriated, 132

HILLSVILLE MILITARY ACADEMY.
Act incorporating, in Carroll county, 141
Powers, 141
How managed, 141
Trustees, 142
Treasurer, 142
Bond to be executed, 142
Mode of subscription, 142

HORE, E. A. W.
Act for the relief of, 122

ILLEGAL ASSESSMENTS.
Penalty for, 36
How enforced, 36
Against whom, 36
Who exempt, 36

ILLEGAL COLLECTION OF TAXES.
See Illegal assessments.

ILLEGAL CURRENCY.
Penalties remitted, 84
Proviso, 85
Act of March 1854 repealed, 85
Proviso, 85

IMPRESSMENTS.
Resolution in relation to, 153

INDIAN TRIBES.
Act concerning bonds held in trust for certain, 34
Preamble, 34-5
Transfer, how made, 35
Certificates, how issued, 35
Interest, how paid, 35

INDIGENT SOLDIERS.
Act for relief of widows and minor children of, 59
Allowances, how made, 59
How chargeable, 59
Who to make allowances, 59
When, 59
Justices to be summoned, 59

INSOLVENT MUSTER FINES.
How certified, 60
To be allowed by auditor, 60

JAILS AND POORHOUSES.
To be used by Confederate States for safe keeping of free negroes, 63
When free negroes to be committed to, 63
Duty of jailor and overseer of poor, 63

JAMES RIVER AND KANAWHA CO.
Act of 23d March 1860 amended, 73
How amended, 73-4
Powers of Kanawha board, 74
Registered stock, how issued, 75
Stock, how deposited, 75
Bond, how executed, 75

JUDGMENT LIENS.
Code amended, 78
Lien of judgment, 78

JURISDICTION OF VIRGINIA.
Resolution relative to, 153

KELLEY, JOHN.
Act to pay to, the amount of a judgment against the board of public works, 123

KERSEY, EDWARD, ET AL.
Act authorizing the granting of a new trial, by the judge of the hustings court of the city of Richmond, to, 122

KIRK, W. N.
See Currell, John S.

LAWSON, C. N., ET AL.
Joint resolution requesting the governor to commission, 145

LESSEES OF WASHINGTON AND SMYTH SALT WORKS.
Joint resolution in relation to, 156

LICENSE.
Who may obtain, 26

LIGHT INFANTRY COMPANY IN HALIFAX.
Joint resolution in relation to, 145

LIGHT INFANTRY COMPANY FROM MIDDLESEX.
Joint resolution authorizing governor to accept, 144

LOYAL CITIZENS.
Act for the protection of, 99
Preamble, 99
Penalty for issuing process, 100
Penalty on sheriff or constable, 100
Judgment, how obtained, 100
Sureties liable, 100
Lien created, 101
Record proof not required, 101
Property of, how restored, 101

LUSK, JOHN A. M.
Act to authorise the auditor of public accounts to settle with sureties of, 120

MANASSAS GAP RAIL ROAD.
See Rail road connection.

MARENGO LODGE No. 109, I. O. O. F.
Act incorporating, at Martinsburg, 138
Property to be held, 138
Powers, 139

178 INDEX.

MARLIN'S BOTTOM AND WEBSTER COURTHOUSE ROAD.
Road to be constructed, 76
Amount appropriated, 76
Proviso, 77

MARYLAND VOLUNTEERS.
To be transferred to Maryland regiments, 56
Preamble, 56
How transferred, 56

MAURY, R. H. & CO.
See Coupon bonds.

McKINNEY, BARNEY, ET AL.
Act authorizing a reassessment of a house and lot in Lynchburg owned by them, and for the repayment to them of certain taxes, 119

MILITIA.
Resolution in relation to, discharged from confederate service, 147

MILITARY FORCES.
See Enrollment.

MILITARY FORCES OF VIRGINIA.
Accurate list and record of, to be made, 53
Record of, to be made, 53
Lists, how made out, 53
Powers of governor, 54

MILITARY CONTINGENT FUND.
Organized, 61
Payments to be made from, on the order of the governor, 61
Amount appropriated for, 61

NEGRO CONVICTS.
When employed on public works, 103
When to be employed in making iron, 103
Governor to prescribe rules, 103

NEW COMPANIES.
Resolution asking secretary of war to decline to receive, 145

NEW RIVER.
Constituted a lawful fence, 136
Board of public works to remove obstructions in navigation of, 72
When work to be completed, 72
Amount appropriated, 72
Engineer to be employed, 72
Proviso, 72

NIMMO, R. M.
Resolution requiring him to execute new official bond, 154

NON-COMMISSIONED OFFICERS AND PRIVATES.
Joint resolution in relation to pay of, 146

NORFOLK BOROUGH.
Act of 1818 amended, 116
Jurisdiction extended, 116
Form of presentment; proviso, 116

NORTHWESTERN BANK OF VA.
See Graziers Bank.

OAK GROVE CHURCH.
Trustees of, to sell and convey property, 139

OFFICIAL SEALS, TAX ON.
See Taxes.

ORDNANCE DEPARTMENT.
Act creating, amended, 52
Officers appointed by governor, 53
Their pay, 54

ORANGE AND ALEXANDRIA RAIL ROAD.
See Rail road connection.

ORGANIZATION OF MILITARY FORCES.
Who to be enrolled, 44
What cities, 44
First class, 44
Second class, 44
Where to perform duty, 45
For what period, 45
FIRST CLASS.
How organized, 45
How rearranged, 45
Regiments, when consolidated, 45
How officers appointed, 45
SECOND CLASS.
How organized, 45
When, may be drilled, 45
Militia laws applicable to, 46
Exemptions, 46

PENITENTIARY STOREKEEPER.
To make quarterly statements, 107
Penalty for failure, 107

PIEDMONT RAIL ROAD COMPANY.
Ordinance of North Carolina incorporating, ratified, 71
Proviso, 71
Further condition, 72

PIKEMEN.
John Scott to raise regiment of, 54
Officers, how elected, 54
Who may be enlisted; proviso, 54
Appropriation, 54
When pay to commence, 55

PITTS, JUDGE E. P.
Joint resolution in relation to, 155

PRISONERS IN CAMP CHASE.
Resolution to enquire into their treatment, 152

PRISONERS.
Resolution concerning, held at Wheeling, 152

PROCESS IN SUITS.
See Taxes.

PROVISIONAL ARMY OF VIRGINIA.
Organization of, 57

INDEX.

Ordinance of convention providing for, amended,	57
Officers of,	57
Regimental officers,	57
Company officers,	57–8
Proviso,	58
General and field officers, how appointed,	58
Aids de camp,	58
Enlistments,	58

PULASKI AND WYTHE COUNTIES.
Lines of, changed,	106

PURCELL, C. W. & CO.
See Coupon bonds.

RAIL ROAD CONNECTION.
Between Orange and Alexandria and Manassas gap rail roads,	67
Preamble,	67
Road, how extended,	67
Capital stock, how increased,	67
Company may borrow money,	67
Amount,	67
Meeting of stockholders,	67
Stock sold, at what price; proviso,	67
Power of councils of Richmond and Fredericksburg,	67–8
Terms of subscription,	68
When road to be commenced,	68
Exemptions from taxation, when to cease,	68
Subject to existing laws,	68
Right of Manassas gap and Orange and Alexandria rail road companies,	68
Time to commence work,	68
How, in cases of partial constructions,	68
Cost, how paid,	68
Between Manassas gap and Winchester and Potomac rail roads,	69
Board of public works authorized to construct road,	69
Powers of board,	69
What may be condemned,	69
Military efficiency,	69
How condemned,	70
Amount, how paid,	70
Amount appropriated,	70
Treasury notes, how issued,	70
Interest,	70
How receivable,	70
Ordinance to apply,	70
Road, how transferred,	70
Stock of commonwealth, how transferred,	71
Road to be under control of board of public works,	71
When board authorised to make other arrangements,	71
Between Richmond and Petersburg,	64
Connection authorized,	64
Proviso,	64
Government, power of,	64
Assent of cities not required,	64
Power of condemnation,	64
Damages,	64
Notice to common council,	64
Surveys to be made,	64
Present connection, how abandoned,	65

RANDOLPH MACON COLLEGE.
Act authorising the establishment of a military school as a part of the instruction at,	139
How managed,	139
Delegated authority,	140
Professors,	140
Terms upon which students may be admitted,	140
Proviso,	140
Duty of officers,	140
Board of visitors,	140
Returns,	140
Powers of governor,	140
Authority to confer degrees,	141
Commissions,	141

RANGER COMPANIES.
Organised,	51
Officers commissioned,	51
Companies, how organised,	51
Pay of officers and privates,	52
Under command of governor,	52
Where companies to act,	52
When to be under confederate authority,	52
Proviso,	52

REMOVAL.
Of records and papers of courts,	79
Code amended,	79
When records may be removed,	79
Penalty,	80

REPAIR AND PURCHASE.
Cannon, how repaired,	46
Small arms to be purchased,	46
Appropriation,	46
Contracts, how made,	46

REQUISITION.
On Virginia by president Confederate States for troops,	41
Governor to ascertain what number of men to be raised,	41
Companies to number 100 men,	41
How apportioned,	41
Volunteers to report,	42
Quotas, how drafted,	42
Levies, how assigned,	42
Re-enlistment,	42
Roll of company,	42
Draft, how made,	42
Draft, how apportioned,	42
Artillery companies,	42
Who discharged,	43
Companies, how reorganised,	43
Officers not re-elected,	43
Field officers, how elected,	43
Company officers; term of service,	43
Substitutes, how furnished,	43
If substitute be drafted,	44
Persons claiming exemption, how examined,	44
Volunteers, how accepted,	44

RICHMOND AND PETERSBURG RAIL ROAD.
Act releasing lien from,	65
Preamble,	65–6
Lien released,	66

RUSSELL COUNTY.
One hundred and seventy-seventh regiment of, attached to 25th brigade, 57
Where to train, 57

SABBATH (VIOLATIONS OF).
Hunting, &c. prohibited, 93
Fines, how recovered, 93-4
Recognizances, how given, 94
Fines, how recoverable, 94
Restraining clause, 94

SALES OF REAL ESTATE.
Under executions in favor of the commonwealth, 78
Code amended, 78
Sale, how made, 78
Time of credit, 78
Fees and commissions, 78
When officer liable, 78

SALT.
Joint resolution in relation to purchase of, 157

SALTVILLE AND TAZEWELL COURTHOUSE ROAD.
Road to be repaired, 77
Amount appropriated, 77

SEAL OF COURTS.
Tax on, when not exacted, 60
When refunded, 61

SHERIFFS.
Act to suspend proceedings against, 37

SINKING FUND.
No further investments to be made, 31

SLAVES.
To prevent escape of, in certain counties, 104
Powers of county courts, 104
Boats to be destroyed, 104
Justices to be summoned, 104

SMALL NOTES.
Authority to issue bank notes, 82
Notes redeemed, 82
Forfeiture, 82
City of Richmond to issue, 83
Amount, 83
Certain towns to issue, 83
State stock banks, 83
Powers of cities, counties and towns to issue, 83
Notes, how redeemed, 83-4
Quarterly returns to be made, 84
Repealing clause, 84
Obligation on real and personal property, 84
See Circulation of small notes.

SMOOT, NORMAN C., ET AL.
Act for relief of, commissioner of revenue of Hampshire county, 129
What appropriated, 129

SOUTH SIDE RAIL ROAD.
Line of road, how changed, 66

SOUTHERN PROTECTION INSURANCE COMPANY.
Joint resolution in relation to changing office of, 158

SPECIE PAYMENTS.
Act of 1861, chapter 57, amended, 86
Privilege suspended, 86
Forfeitures remitted, 86
Proviso, 86

SPECIAL MESSENGERS.
Joint resolution authorizing governor to send, to obtain enrollments, 147

STAY LAW.
Act re-enacting ordinance of convention, 94
Act to suspend sales, &c. 95
Execution not to issue, 95
Infancy, &c. 95
Proviso, 95
Proviso as to attachments, 95
Execution, how issued, 95
How quashed, 95
Property, how retained, 95
Cases which may be tried by a jury, 96
Other cases not to be tried, 96
Issues out of chancery, 96
Writs of ad quod damnum, 96
Misdemeanors, 96
Limitation, 96
Liabilities of public officers, 96
Interest, when collected, 96
Interest and alimony, 96
Payment of interest, how enforced, 97
Execution, how directed, 97
No security to be taken, 97
Ordinance repealed, 97
Who may have benefit of such act, 97

SUPERINTENDENT OF WEIGHTS AND MEASURES.
Office of, abolished, 106
Register to perform duties of, 106

SUSPENSION OF SALES, ETC.
See Stay law.

TAXES.
On land, 3
What included therein, 3
On personal property, 3
What included, 3
What exempted, 3
On free negroes, 4
On white male, 4
On public bonds, 4
On bank dividends, 4
On dividends of other incorporations, 5
On dividends of corporations not chartered by this state, 5
On income, 5
Exception, 5
Taxes of officers, how paid, 5
On toll bridges and ferries, 5
On collateral inheritances, 5
On estates passing under sequestration acts, 5-6
On internal improvement companies, 6

Companies, when to report,	6	Theatrical performances,	15
What to report,	6	Theatre,	15
When only partly in state,	6	Tax for twenty-four hours,	15
Report made on oath,	6	For three months,	15
Penalty for failure,	6	Refreshments in theatres,	15
Tax on passengers,	6	Ardent spirits,	15
To be exempt from tax on land,	6	Shows, circuses, &c.	15–16
In case of failure to pay tax,	6–7	Manufacture of malt liquors,	16
Express companies,	7	Sale of malt liquors, how licensed,	16
Semi-annual reports,	7	Brokers,	16
Returns on oath,	7	Insurance companies,	16
On receipts,	7	Physicians, attorneys, &c.	16–17
Exception,	7	Daguerreian artists,	17
Penalty for failure to report,	7	Horses brought into the state,	17
On original suits,	7	Horses, mules, &c. sold for profit,	17
On appeals, &c.	7	Carriages, buggies and other vehicles,	17
On seals,	8	Slaves bought or sold for profit,	17
On wills and administrations,	8	General provisions,	17
On deeds,	8	Tax on corporations,	18
On bank corporations,	8	When acts to be published,	18
On manufacturing companies,	8	When not,	18
On gas light and other companies,	9	Tax tickets, when made out,	18
On savings institutions,	9	Penalty for failure to obtain license,	18
On private corporations,	9	Limitation of license,	18
Exceptions,	9	Where licensed privilege to be exercised,	19
Unorganized companies, how taxed,	9	Forms for tax payers,	19
LICENSES.		Market value of stocks to be taxed,	19
Ordinaries,	10	When double tax imposed,	19
Retailing,	10	When deductions made from commis-	
Cook shops and eating houses,	10	sioner's compensation,	19
Private entertainment,	10	Slaves and similar subjects, how taxed,	19
Bowling alleys,	10	Value of lands and lots not to be	
Billiard tables,	10	changed,	20
Bagatelle tables,	11	When agricultural products to be	
Livery stables,	11	taxed,	20
Distilleries,	11	Domestic manufactures, how taxed,	20
Tax for distilling,	11	Licenses, how granted,	20–21
Rectifying ardent spirits,	11	Change of firm,	21
Tax,	11	Insolvents, how collected,	21
Additional tax, if continued,	11	Commission,	21
Merchants,	11	Penalty on officers,	21
Merchant's specific tax,	11	License to sutlers,	21–2
When tax proportioned to sales,	12	License to a merchant who is a be-	
Merchant's permission to sell ardent		ginner,	22
spirits,	12	Commissions to commissioners,	22
License to beginners,	12	Repealing clause,	22
To continue business,	12		
Merchant tailors and others,	12	TAXES ON DIVIDENDS, ETC.	
Commission merchants,	13	Banks to declare dividends,	22
Tobacco auctioneers,	13	When and for what period,	23
Ship brokers,	13	Cashier to report to auditor,	23
Auctioneers,	13	In case of no dividend, report to be	
Scale of license,	13	made,	23
Real estate auctioneers,	13	Penalty for failure to report,	23
Per centage, when charged,	13	Dividends to be paid into the treasury,	23
Where sales to be made,	13	On certain estates of decedents,	23
Exceptions,	13	Tax on collateral inheritances,	23
When goods may be consigned,	13	Duty of commissioners to assess tax,	23
Taxable sales,	13	Rate of tax,	23
Common crier,	13	Where annual tax to be placed,	23
Sample merchants,	14	Specific tax,	23
Express and telegraph companies,	14	Sheriff to collect and pay tax,	23
Patent rights,	14	Exception,	23
Quack medicines,	14	When estate deemed paid or delivered,	24
Book agents,	14	Personal representative liable to da-	
If non-residents,	14	mages,	24
Religious books,	14	Sheriff to collect,	24
Agents for renting houses,	14	The per centum on tax,	24
Agents for hiring negroes,	15	Personal representative to sell property	
Stallions and jackasses,	15	to pay tax,	24

Writ tax; tax on seals, &c. 24
Tax on process to be paid to the clerks
  of courts, 24
When tax on seals not to be charged, 25
Deeds not to be admitted to record
  until tax is paid, 25
Will not admitted to probate until
  tax is paid, 25
No administration to be granted until
  tax is paid, 25
How clerks, &c. to account and pay, 25
Correctness of, to be sworn to, 25
Commissions for collecting, 25
Penalty for failure, 25
For continued failure, 25
No money to be drawn by any clerk
  until report is made, 25
Where money to be paid; when, 25
Judgment in case of default, 25
How and where taken, 26
Judgment to be without notice, 26

TEMPORARY DEFICIENCIES.
Money, how borrowed, 31
Act of 1851 inoperative, 31

TREASURY NOTES.
Issue authorized; amount, 30
Denomination, 30
Receivable in payment of taxes, 30
Ordinance of convention, 30
How signed, 30

THORN ROSE CEMETERY.
Act amending second section of act of
  incorporation, 138

TRIAL.
Of persons in certain cases, 93
When offence committed in counties
  in the hands of the enemy, &c. 93
Duty of judge, 93
Examining court, 94
Venue, how changed, 94
Where confined, 94

TURNPIKE AND PLANK ROAD COMPANIES.
Dead timber, how to be removed, 75
Fines, 76

UNION (TOWN OF).
Act of 1861 amended, 117
Delegated powers, 117
Bonds to be given; liabilities, 117
Record preserved, 117
Liable to taxation, 117
Oath of office of mayor, 117
Powers of mayor; fees, 117
Patrols, 117

VACANCIES.
To be filled pro tempore in certain cases, 105

VAUGHAN, JOHN W., ET ALS.
Act for the relief of, 121

VIRGINIA CANAL COMPANY.
Act 29th March 1861 amended, 73
How amended, 73

VIRGINIA FORCES.
Complete lists of, to be filed, 53
Lists, how made, 53
Powers of governor, 54

VIRGINIA MILITIA.
Joint resolution concerning the discharge
  of a portion thereof, 147

VIRGINIA'S QUOTA OF THE CONFEDERATE ARMY.
Joint resolution in relation to, 144

VOLUNTEER COMPANY IN THE CITY OF PETERSBURG.
Joint resolution concerning, 146

VOLUNTEER COMPANIES.
From any county or corporation which
  may have furnished its quota to the
  confederate army, 144
Resolution authorizing the governor to
  receive, 144

VOLUNTEER FORCES OF THE STATE.
Resolution in relation to, 143

WARM SPRINGS AND HUNTERSVILLE ROAD.
Road to be repaired; amount appropriated, 76

WASHINGTON, JOHN.
Governor to sell convicted slave named
  Richard to, 133
Amount required to be paid, 133

WAR TAX.
See Confederate States war tax.

WESTERN VIRGINIA.
Resolution for joint committee to confer
  with confederate authorities in relation to defence of, 154

WHITEHEAD, A. J.
Act for relief of, 128
Amount appropriated, 128

WILLEY, COL. W. J.
Resolution in relation to, 148

WILLS.
See Taxes on dividends, &c.

WINCHESTER AND POTOMAC RAIL ROAD.
See Rail road connection.

WISE COUNTY.
Attached to 17th brigade, 57

WOOLDRIDGE, A. S.
An act to authorize the county court of
  Powhatan county to correct the assessment of the lands of, 119

YORK SPIT LIGHT VESSEL.
Act for relief of officers and crew of, 124
Appropriation limited, 124
How appropriated, 124

ACTS

OF THE

GENERAL ASSEMBLY

OF THE

STATE OF VIRGINIA,

PASSED AT EXTRA SESSION, 1862,

IN THE

EIGHTY-SIXTH YEAR OF THE COMMONWEALTH.

RICHMOND:
WILLIAM F. RITCHIE, PUBLIC PRINTER.
1862.

ACTS

PASSED AT THE

EXTRA SESSION IN 1862.

Chap. I.—An ACT prescribing the mode of obtaining Judgment against defaulting Collectors of Taxes and other Public Dues.

Passed May 17, 1862.

1. Be it enacted by the general assembly, that the twenty-third section of chapter fourth, entitled an act for the collection of taxes on persons and property, passed March twenty-eighth, eighteen hundred and sixty, and the fifty-third and fifty-fourth sections of chapter second, entitled an act making regulations concerning licenses, passed March thirtieth, eighteen hundred and sixty, and the twenty-fourth section of chapter second, entitled an act amending and re-enacting the thirty-ninth chapter of the Code, in relation to taxes on dividends, certain estates of decedents, process on suits, official seals, deeds, wills, administrations and foreign insurance companies, passed March thirty-first, eighteen hundred and sixty-two, be reduced into one section, amended and re-enacted so as to read as follows: *Acts of 1860 amended / Act of 1862 amended*

"In case any sheriff, clerk or other collector of taxes, or any person or corporation charged with the collection or payment of taxes, militia fines or other public dues, fail to pay the same into the treasury at the time and in the manner prescribed by law, the auditor of public accounts may file in the clerk's office of the circuit court of the city of Richmond, or of the county, city or town within which the auditor of public accounts shall at the time be authorized to perform the duties of his office, with the clerk thereof, an accurate statement of the amount with which any such collector may be chargeable on account of such taxes, militia fines or other public dues; and thereupon such clerk shall enter up judgment against such collector and his sureties (where any has been given), jointly or severally, or against any one or more of them, for the amount wherewith he is chargeable, with interest thereon, at the rate of twelve per centum per annum, from the time of the failure to pay until payment, and fifteen per centum damages in addition thereto, unless the auditor of public accounts shall in his discretion, for good cause, accept a judgment with a less per centum of damages. A judgment so rendered *Sheriffs and collectors / Judgment, how obtained / Interest / Damages*

FINANCIAL.

New trial, when shall have the same validity, and he subject in all respects to the like proceedings thereupon, as if it had been rendered by the court, and may, within two years after it has been so rendered, for good cause, and upon such terms as the court may prescribe, be set aside, and a trial had thereon as upon a motion."

Commencement 2. This act shall be in force from its passage.

CHAP. 2.—An ACT authorizing a Change of Licenses.

Passed May 15, 1862.

License, how changed 1. Be it enacted by the general assembly, that in case any person has obtained a license authorizing any business or performance in any specified county or corporation, it shall be lawful, during the existing war, to have such license changed in the same manner now authorized in a county or corporation, so as to authorize the business or performance licensed in any other county or corporation; and if such person shall have been engaged in business in any county or corporation in this state during the preceding year, such person may obtain a license in any other county or corporation upon the same terms and at the same rate of tax, and not otherwise, as if the application had been made in the county or corporation where the former license was granted: provided, that the business or performance shall not extend to a greater number of counties or corporations than allowed by existing laws. But this act shall not be construed to apply so as to authorize any person to do business under his license in any county, city or town other than that for which it was obtained, unless he was so prevented from conducting his business or performance by reason of the presence of the public enemy.

Restriction

Commencement 2. This act shall be in force from its passage.

CHAP. 3.—An ACT concerning Treasury Notes.

Passed May 14, 1862.

Treasury notes, how issued 1. Be it enacted by the general assembly, that all or any portion of the treasury notes authorized to be issued in pursuance of the act entitled an act authorizing the issue of treasury notes, passed March thirty-first, eighteen hundred and sixty-two, may be issued in the denomination of one dollar, or the multiples of one dollar.

Commencement 2. This act shall be in force from its passage.

CHAP. 4.—An ACT prescribing the effect of a Judgment in favor of the Commonwealth against a deceased person.

Passed May 9, 1862.

1. Be it enacted by the general assembly, that if a judgment in favor of the commonwealth be rendered against any person who is dead at the time of rendering the same, the said judgment shall not be invalidated by reason of the death of such person, but that the same shall operate to all intents and purposes, and have the same effect as if it were a judgment against the personal representative of such deceased party; but the time within which the right to review the judgment or appeal therefrom, and the time within which the distribution of assets shall be made, shall commence at the time personal notice is given to such personal representative of the rendition of such judgment. *Judgment not invalidated by death of party* *Right of appeal*

2. This act shall be in force from its passage. *Commencement*

CHAP. 5.—AN ACT to authorize a Force of Ten Thousand Men to be raised for the Defence of the Commonwealth.

Passed May 15, 1862.

1. Be it enacted by the general assembly, that the governor of this commonwealth be and he is hereby authorized to commission John B. Floyd a major general of the state of Virginia, with authority to raise, by voluntary enlistment, a force not exceeding ten thousand men, who are not in the service of this state or of the Confederate States, or liable to draft under the act of congress, commonly called the "conscription law," approved on the sixteenth day of April eighteen hundred and sixty-two. *John B. Floyd a major general* *Force to be raised*

2. That the said force shall be divided into two brigades, to be composed of five regiments of not less than one thousand men each; for which brigades the governor is authorized to appoint and commission two brigadier generals; and such appointment may be made for either brigade when three regiments in such brigade shall have been raised, organized and officered. *How divided*

3. The governor shall appoint and commission forthwith, ten captains for each regiment in each brigade, with authority to raise, by opening recruiting stations or otherwise, companies of one hundred men each, including commissioned, non-commissioned officers and privates; and whenever ten companies are raised and mustered into service as required by law, the governor shall cause the same to be organized into a regiment, and shall appoint and commission therefor one colonel, one lieutenant colonel and one major to command the *Captains to be commissioned* *Regiment, how organized*

same. Each of the said companies shall be and is hereby authorized to elect one first and two second lieutenants; the said elections to be superintended by the captains, and to be certified to the governor, and commissioned by him. The captain of each of said companies is authorized to appoint therefor five sergeants and four corporals.

<small>Vacancies</small>

<small>In lowest grade</small>

4. That all vacancies shall be filled by the governor from the company, battalion, squadron or regiment in which such vacancies shall occur, by promotion according to seniority, except in cases of disability or other incompetency; and whenever a vacancy shall occur in the lowest grade of commissioned officers of a company, said vacancy shall be filled by election, as herein before provided.

<small>Cavalry and artillery</small>

5. In each brigade the governor is hereby authorized to appoint and commission as many captains of cavalry and as many captains of artillery as he in his discretion may think proper.

<small>Staff of major general</small>

6. The staff of the major general shall consist of two aids de camp, one assistant adjutant general, one division quartermaster, who shall act as commissary; each with the rank of like officers in the service of the Confederate States: provided, however, that the division quartermaster shall not be appointed, unless two brigades of not less than three regiments each have been raised.

<small>Staff of brigadier general</small>

7. The staff of each brigadier general shall consist of one aid de camp, one assistant adjutant general, and one quartermaster, who shall act as commissary; each with the rank and pay of first lieutenant of cavalry.

<small>Staff of colonel</small>

8. The staff of a colonel shall consist of one quartermaster, who shall act as commissary, one surgeon, two assistant surgeons, one adjutant, with the rank of similar officers in the confederate service, one sergeant major, one quartermaster's sergeant and two musicians.

<small>How armed and equipped</small>

9. The governor shall cause the said division hereby authorized to be raised to be armed and equipped according to the description of the force, whether artillery, cavalry, riflemen or infantry, with the best description of arms and ordnance possible to be procured, and to furnish them with the necessary equipments, ammunition and munitions of war, with suitable camp equipage and transportation. The cavalry, however, shall furnish their own horses, on the same terms as in the confederate service.

<small>Force, how governed</small>

10. The said force, as soon as they are mustered into service, which shall be for the term of twelve months, shall be governed by the articles of war which may be in force at the time for the government of the troops of the Confederate States, and shall be subject to the orders of the governor of Virginia, for such duty as he may re-

quire, not inconsistent with the constitution and laws of this state or of the Confederate States. The officers and privates of the forces herein authorized to be raised shall receive the same pay, allowance and rations as officers and privates of the same grade and in like service are entitled to in the service of the Confederate States, except that they shall receive no bounty; and no officer authorized to be commissioned by this act, nor non-commissioned officer or private, shall receive pay before being mustered into the service of the state, subject to the orders of the governor.

11. To carry into effect the provisions of this act, the sum of two millions five hundred thousand dollars shall be and the same is hereby appropriated out of any money in the treasury not otherwise appropriated: and the governor and auditor of public accounts are authorized, if necessary, to borrow from time to time, at a rate of interest not exceeding six per centum, parts of said sum of money, or to cause registered stock of the commonwealth to be issued and sold at par, for the purpose of raising from time to time parts of said sum of money; or if the necessary amount of money should not be so obtained, to cause to be issued treasury notes of the commonwealth in the manner as provided for in the ordinance of the convention authorizing the issue of treasury notes, but without interest. *Amount appropriated*

12. The governor may authorize such portion of the said ten thousand men as he may deem proper, to be raised for service in particular sections of the state, or for co-operation with particular departments of the confederate army, so long as they may be needed in such district; and for this purpose may confer special authority on such number of officers as he may deem expedient, who, when the requisite number of men are raised, shall be commissioned by him; but the troops thus raised shall at all times be subject to the orders of the governor, and may, whenever in his opinion it is proper, be ordered for service to any portion of the commonwealth. *How force to co-operate with an army* *Subject to orders of governor*

13. In enacting the foregoing bill, the general assembly does not, to any extent whatever, intend to censure the recent action of the confederate executive in reference to General John B. Floyd, or to express, by implication or otherwise, any opinion on that subject. *Proviso*

14. This act shall be in force from its passage. *Commencement*

CHAP. 6.—An ACT amending and re-enacting the first section of an act passed 15th May 1862, entitled an act to authorize a Force of Ten Thousand Men to be raised for the Defence of the Commonwealth.

Passed May 17, 1862.

1. Be it enacted by the general assembly, that the first section of an act entitled an act to authorize a force of ten thousand men to be *Act of May 15, 1862, amended*

raised for the defence of the commonwealth, passed May fifteenth, eighteen hundred and sixty-two, be amended and re-enacted so as to read as follows:

John B. Floyd a major general

"§ 1. Be it enacted by the general assembly, that the governor of this commonwealth be and he is hereby authorized to commission John B. Floyd a major general of the state of Virginia, with authority to raise, by voluntary enlistment, a force not exceeding ten thousand men, who are not in the service of the state of Virginia or of the Confederate States, or liable to draft under the act of congress, commonly called the 'conscription law,' approved on the sixteenth day of April eighteen hundred and sixty-two: provided, that the governor shall have authority to appoint, to the offices herein after authorized to be filled by him, any persons in the confederate service, or liable thereto under the 'conscription law' aforesaid, whom the president of the Confederate States may consent to discharge from the confederate service."

Who may be appointed officers

Commencement

2. This act shall be in force from its passage.

CHAP. 7.—An ACT to organize a Home Guard.

Passed May 14, 1862.

Who may organize companies

1. Be it enacted by the general assembly, that the citizens of each of the counties of this commonwealth, who are not subject to, and those who are exempt from military duty by the laws of this state or of the Confederate States, be and the same are hereby authorized to raise, by voluntary enlistment, one or more companies of not less than fifty nor more than one hundred men, rank and file, to act as a home guard for said counties: and whenever a sufficient number shall be raised to form a company, they are hereby authorized, under the superintendence of a commissioned officer of a county, or of such person as the governor may designate, to elect a captain and two lieutenants, whose election shall be certified by the officer or person conducting the same, to the governor of this commonwealth, who shall thereupon commission said officers. The captain of each company is hereby authorized to appoint therefor four sergeants and four corporals.

Commissions, how issued

By-laws, &c

2. The said companies are hereby authorized to adopt such by-laws and regulations for their government as they may choose, not inconsistent with the constitution and laws of this state or of the Confederate States. Said force, when in actual service, shall be governed by, and be subject to all rules, regulations and articles of war which may be in force at the time for the government of the troops of the Confederate States.

MILITARY AFFAIRS. 9

3. The said companies shall operate as a guard and police for their respective counties during the war; and the officer in command is hereby authorized to order such force to rendezvous at any point that he may determine upon, whenever in his opinion the safety of the county may require it. Whenever two or more companies shall be organized in a county, they may elect a major, who shall be commissioned by the governor, to command the whole: provided, however, that the troops hereby authorized to be raised shall not be marched beyond the limits of their respective counties against their consent, or kept in active service for more than thirty days at any one time. *Guard and police* *When major may be elected*

4. The troops hereby authorized to be raised shall furnish their own weapons, and shall not be entitled to compensation for their services, except that they shall be furnished with rations authorized by law when in actual service: but the governor shall provide them with such ammunition as the exigency of the service may require; to be deposited with the senior officer of said corps in each county, who shall give bond and security for the proper disposition of the same. *Weapons, how furnished* *Compensation* *Rations*

5. The officer in command shall have power, when in active service, to appoint a quartermaster, who shall act as commissary, and who shall give bond and security for the faithful performance of his duty, in such penalty as the officer aforesaid shall require. *Quartermaster, how appointed*

6. This act shall be in force from its passage. *Commencement*

CHAP. 8.—An ACT to authorize the Governor of Virginia to co-operate with the Confederate Government in and about the Defences of Richmond and Petersburg.

Passed May 15, 1862.

1. Be it enacted by the general assembly, that the sum of two hundred thousand dollars be and the same is hereby appropriated, out of any money in the treasury not otherwise appropriated, to enable the governor to co-operate with the president of the Confederate States on consultation in and about the most effectual ways and means of promoting the defences of the cities of Richmond and Petersburg, or either of them: provided, that the money herein appropriated shall only be expended in obstructing the water approaches to said cities. *Amount appropriated* *Proviso*

2. That the governor be and he is hereby required to make in detail a report to the general assembly of all sums and for what purposes expended in virtue hereof, and that he make the same, by demanding reimbursement thereof to the state by the confederate government, a charge on that government. *Power and duty of governor*

3. This act shall be in force from its passage. *Commencement*

CHAP. 9.—An ACT to amend and re-enact the 1st section of chapter 108 of the Code of Virginia.

Passed May 9, 1862.

Code amended

1. Be it enacted, that the first section of chapter one hundred and eight of the Code of Virginia be amended and re-enacted as follows, viz:

License for marriage
How issued

"§ 1. Every license for a marriage shall be issued by the clerk of the court of the county or corporation in which the female to be married usually resides, or if the office of clerk be vacant, by the senior justice of such county or corporation, who shall make return thereof to the clerk, so soon as there may be one; or in case of the presence of the public enemy in such county or corporation, by the clerk or senior justice, as the case may be, of any county or corporation in which the female to be married may have resided for thirty days next preceding the issuing of the license."

Commencement

2. This act shall be in force from its passage.

CHAP. 10.—An ACT to amend and re-enact section 13, chapter 207 of the Code of Virginia.

Passed May 9, 1862.

Code amended

1. Be it enacted by the general assembly, that section thirteen of chapter two hundred and seven of the Code of Virginia be amended and re-enacted so as to read as follows:

When person may be discharged

Witnesses

"§ 13. Except in time of war, a person in jail on a criminal charge shall be discharged from imprisonment, if he be not indicted before the end of the second term of the court at which he is held to answer, unless it appear to the court that material witnesses for the commonwealth have been enticed or kept away, or are prevented from attendance by sickness or inevitable accident, and except also in the case provided in the following section."

Commencement

2. This act shall be in force from its passage.

CHAP. 11.—An ACT to amend and re-enact section 1, chapter 162 of the Code of Virginia (edition of 1860).

Passed May 12, 1862.

Code amended

1. Be it enacted by the general assembly, that the first section of chapter one hundred and sixty-two of the Code of Virginia of

eighteen hundred and sixty be amended and re-enacted so as to read as follows:

"§ 1. All free white male persons, twenty-one years of age, shall be liable to serve as jurors, except as herein after provided." _{Who may be grand jurors}

2. This act shall be in force from its passage. _{Commencement}

CHAP. 12.—An ACT to amend and re-enact section 7, chapter 103 of the Code.

Passed May 17, 1862.

1. Be it enacted by the general assembly, that the seventh section of chapter one hundred and three of the Code be amended and re-enacted so as to read as follows: _{Code amended}

"§ 7. If any tenant for life of a slave shall remove him, or permit his removal out of the state, without the consent of those in reversion or remainder, he shall forfeit such life estate and the full value of such slave to the person in reversion or remainder: and should such tenant for life be one of several remaindermen or reversioners in such slave, the others may recover either jointly or severally their shares in remainder or reversion in such slave from any person claiming from or under such tenant for life: provided, if such tenant for life in any county, city or town in the possession of, or likely to be overrun by the public enemy, shall remove temporarily, or cause to be removed temporarily any such slave out of the state and within the Confederate States, with the bona fide intention of preventing such property from falling into the hands of the public enemy, then none of the penalties imposed shall be incurred." _{Tenant for life of a slave} _{When slave may be removed}

2. This act shall be in force from its passage. _{Commencement}

CHAP. 13.—An ACT amending the 19th section of chapter 14 of the Code, concerning Salaries.

Passed May 14, 1862.

1. Be it enacted by the general assembly, that the nineteenth section of chapter fourteen of the Code, edition of eighteen hundred and sixty, be amended and re-enacted so as to read as follows: _{Code amended}

"§ 19. All the annual salaries mentioned in the preceding sections shall be paid out of the treasury monthly, after being duly audited. All the other allowances and the mileage mentioned in the preceding sections shall in general be payable when the services and _{Salaries, how paid}

Pay of members of assembly — travel shall have been performed. But members of the general assembly and others traveling to the seat of government, who would be entitled to mileage for traveling home, may receive the mileage last mentioned before going home."

Commencement — 2. This act shall be in force from its passage.

CHAP. 14.—An ACT to amend and re-enact section 5, chapter 205 of the Code of Virginia.

Passed May 9, 1862.

Code amended — 1. Be it enacted by the general assembly, that section fifth, chapter two hundred and five of the Code of Virginia be amended and re-enacted so as to read as follows:

Examination, how adjourned

When witnesses kept away

"§ 5. The court, at any such special session, may adjourn the examination to the next regular term, quarterly or monthly, or to an earlier day, and at a regular term may continue any examination from term to term, so that such continuance, except on the motion of the accused, or in time of war, or by reason of the witnesses for the commonwealth being enticed or kept away, or prevented from attending by sickness or some inevitable accident, shall not be beyond the third regular term after the examination was ordered. But if an examination be commenced at any term, such term may be extended until the examination is concluded."

Commencement — 2. This act shall be in force from its passage.

CHAP. 15.—An ACT to authorize the Sale of the Roanoke Valley Rail Road.

Passed May 14, 1862.

Sale authorized

Sanction of board of public works

1. Be it enacted by the general assembly, that the Roanoke valley rail road company shall have power to sell their road, together with all their property of every sort and description, either to the Raleigh and Gaston rail road company or to the Richmond and Danville rail road company; subject, however, to the approval and sanction of the board of public works; and the purchaser under this act shall have and enjoy all the rights, privileges and immunities which the said Roanoke valley rail road company had under their charter and the several acts amendatory thereof: provided, however, that the purchaser under this act shall give satisfactory guarantees that the extension of said Roanoke valley rail road shall be completed to Keysville, in the county of Charlotte in this state, within the present

MISCELLANEOUS.   13

year, and that motive power and rolling stock sufficient to meet the wants of the public along the line of said road shall be provided for and put thereon within the same period: provided further, that the purchaser of said Roanoke valley rail road shall have no power or right to discriminate, by its tolls or otherwise, against the interests of any other work of internal improvement in this commonwealth. Restrictions

2. Be it further enacted, that out of the proceeds of such sale the debts of said company shall first be paid; and then shall be paid to the state of Virginia the preferred stock held by said state in the said company; and what remains of the proceeds of said sale shall be divided ratably among the stockholders of said Roanoke valley rail road company. Debts to be paid

3. This act shall be in force from its passage. Commencement

CHAP. 16.—An ACT to authorize the County Courts to purchase and distribute Salt amongst the people, and provide payment for the same.

Passed May 9, 1862.

1. Be it enacted by the general assembly, that the courts of the several counties of this commonwealth, when a majority of the acting justices of the county is present, or when the justices have been summoned to attend to act upon the matter, are hereby authorized and empowered to order the purchase, for the use of the people of said counties respectively, such quantities of salt as the said courts may deem necessary, and to provide for the payment of the same by county levies, or by loans negotiated upon the bonds of the said counties, to be redeemed by county levies or otherwise. When county courts may purchase salt

2. The said courts shall have power and authority to distribute the salt thus purchased, amongst, or dispose of the same to the people of their respective counties, in such quantities, upon such terms, and under such regulations as the said courts may prescribe. Salt, how distributed

3. For the purpose of carrying out the provisions of this act, the said courts may appoint or employ agents or commissioners, and take from them bonds with approved security, payable to their respective counties, in such penalties as the said courts may prescribe, with conditions for the faithful performance of their duties as such agents or commissioners. The bonds so taken shall be filed in the clerk's office of the court in which they are taken, and may be put in suit from time to time by the said court, in behalf of the said counties, or by any persons injured by the breach of the said conditions. Agents, how appointed Bonds Breach of conditions

4. This act shall be in force from its passage. Commencement

CHAP. 17.—An ACT making an Appropriation, in a certain contingency, for the protection of certain Inhabitants of the City of Richmond.

Passed May 15, 1862.

Preamble

Whereas a resolution, by the proper authorities, to hold this city to the last extremity, rather than surrender to a bombarding force, would necessarily expose the lives of numbers of women, children and decrepit persons, resident at the seat of government, and unable, by reason of their poverty or other cause, to remove themselves to a place of safety: Therefore,

Amount appropriated

1. Be it enacted by the general assembly, that the sum of two hundred thousand dollars be and is hereby made subject to the order of the governor, to be paid out of any money in the treasury not otherwise appropriated, to be placed by him at the disposal of the authorities, mayor and council of the city of Richmond, on such terms and in such amounts as he may deem expedient, for the purpose of aiding the removal and temporary maintenance of such persons as may by reason of their poverty or other cause, be unable to withdraw from the effects of such bombardment:

Proviso

provided, that no portion of the money hereby appropriated shall be expended until due notice is given by the proper authorities for the removal of such persons.

Commencement

2. This act shall be in force from its passage.

CHAP. 18.—An ACT to punish Purchasers of Property, falsely representing themselves authorized to impress or purchase the same.

Passed May 14, 1862.

When persons to be considered guilty of misdemeanor

1. Be it enacted by the general assembly of Virginia, that if a free person buy property of any person, falsely representing himself to be duly authorized to impress or buy the same for the use of the state or Confederate States, he shall be deemed guilty of a misdemeanor, and upon conviction, shall be fined in a sum double the value of the property purchased, and confined in jail not exceeding one year.

Commencement

2. This act shall be in force from its passage.

CHAP. 19.—An ACT fixing the Compensation of the Clerks of the Senate and House of Delegates during Extra Sessions.

Passed May 14, 1862.

Compensation allowed

1. Be it enacted by the general assembly, that the clerk of the house of delegates and the clerk of the senate be each allowed the

sum of eight dollars per day for services rendered during extra sessions of the general assembly; and that the auditor of public accounts be directed to issue his warrant upon the treasury for said sums.

2. This act shall be in force from its passage.   Commencement

---

CHAP. 20.—An ACT declaring the standard of a Cord Measure.

Passed May 14, 1862.

1. Be it enacted by the general assembly, that a cord contains one hundred and twenty-eight cubic feet, being eight feet long, four feet high and four feet wide, or the equivalent thereof; and that in all measurements of wood, tan-bark or other things subject to such measurements, the foregoing shall be the true and legal standard: any usage, by-law or ordinance of any corporation, rail road or other company, to the contrary notwithstanding.   Standard declared

2. This act shall be in force from its passage.   Commencement

---

CHAP. 21.—An ACT authorizing a Temporary Change in the Seat of Government in a certain contingency.

Passed May 17, 1862.

1. Be it enacted by the general assembly, that in the event of the occupation by the public enemy of the seat of government, or under any public emergency, which, in the opinion of the governor, may render it necessary, the governor is hereby authorized by proclamation to declare and make known some other place within the limits of Virginia, and to change the same from time to time, as may be necessary, as the temporary seat of government, and all things now required by law to be done at the existing seat of government, may be rightfully and legally done at the seat of government thus declared and made known by the governor's proclamation.   When seat of government may be changed

2. This act shall be in force from its passage.   Commencement

---

CHAP. 22.—An ACT providing for the execution of Sentence of Death in certain cases.

Passed May 9, 1862.

1. Be it enacted by the general assembly, that whenever, during the existing war, sentence of death pronounced by any court cannot   Sentence of death, how executed

be executed in the county in which it was pronounced, by reason of the presence of the public enemy, such sentence may be executed in any county in this commonwealth, upon the warrant of the governor, directed to any sheriff or other officer appointed by the governor to execute such sentence.

Commencement   2. This act shall be in force from and after its passage.

CHAP. 23.—An ACT authorizing Insurance Companies to change their Place of Business.

Passed May 14, 1862.

When insurance companies may change place of business   1. Be it enacted by the general assembly, that whenever the president and directors of any insurance company shall consider the place of business of any such company unsafe, or that access thereto is interrupted by reason of the public enemy, and shall appoint some other place for the custody of its books and effects, and the trans-
What, when removed action of its business, it shall be lawful for the board or president thereof to remove thereto, and thereat exercise its corporate rights until the danger be over, when it shall return to its original place of business: and bills of exchange, checks and all other claims payable at the domicil of such insurance company, shall be held and treated as payable at the place to which said company shall have removed. The board or president thereof shall cause notice to be given of the removal of such company, by advertisement and other means likely to make the fact public.

Prior removal   2. Be it further enacted, that the removal of all said companies heretofore made, and all the acts thereof in accordance with the charter, be and are hereby legalized and made valid.

Commencement   3. This act shall be in force from its passage.

CHAP. 24.—An ACT to amend the 81st section of an act entitled an act to amend the Charter of the City of Richmond, passed March 18, 1861.

Passed May 15, 1862.

Charter amended   1. Be it enacted by the general assembly, that section eighty-one of the act entitled an act to amend the charter of the city of Richmond, be and the same is hereby amended and re-enacted so as to read as follows:

Jurisdiction of court   "§ 81. A term of the said court, not exceeding twenty days, shall also be held by the said judge in every month, except the month of

August, at such time and place as the council of the said city shall prescribe; at which term the said court shall exercise exclusively the jurisdiction now vested in it over all attachments, appeals in civil cases, civil actions, motions, and suits at law and in chancery, all matters concerning the probate of wills, the appointment, qualification and removal of fiduciaries, and the settlement of their accounts: and the court so held, or the judge thereof, may appoint commissioners in chancery, commissioners to take depositions, receivers and any other officers or agents for the conducting of its business, which a circuit court or judge may appoint in similar cases, and whose appointment is not otherwise provided for by this act, or ordinances of the city; and the said court, when held by the judge thereof, may exercise the power which a circuit court may exercise under section thirty-five, chapter one hundred and eighty-four, and sections one, two and three of chapter two hundred and ten of the Code of eighteen hundred and forty-nine: provided, however, that during the existing war it shall be lawful for the judge of the said court to adjourn the court from time to time, not exceeding six months at a time, and to hold the terms thereof not exceeding twenty days for a term, and at such terms to possess and exercise all the jurisdiction, civil and criminal, now vested in it by law: and the judge of the said court shall have the same power to appoint and hold special terms as is now possessed by the judges of the circuit courts, and to order a grand jury or any venire to be summoned to attend such terms. No person charged with felony, and remanded to said court for trial, shall be discharged from prosecution for the said offence, by reason of there being three regular terms of said court without a trial. That during the existence of the present war it shall not be requisite for the judge of the said court to reside in the city of Richmond." *Powers of court* *When judge may adjourn court* *Residence of judge*

2. This act shall be in force from its passage. *Commencement*

CHAP. 25.—An ACT to amend the first section of an act entitled an act to amend and re-enact the 63d ordinance of the Convention, authorising Banks to change their Place of Business, passed 31st March 1862.

Passed May 16, 1862.

1. Be it enacted by the general assembly, that the first section of an act entitled an act to amend and re-enact the sixty-third ordinance of the convention authorizing banks to change their place of business, passed March thirty-first, eighteen hundred and sixty-two, be amended and re-enacted so as to read as follows: *Act 31st March 1862 amended*

"§ 1. That whenever the president and directors of any bank or of any branch of any bank shall consider the domicil of the bank unsafe, or that access thereto is interrupted by reason of the public enemy, and shall so enter on their minutes, and appoint some other *When bank may change place of business* place for the custody of its books and effects and the transaction of its business, it shall be lawful for the board to remove thereto, and thereat to exercise its corporate rights until the danger be over, when it shall return to its original domicil; and bills of exchange, checks and negotiable notes payable at the domicil of such bank, shall be held and treated as payable at the bank in the place to which it is removed.

Advertisement thereof

The president and directors shall cause notice to be given of the removal of such bank, by advertisement and other means likely to make the fact public; and that whenever the domicil of any such bank or branch bank has been so changed, and the quorum of the board of directors shall fail to accompany such bank or branch bank to its new domicil, any one or more of such directors, or

Who to exercise power of board of directors

in case there be none present, the cashier, and such of the officers of the bank or branch bank as may be with him, shall have the power of a board of directors to transact its business and provide for its safety, by further removals whenever they shall consider such new domicil unsafe; that access thereto is interrupted; and the business transacted at such new domicil shall be as valid as if transacted at its original place of business. That whenever, by the presence or threatened approach of the enemy, access by mail, to or from any bank or branch, be interrupted, or any such bank or

Parties, when bound

branch be in the act of changing its domicil, the parties to negotiable notes, bills and checks, payable at such bank or branch, and maturing during such interrupted access or such change of domicil, shall remain bound after the maturity of such notes, bills and checks, without demand, protest or notice, as if the requirements of law in

Notice

that behalf had been complied with; provided, however, that notice, as now required by law, be given to the parties thereto, within ten days after the removal of the disabilities therein set forth."

Commencement

2. This act shall be in force from its passage.

CHAP. 26.—An ACT to amend and re-enact the 1st section of the act passed March 29, 1862, entitled an act to provide a Currency of Notes of less denomination than Five Dollars.

Passed May 16, 1862.

Act 29th March 1862 amended

1. Be it enacted by the general assembly, that the first section of the act entitled an act to provide a currency of notes of less denomination than five dollars, passed March twenty-ninth, eighteen hundred and sixty-two, be amended and re-enacted so as to read as follows:

Notes, how issued

"§ 1. That the several banks of circulation of this commonwealth be and they are hereby authorized to issue notes of a less denomination than five dollars, and not less than one dollar, including fractional amounts between one and five dollars, to an amount not exceeding ten per centum of the capital of said banks respectively; and every bank or branch shall, after the expiration of ninety days from the twenty-ninth day of March eighteen hundred and sixty-two, pay all sums less than five dollars, and redeem all notes of five dollars, either in specie or in its own notes of less denomination than five dollars, unless said bank or branch shall have issued and have in circulation notes of the denomination hereby authorized, to the amount herein before specified; and every bank or branch failing to pay in specie or in small notes as aforesaid, shall pay to the person demanding such payment or redemption, the sum of fifty dollars for each offence: provided, that in case any bank or branch shall have changed its domicil under existing laws before the said ninety days expire, such bank or branch shall have the further period of sixty days within which to comply with this act: and provided further, that if any bank be disabled from complying with this act by reason of its being within the lines of the enemy, each branch of such bank not within the lines of the enemy, is required, under the penalties aforesaid, within ninety days from the passage of this act, to issue such notes to an amount equivalent to ten per centum of the capital of such branch, independently of the bank of which it is a branch. The notes hereby authorized to be issued may be signed by such officer or officers of said bank or branches as may be designated for that purpose by the respective boards of directors; and any of said banks or branches which may have preserved notes of less denomination than five dollars, heretofore issued under authority of law, shall be at liberty to circulate the same, so that the amount shall not exceed the amount authorized by this act."

Notes of five dollars, how redeemed

Penalty

Proviso

Notes, how signed

2. This act shall be in force from its passage. *Commencement*

CHAP. 27.—An ACT to amend and re-enact the 3d section of an act entitled an act to provide a Currency of Notes of less denomination than Five Dollars, passed March 29th, 1862.

Passed May 19, 1862.

1. Be it enacted by the general assembly, that the third section of an act entitled an act to provide a currency of notes of less denomination than five dollars, passed March twenty-ninth, eighteen hundred and sixty-two, be amended and re-enacted so as to read as follows:

Act 29th March 1862 amended

"§ 3. Be it further enacted, that the lawfully constituted authorities of the city of Richmond be and they are hereby authorized to issue, as currency, notes of a less denomination than one dollar, to an amount not exceeding five hundred thousand dollars; and the authorities of all the other cities and the towns of this commonwealth con-

City of Richmond authorised to issue notes

What cities and towns authorised to issue

taining a population of two thousand, and of the towns of Leesburg, Lewisburg and Warrenton, are hereby authorized to issue notes, as currency, of a like denomination, to an amount double the amount of state tax assessed on property, real and personal, within such city or town for one year, taking therefor the average of the last preceding three years; and the notes issued as aforesaid shall be receivable in payment of all dues to the corporation issuing them: and the banks of the commonwealth are hereby authorized to receive and pay out the same: provided, however, that all notes under the denomination of five dollars, heretofore issued by the cities and towns referred to in this section, and now in circulation, may be held and accounted a part of the amounts herein authorized to be issued by them respectively, subject to redemption in the mode prescribed by the said act of March twenty-ninth, eighteen hundred and sixty-two."

As to notes heretofore issued

Commencement 2. This act shall be in force from its passage.

CHAP. 28.—An ACT to amend and re-enact the 5th section of an act passed 29th March 1862, entitled an act to provide a Currency of less denomination than Five Dollars.

Passed May 15, 1862.

Act of March 1862 amended

1. Be it enacted by the general assembly, that the fifth section of the act passed on the twenty-ninth day of March eighteen hundred and sixty-two, entitled an act to provide a currency of less denomination than five dollars, be amended and re-enacted so as to read as follows:

Notes, how and when redeemed

"§ 5. That for the purpose of redeeming the notes issued by the counties, cities and towns of the commonwealth, under the provisions of this act, the courts of such counties and the councils of such cities and towns as may issue such notes, are required at their levy terms for the year eighteen hundred and sixty-three, to levy upon the subjects of taxation mentioned in the fifth section of chapter fifty-three of the Code of eighteen hundred and sixty, an amount sufficient to redeem sixteen and two-thirds per cent. of the amount of such notes in circulation at the time of such levy: and at the time of the annual levy in each year thereafter, the courts of the said counties and councils of such cities and towns shall levy upon the said subjects of taxation an amount sufficient to redeem a like per centage of such notes as may be in circulation at the time of said levy, until the entire amount issued by any county, city or town, is redeemed: provided, that the redemption of the entire issue shall not be postponed for a longer time than six years from the levy courts of the year eighteen hundred and sixty-three of the respective counties, cities and towns. Such redemption to be made in such funds as are receivable in payment of dues to the commonwealth."

Proviso

Commencement 2. This act shall be in force from its passage.

CHAP. 29.—An ACT to re-establish an Inspection of Tobacco at the Farmville Warehouse in the Town of Farmville.

Passed May 13, 1862.

1. Be it enacted by the general assembly, that an inspection of tobacco be and hereby is established at the Farmville warehouse in the town of Farmville, agreeably to the provisions of chapter eighty-seven of the Code of eighteen hundred and sixty. *Warehouse established*

2. This act shall be in force from its passage. *Commencement*

CHAP. 30.—An ACT providing Payment for Horses taken in the Service of the State.

Passed May 14, 1862.

1. Be it enacted by the general assembly, that the auditing board, established for the settlement of military claims, shall be authorized to pay, as other claims are paid, when allowed by said board, if in the opinion of the board, on a full examination of the evidence, the claim against the commonwealth appear to be just and right, to William H. Gooding, his heirs or assigns, the sum of one hundred and fifty dollars; to R. J. Simpson, his heirs or assigns, the sum of one hundred and twenty-five dollars; and to S. J. Beach, his heirs or assigns, the sum of one hundred dollars: the said amounts being the value of three horses, the property of said individuals, which were impressed by the military officers of Virginia, for the defence of the state prior to its secession, and its union, under the provisional government, with the Confederate States of America. *Amount appropriated*

2. This act shall be in force from its passage. *Commencement*

CHAP. 31.—An ACT authorizing the Payment of a certain Coupon.

Passed May 14, 1862.

1. Be it enacted by the general assembly, that upon due and satisfactory evidence of the loss of a coupon, number fourteen hundred and fifty-nine, due July first, eighteen hundred and sixty-one, being given to the second auditor, he is hereby authorized and required to pay the amount of said coupon to Miss Ann M. Fleming: provided, that before paying the same, the said Ann M. Fleming shall file with the said auditor proof of advertisement of the loss of said coupon, and a bond with approved security, indemnifying the state against all losses which she may in any manner be liable for on account of the payment of said coupon. *Coupon, how issued*

2. This act shall be in force from its passage. *Commencement*

MINING AND MANUFACTURING COMPANY.

Chap. 32.—An ACT incorporating the Victoria Mining and Manufacturing Company of the County of Louisa.

Passed March 27, 1862.

Company incorporated

1. Be it enacted by the general assembly, that Thomas A. Curtis, John E. Tackett, James W. Ford, William Warren, junior, William H. Hill and B. B. Warren, and such other persons as may be hereafter associated with them, shall be and are hereby incorporated and made a body politic and corporate, by the name and style of The Victoria Mining and Manufacturing Company; for the purpose of mining iron ore, and of working and of smelting the same into pig iron or otherwise; and also for the purpose of manufacturing iron in all its various branches and uses in said county of Louisa; and of transporting to market and selling iron ores or other products of their mines and manufactory; and of transacting the usual business of companies engaged in mining, manufacturing and of transporting to market and selling the products of their mines and manufactory.

Name

Powers and privileges

2. The said company and their successors are hereby invested with all the rights, privileges and powers, and made subject to the restrictions and regulations now provided by law for the general regulation of bodies politic and corporate, and of the mining and manufacturing companies of this commonwealth, so far as the same may apply, and are not inconsistent with the provisions of this act.

Capital stock

3. Be it further enacted, that the capital stock of said company shall consist of not less than eight nor more than one hundred thousand dollars, to be divided into shares of one hundred dollars each; and the said company shall have the right to purchase and to hold land not exceeding three thousand acres.

Commencement

4. This act shall be in force from the passage thereof, and shall be subject to any amendments, alteration or modification, at the pleasure of the general assembly.

RESOLUTIONS.

No. 1.—Resolution in relation to the Duration of Special Sessions.

Adopted April 1, 1862.

1. Resolved, that the constitutional limitation on the duration of the sessions of the legislature, applies to special as well as regular sessions. *Sessions of legislature; their duration*

2. Resolved, that when the legislature adjourns to-day, it will be to meet again on the first Monday of May eighteen hundred and sixty-two, unless sooner called together by the governor; and then, upon such day as he shall designate. *Adjournment*

No. 2.—Resolution as to the Adjournment of the General Assembly.

Adopted May 17, 1862.

Resolved, that when the general assembly adjourns, it will adjourn to meet on the first Monday in December eighteen hundred and sixty-two, unless sooner convened by the governor. *Adjournment*

No. 3.—Joint Resolution as to Mileage, &c.

Adopted April 1, 1862.

Resolved by the general assembly, that the members of the general assembly convened in session under the proclamation of the governor of the first day of April eighteen hundred and sixty-two, shall not be entitled to receive mileage, except for attendance upon any adjourned session; nor shall they be entitled to receive pay for attendance during the time of any recess in the session held under said proclamation. *Mileage*

No. 5.—Resolutions to increase the Production of Lead and Saltpetre.

Adopted May 15, 1862.

Preamble

Whereas it is deemed of great importance in the prosecution of the war, that the increase of the production of lead should be facilitated by all the means necessary for that purpose: Therefore,

Powers of governor

1. Be it resolved by the general assembly, that the governor is hereby authorized to aid in the production of the mines now in operation in this state, by furnishing, so far as he may be able, labor, by hiring, or impressment, if deemed expedient by him, or by such other means as he may deem proper, and upon such terms with the owners of said mines as he may deem equitable.

Lead

2. Be it further resolved, that the governor be authorized to contract for lead for the use of the state, in such quantities as he may deem expedient, so as not to interfere with the supply to the confederate government; and he is requested to confer with the confederate authorities on this subject, with a view to a concert of action.

Saltpetre

3. Be it further resolved, that the governor be requested to aid, by all the means necessary for that purpose, and in such manner as he may deem expedient, the production of saltpetre.

Saltpetre

4. Be it further resolved, that the governor be directed to authorize any person whom he may deem to be discreet and reliable, to take, for the public use, wood, earth and other material off of any lands in this state necessary to the manufacture of saltpetre, under such rules and regulations as he may adopt; and the value of such wood, earth and other material is hereby made a charge on the treasury of the state. The saltpetre so manufactured to be for the use of the state, or to be disposed of to the Confederate States; and in either case, the finder and manufacturer shall be paid therefor such price as the governor may deem reasonable.

No. 6.—Resolution authorizing the Payment of a sum of Money to L. D. Haymond.

Adopted May 10, 1862.

Amount to be paid

Resolved by the general assembly, that the board of public works be and they are hereby directed to pay to L. D. Haymond, or his legal representatives, the sum of one hundred and sixteen dollars, for locating parts of the Elk river turnpike road, out of the appropriation made to said road by act of assembly.

No. 7.—Resolution directing the Second Auditor to issue a warrant to L. D. Haymond.

Adopted May 17, 1862.

Resolved by the general assembly, that the second auditor is directed to issue his warrant upon the treasury in favor of L. D. Haymond, payable out of the internal improvement fund, for the one hundred and sixteen dollars authorized to be paid to him by a joint resolution of the present session. *(Warrant to be issued)*

No. 8.—Resolution in relation to the Defence of James and Appomattox Rivers.

Adopted May 10, 1862.

Resolved, that the governor be and he is hereby authorized to co-operate with the confederate authorities in the obstruction and defence of the James and Appomattox rivers; and with a view of accomplishing that object in the most speedy and effectual manner, he is hereby empowered to tender to the president of the Confederate States all the power and resources of the state; and if necessary to make such tender effectual, he is authorized to impress or otherwise procure such property and number of men as may be required to effect the object aforesaid. *(Governor authorised to co-operate with confederate authorities)*

No. 9.—Resolution extending the Time for the Examination and Return of the Books of Commissioners of the Revenue.

Adopted May 15, 1862.

Be it resolved by the general assembly, that the auditor of public accounts be and he is hereby authorized, in such cases as he may be satisfied there has been no neglect of duty, to grant to commissioners of the revenue such extension of the times prescribed by law for the examination and return of the land and property books, as he may deem just to the commissioners of the revenue, and not inconsistent with the public interest; and in cases of peculiar difficulty in the execution of their duties, the auditor, with the consent and approval of the governor, shall forbear to institute legal proceedings against commissioners of the revenue for failure to comply with the requirements of law. *(Time extended)*

No. 10.—Preamble and Resolution authorizing the Governor to appoint a Commission to enquire into the Condition of the Penitentiary and into the best means to render the Institution productive.

Adopted May 15, 1862.

Preamble

Whereas the penitentiary of Virginia has for many years been a charge upon the treasury of Virginia: And whereas it is probable that by a change in the laws regulating the said penitentiary, it may be made self-supporting, and it is believed by many that it would, under proper management, be a source of revenue: And whereas past experience has shown that committees appointed by the legislature to examine the penitentiary (in the nature of the case) cannot spare the time from other representative duties to investigate the whole subject, so as to recommend such reforms or improvements as might be the result of a thorough investigation into all the details of the laws regulating the institution, and more especially into the manner and details of all the various mechanical and other operations of the convicts, the mode of purchasing and otherwise obtaining supplies of raw material, provisions, &c.; and furthermore, the accommodations of the convicts, the necessity or not of enlarging the buildings and workshops, and of providing proper safegnards to prevent attempts to escape, or mutiny among the convicts: Therefore,

Commission to be appointed

Be it resolved by the general assembly of Virginia, that the governor be empowered, at such time as in his discretion may seem proper, to appoint a commission of three discreet persons, whose duty it shall be to investigate the entire subject of the penitentiary, in its details; the laws regulating the same; its interior management; mode of obtaining supplies; and any and every thing connected with the penitentiary system, which in their judgments may conduce to the prosperity of the institution, and report to the next meeting of the legislature.

No. 11.—Joint Resolution in relation to the Destruction of Canceled Coupon Bonds and Treasury Notes.

Adopted May 14, 1862.

Coupon bonds to be destroyed

Resolved by the general assembly of Virginia, that the treasurer of this commonwealth be instructed to destroy such coupon bonds and treasury notes in his office as have been canceled, and are now registered by law.

RESOLUTIONS. 27

No. 12.—Resolution for the Destruction of certain Coupon Bonds.

Adopted May 15, 1862.

Resolved by the general assembly, that the treasurer and the second auditor be authorized and required to cause to be destroyed any canceled coupon bonds that may have been guaranteed by the state, of which a register has been kept. Coupon bonds to be destroyed

---

No. 13.—Preamble and Resolutions in respect to the Nature and Conduct of the pending War.

Adopted May 9, 1862.

The general assembly of Virginia, now convened in extraordinary session, deem this a fit occasion briefly to review the nature and conduct of the pending war, and solemnly to reaffirm the sentiments which animate them, and those principles of civil liberty which the people of this state and of the Confederate States have maintained from the commencement of the contest, and which, with the blessing of God, they will continue to maintain with unshaken constancy to its close. Preamble

For more than a year the government and people of the north have waged a cruel, unjust and unrelenting war against us. They deny to us the inalienable right of self-government, in defence of which, in the war of the revolution of seventeen hundred and seventy-six, they pledged their lives, their fortunes and their sacred honor. With professed regard for the rights of man, they have at different periods sympathized with the Greeks, the Poles, the Irish, the Hungarians, the South American states, and all others who have at any time sought by force to dissolve their subsisting political ties, and to establish a separate nationality; yet they deny to those whom they call their brethren, the right, which clearly belongs to them as sovereign states, to withdraw peaceably from their union, and to govern themselves; which right the people of the Confederate States have declared their solemn purpose to exercise, with a unanimity without a parallel in the history of civil revolutions.

In prosecuting the war they have violated without scruple the constitution which they profess to defend. They have suspended by executive proclamation and without law, the writ of habeas corpus; imprisoned, without legal warrant or military necessity, thousands of respectable citizens of both sexes; violated their obligations to the state of Maryland, and their solemn compact in the compromise resolutions of eighteen hundred and fifty, by abolishing slavery in the district of Columbia. They have trampled on private rights, by depredating upon private property, and now meditate, by a wholesale act of legal robbery, the confiscation of the property of nearly every citizen of the southern states.

Professing to be the peculiar friends of the black race, they have destroyed their peace and happiness; seducing them by false promises from the kind care and protection of their hereditary owners, and having found them burdensome to their benevolence, have cruelly cast t' 'm off by thousands, without protection or support, to starve and die. The civilized world cannot fail to contrast the acts of these pretenders with their professions, and to see, in their seemingly anxious desire to uphold the constitution, their true motives—the greed of avarice and the lust of power.

Be it resolved, as the solemn and deliberate sense of the general assembly of Virginia:

Separation

1. That the separation between the north and south is final and eternal; that it was declared by the people of the Confederate States, each acting for itself, with unexampled unanimity; and whatever reverence for the Union may have lingered for a time in some minds, has been entirely dissipated by the cruel, rapacious and atrocious conduct of our enemies.

Confidence in our armies

2. That we have full confidence in our gallant armies now in the field, which have achieved many glorious victories, and never sustained a disgraceful defeat; yet should the tide of battle turn against us, we will not be discouraged, but summoning new energy to meet the exigencies, struggle on until, with the blessing of God, we shall conquer an honorable peace, and finally establish our independence.

Coast defences

3. That ordinary coast defences cannot be expected to withstand the powerful armaments of modern naval warfare; and whilst the fall of New Orleans is to be regretted as a calamity, it is no cause for despondency. In the language of our own Washington on a similar occasion, "We should never despair. If new difficulties arise, we must only put forth new exertions, and proportion our efforts to the exigency of the times."

Resources of state pledged to war

4. That in defence of our liberties, we solemnly pledge, for ourselves and our constituents, to the government of the Confederate States, our whole resources, public and private, and deliberately declare to our enemies and to the world, that we will never submit, under any circumstances, to a reunion with the north, nor abandon this contest so long as a hostile foot rests upon our soil.

RESOLUTIONS.

No. 14.—Resolution in relation to Partisan Service.

Adopted May 17, 1862.

Preamble

Whereas this general assembly places a high estimate upon the value of the ranger or partisan service, in prosecuting the present war to a successful issue, and regards it as perfectly legitimate; and it being understood that a federal commander on the northern border of Virginia has intimated his purpose, if such service be not discontinued, to lay waste, by fire, the portions of our territory at present under his power:

Policy to be carried out

Resolved by the general assembly, that in its opinion the policy of employing such rangers or partisans ought to be carried out energetically both by the authorities of this state and of the Confederate States, and without the slightest regard to such threats.

No. 15.—Resolution establishing a Board of Manufactures.

Adopted May 14, 1862.

Board of manufactures

Resolved by the general assembly, that the auditor of public accounts, the second auditor and the general agent and storekeeper of the penitentiary be constituted a board of manufactures, and charged with the duty of reporting to the next session of the general assembly upon the following points:

Its duties

1st. The present condition of manufactures in the state of Virginia.

Authority of board

2d. Such plans as may seem to them proper for promoting the manufacture, production or increased production of articles of prime necessity or of general utility. Said board to have authority to call for information and require reports from any officer in this state.

No. 16.—Resolution as to the Defence of the City of Richmond.

Adopted May 14, 1862.

Capital of state to be defended

1. Resolved by the general assembly of Virginia, that the general assembly hereby express its desire that the capital of the state be defended to the last extremity, if such defence is in accordance with the views of the president of the Confederate States; and that the president be assured that whatever destruction and loss of property of the state or individuals shall thereby result, will be cheerfully submitted to.

Destruction of property

RESOLUTIONS.

Resolution communicated to president

2. *Resolved*, that a committee of two on the part of the senate, and three on the part of the house, be appointed to communicate the adoption of the foregoing resolution to the president.

No. 17.—Resolution as to the Distribution of the Acts of the General Assembly.

Adopted May 15, 1862.

Secretary of commonwealth to have unbound copies of Acts, &c. distributed

Resolved, that the secretary of the commonwealth be authorized to cause unbound copies of all acts and resolutions of the general assembly, passed at the session of eighteen hundred and sixty-one and two, to be circulated as prescribed by law, if circumstances should not permit the distribution of bound copies of the same at an early day, and that he take the same course in relation to the acts and resolutions of the present session.

No. 18.—Resolution relative to the Publication of the Constitution and Schedule and Ordinances of the third session of the Convention.

Adopted April 1, 1862.

Constitution and schedule to be printed

Resolved by the general assembly, that the public printer cause to be printed and published with the acts of the late session, the constitution and schedule submitted by the late convention to a vote of the people, if the same shall be declared by the governor to have been adopted, and the ordinances of the third session of the convention.

No. 19.—Resolution in relation to the care, custody and maintenance of Prisoners confined in the Jail of the City of Richmond.

Adopted May 19, 1862.

Maintenance of persons confined in jail of Richmond city

Resolved by the general assembly, that the governor be and is hereby authorized, in conjunction with the judge of the hustings court, to take such order in respect to the care, custody and maintenance of persons confined in the jail of the city of Richmond, as circumstances may render expedient, and pay any necessary expenditure occasioned thereby, out of any contingent fund under his control:

Expenses, how paid

but prisoners charged with, or convicted of violation of any ordinances of the city, shall be supported, removed or maintained at the expense of the city, should any expense be incurred in and about them, under this resolution.

No. 20.—Resolution to provide for the care and comfort of the Inmates of the Lunatic Asylum at Williamsburg.

Adopted May 17, 1862.

Whereas the hospital of the insane at Williamsburg has fallen into the possession of the enemy, and the general assembly cannot but feel solicitude for its unfortunate inmates, who are incapable of taking care of themselves, or of making known their wants and sufferings, and who are or may be deprived of the care and control of their natural friends and guardians: *[Preamble]*

Resolved by the general assembly, that the governor be authorized to appoint one or more persons to visit (through the intervention, if necessary, of the proper military authorities) the hospital, if permitted by the enemy, and upon their report, to adopt such measures as may be in his power for the preservation of the institution and the care and comfort of its patients, and to use for that purpose the funds appropriated for the institution, or if required, the contingent fund. *[Governor to appoint persons to visit hospital]*

No. 21.—Joint Resolution concerning an Address to the People and our Soldiers.

Adopted May 16, 1862.

Resolved by the general assembly, that the joint committee on the state of the country be instructed to prepare an address to the people and our soldiers, and submit it to the general assembly, for its approval. *[Committee to prepare address]*

No. 22.—Resolution as to the Lessees of the Washington and Smyth Salt Works.

Adopted April 1, 1862.

Whereas the general assembly having failed, at its recent session, to pass a law to carry into effect the contract entered into between the lessees of the Smyth and Washington salt works and the joint committee of the general assembly, for the sale to the state of four hundred thousand bushels of salt: Therefore, *[Preamble]*

Be it resolved by the general assembly, that the lessees aforesaid be released from the obligations of said contract. *[Lessees released from contract]*

No. 23.—Resolutions in relation to Confederate Money.

Adopted May 19, 1862.

Notes of Confederate States

1. Resolved by the general assembly of Virginia, that it is the sacred and patriotic duty of every good citizen of the Confederate States, not under duress of the enemy, to receive in his business transactions the notes of the Confederate States. To refuse to receive them, must depreciate their credit, and will tend to deprive the confederate government of the means of defending our liberty and independence; and such conduct cannot be too strongly denounced, as most effectually affording aid and comfort to the public enemy.

Confederate stock to be guaranteed

2. Resolved, that the confederate stock should be guaranteed by the several states of the Confederacy, according to their respective confederate proportions, and that congress be requested to bring the subject to the attention of the legislatures of the several states.

INDEX.

ACTS OF ASSEMBLY.
Resolution for distribution of, 30

ADDRESS.
Resolution as to, 31

BANKS.
Act of 1862 amended, 17
When bank may change place of business, 17–18
Advertisement, 18
Who may exercise powers of board of directors, 18
Parties, when bound; notice, 18

BOARD OF MANUFACTURES.
Resolution as to, 29

CANCELED COUPONS AND TREASURY NOTES.
Resolution for destruction of, 26–7

CHANGES IN CODE.
Sect. 1, chap. 208, amended, 10
Licenses for marriage, 10
How issued, 10
Sect. 13, chap. 207, amended, 10
When person may be discharged, 10
Witnesses, 10
Sect. 1, chap. 162, amended, 10
Who may be grand jurors, 11
Sect. 7, chap. 103, amended, 11
Tenure for life of slave, 11
When slave may be removed, 11
Sect. 19, chap. 14, amended, 11
Salaries, how paid, 11
Pay of members of general assembly, 12
Sect. 5, chap. 205, amended, 12
Examination, how adjourned, 12
When witnesses kept away, 12

CODE.
See Changes in Code.

COMMISSIONERS OF REVENUE.
Resolution as to time of examining books of, 25

COMPENSATION TO CLERKS OF SENATE AND HOUSE OF DELEGATES.
Compensation allowed, 15

CONFEDERATE MONEY.
Resolution as to, 32

CONSTITUTION.
Resolution for publication of new, 30

CORD MEASURE.
Standard of, declared, 15

DEFAULTING COLLECTORS.
Acts of 1860 amended, 3
Act of 1862 amended, 3
Sheriffs and collectors, 3
Judgment, how obtained, 3
Interest, 3
Damages, 3
New trial, 3

DEFENCE OF THE STATE.
John B. Floyd, a major general, 5
Forces, how raised, 5
How divided, 5
Captains to be commissioned, 5
Regiments, how organized, 6
Vacancies, 6
In lowest grade, 6
Cavalry and artillery, 6
Staff of major general, 6
Staff of brigadier general, 6
Staff of colonel, 6
How armed and equipped, 7
Force, how governed, 7
Amount appropriated, 7
Co-operation, 7
Subject to orders of governor, 7
Act amended, 7–8
Who may be officers, 8

DURATION OF EXTRA SESSION.
Resolution as to, 23

FARMVILLE WAREHOUSE.
Act establishing, 21

FLEMING, ANN M.
Act for relief of, 21

GOVERNMENT, SEAT OF.
When, may be changed, 15

HAYMOND, L. D.
Resolution for relief of, 24, 5

HOME GUARD.
Who may organize companies, 8
Commissions, how issued, 8
By-laws, 8
Guard and police, 9
When major may be appointed, 9
Weapons, how furnished, 9
Compensation, 9
Rations, 9
Quartermasters, 9

INDEX.

HORSES TAKEN IN SERVICE.
Amount appropriated, 21

IMPRESSMENTS.
Who guilty of misdemeanor, 14

INSURANCE COMPANIES.
When may change place of business, 16
What, when removed, 16
Prior removal, 16

JAMES AND APPOMATTOX RIVERS.
Resolution as to defence of, 25

JUDGMENT AGAINST DECEASED PERSON.
Judgment not invalidated by death, 5

LEAD AND SALTPETRE.
Preamble, 24
Powers of governor, 24
Lead, 24
Saltpetre, 24

LICENSES, CHANGE IN.
License, how changed, 4
Restriction, 4

LUNATIC ASYLUM AT WILLIAMSBURG.
Resolution as to, 31
Commission to visit hospital, 31

MILEAGE.
Resolution as to, 23

NATURE AND CONDUCT OF PENDING WAR.
Preamble and resolutions as to, 27–8
Separation, 28
Confidence in armies, 28
Coast defences, 28
Resources of state, 28

PARTISAN SERVICE.
Preamble and resolution as to, 29

PENITENTIARY.
Preamble and resolution as to, 26
Commission to be appointed, 26

PRISONERS IN RICHMOND.
Resolution as to maintenance of, 30

PROTECTION OF CITIZENS.
Preamble, 14
Amount appropriated, 14
Proviso, 14

RICHMOND CITY.
Resolution as to defence of, 22
Charter amended, 16
Jurisdiction of court, 16
Powers of court, 17
When judge may adjourn court, 17
Residence of judge, 17

RICHMOND AND PETERSBURG.
Act as to defences of, 9
Amount appropriated, 9
Proviso, 9
Power and duty of governor, 9

ROANOKE VALLEY RAIL ROAD.
Sale of, authorized, 12
Sanction of board of public works, 12
Restrictions, 13
Debts, how paid, 13

SALT.
When county courts may purchase, 13
How distributed, 13
Agents, how appointed, 13
Bond, and breach of, 13

SENTENCE OF DEATH.
How executed, 15–16

SMALL NOTES.
Act of 29th March 1862 amended, 18
Notes, how issued, 18
How redeemed, 19
Penalty; proviso, 19
Notes, how signed, 19
Act of 29th March 1862 amended, 19
City of Richmond to issue, 19
Cities and towns, 19
Notes heretofore issued, 20
Act of 29th March 1862 amended, 20
Notes, how redeemed; proviso, 20

SMYTH AND WASHINGTON SALT WORKS.
Resolution releasing lessees of, from contract, 31

SPECIAL SESSIONS.
Resolution as to, 23

TREASURY NOTES.
How issued, 4

VICTORIA MINING AND MANUFACTURING COMPANY.
Company incorporated; name, 22
Powers and privileges, 22
Capital stock, 22

ORDINANCES

ADOPTED BY

THE CONVENTION OF VIRGINIA,

AT THE

ADJOURNED SESSION

IN

NOVEMBER AND DECEMBER 1861.

ORDINANCES.

No. 89.—An ORDINANCE to amend an Ordinance for the Apportionment of Representation in the Congress of the Confederate States.

Passed November 20, 1861.

Be it ordained, that the ordinance, entitled an ordinance for the apportionment of representation in the congress of the Confederate States, be and the same is hereby amended so that the third section thereof shall read as follows: Norfolk city, Norfolk county, Princess Anne, Nansemond, Isle of Wight, Southampton, Sussex, Surry, Greenesville and the city of Portsmouth shall be the second district.

No. 90.—An ORDINANCE authorizing Officers in the service of the State to accept Commissions from the Government of the Confederate States.

Passed November 23, 1861.

Be it ordained, that during the existing war officers of the volunteers and militia shall be eligible to seats in the general assembly, and that any person holding office in this commonwealth, may hold any military appointment under the confederate government during the war without vacating such office.

Be it further ordained, that Colonel Henry Hill, the paymaster of the Virginia forces, be and he is hereby authorized to accept a commission in the army of the Confederate States, without vacating his commission as paymaster of the Virginia forces.

Be it ordained, that so much of section 2, chapter 12 of the Code of Virginia, as forbids an officer under the government of Virginia from holding office or appointment under the government of the Confederate States of America, be and the same is hereby declared to be inoperative as to such officers of this commonwealth as have been or may be driven from their homes, deprived of their offices, and the means of supporting themselves and their families, until the close of the war.

This ordinance shall be in force from its passage.

No. 91.—An ORDINANCE relative to the Proceedings against Judges.

Passed November 30, 1861.

Be it ordained, that in any proceeding against a judge, under the seventeenth section of the sixth article of the constitution of this commonwealth, if it shall from any cause be impossible to give notice by personal service of process on such judge, that the general assembly may cause notice to be given by publication, once a week for four successive weeks, in one of the newspapers published at the capital of the state, in which publication the causes alleged for his removal shall be stated; which publication shall be equivalent to personal service of the notice.

No. 92.—An ORDINANCE for the trial of persons offending against the laws of the Commonwealth, in Counties in possession of the Common Enemy.

Passed November 30, 1861.

1. Be it ordained, that offenders against the criminal laws of this commonwealth, when the offence shall have been committed in a county in the possession of the public enemy, or is threatened with invasion, whereby the laws cannot be safely or conveniently administered therein, may be prosecuted, tried and punished in any other convenient county; and no question of jurisdiction as to the place of trial shall be sustained by the court: provided, however, that the venue may be changed in such as in other cases.

2. Be it further ordained, that when any soldier is charged with any offence against the criminal laws, he may be arrested not only by any officer now authorized by law to make such arrest, but by any officer of the army, and may be carried before any justice of the peace of the commonwealth, whether in or out of his county, with the charge and evidence against the accused; and such justice is hereby authorized to hear such case; and if in his opinion the accused should be further tried, he shall also decide to what county he will send him for trial. Such justice shall have power and it shall be his duty to bind the witnesses in a recognizance for their appearance in court to testify, and in default of such recognizance, to commit them to jail for safe keeping.

3. Be it further ordained, that during the present war rape committed upon a white woman shall be punished with death.

No. 93.—An ORDINANCE for Reorganizing the Militia.

Passed November 29, 1861.

Be it ordained, that all persons subject to military duty in this commonwealth shall be classed as follows: All over twenty-one years of age and under thirty-one years of age, shall constitute the active class: all the rest shall constitute the reserve.

Regimental and company districts.

2. The governor shall forthwith cause the regimental and company districts to be rearranged by uniting two districts in one, and by such changes of boundary as may be necessary to equalize them. The said rearrangement of company dis-

triots shall be made by the regimental boards as at present organized, each board acting for its present district, or in case of their absence, inability, refusal or failure to act, by such other persons as the governor shall appoint. After the active regiments and battalions are organized, battalion and company districts shall only be altered by the boards of officers of those regiments and battalions.

Divisions and brigades.

3. The governor may rearrange the divisions and brigades of the militia so as to make them conform to the change of organization herein after prescribed.

Enrollment.

4. The governor, so soon as the company and regimental districts are rearranged as above directed, shall cause a company of the active class and one of the reserve to be enrolled in each company district. The enrollment shall be made by the commandants of companies under the present organization, acting together for the enlarged company districts, or in case of their absence, inability, refusal or failure to act, by such persons as the governor may appoint, who shall be allowed therefor such compensation as is allowed by law for the registration of voters. The form of the enrollment shall be as at present prescribed by law, with the addition of columns, giving the ages of the persons enrolled and the expiration of the term of service of such of them as are serving as volunteers; and it shall specify that the company is of the active class or the reserve, as the case may be. In all counties situated within the ebb and flow of the tide, the enrollment shall also specify all seamen and mariners. In time of war commandants of regiments may cause enrollments to be made whenever recruits are needed for their respective commands. Notices requiring enrollment shall be posted at three or more places of public resort in each company district not less than thirty days before the organization of a company. Persons subject to service under this ordinance belonging to districts occupied by the enemy, may be enrolled and called into service under temporary regulations to be prescribed by the governor of the commonwealth, in his discretion.

Organization.

5. The militia of the state shall continue to be organized into divisions, brigades, regiments, battalions and companies, but the organization of each class shall be distinct and separate from that of the other class. In each company district the governor shall cause to be organized two companies, one of the active class and one of the reserve; and in each regimental and battalion district, where there is a battalion district not comprised within a regimental district, he shall cause to be organized two regiments or battalions, one of the active class and one of the reserve, and he shall then organize brigades and divisions of the active class and brigades and divisions of the reserve, assigning not less than four regiments to a brigade, and not less than two brigades to a division. The governor may distribute the militia as infantry, cavalry, and light and heavy artillery, at his discretion, not exceeding, however, the proportion of one battery of artillery and one troop of cavalry to each regiment of infantry. He may organize the artillery and cavalry into regiments and battalions, and he may assign men to the cavalry and artillery service without confining a troop or company to one company district. No officer,

non-commissioned officer or private, assigned to cavalry or artillery service, shal be required to furnish his own horse. The governor shall cause the regiments of infantry, cavalry and artillery to be numbered, assigning the same number to the active regiment, and the reserve regiment of infantry in the same regimental district, and distinguishing them as active or reserve regiments.

Coast defence.

6. The governor may assign all enrolled seamen and mariners to the defence of the coast and rivers of the commonwealth, and may require them to serve afloat or on shore, but their term of service shall not differ from that of the class to which they belong. He may organize them as infantry or artillery or as seamen and marines for service afloat; and in the latter organization he shall follow as nearly as practicable that of the Confederate States navy, and may appoint and commission the officers necessary under the said organization: and when the militia are organized for service afloat, and actually serve in that manner, without being accepted and paid by the Confederate States, their rate of pay received from this commonwealth shall be the same as that allowed in the Confederate States navy. It shall be competent for the governor to officer the said marine force in whole or in part with such officers of the Confederate States navy as may be permitted by the confederate government to enter the said service. Instead of enrolling and organizing seamen and mariners with the militia, the governor may cause a separate enrollment and organization to be made of all such persons resident in the commonwealth, whether of military age or not, for a term of service not exceeding three years; and they shall be excused from all other military duty.

Officers.

7. General and field officers of the militia and volunteers shall be appointed by the governor. The reserve shall have no general officers, but shall serve under the general officers of the active class. In time of war, however, the governor may refrain from making appointments of general officers, or from calling them into service, and may permit the troops to serve under general officers appointed by the president of the Confederate States, but without prejudice to the constitutional rights of this commonwealth. Volunteer companies at the time of their organization shall elect a captain and one first and two second lieutenants, or two first and one second lieutenant, as in corresponding arms of the confederate army, who shall be commissioned by the governor. Vacancies among commissioned officers of volunteers and militia companies, occurring before and after they have been mustered into the service, shall be filled as heretofore. The company officers of the militia shall be of the same grade as those of the volunteers. Appointments of generals and field officers shall be submitted to the senate for confirmation at its next session. Such appointments shall continue valid until rejected. Each commandant of a regiment or battalion shall appoint his adjutant and sergeant major. So soon as the enrollment in two company districts in the same regimental or battalion district is complete for either the active or the reserve class, the governor shall appoint the colonel of the regiment or the major of the battalion containing the said two enrolled companies; and the colonel or major so appointed shall order the election of company officers as the enrollment of the companies in his regiment or battalion shall be completed, and shall organize forthwith his regi-

ment or battalion, and report the same to the governor. But no colonel or major of cavalry or artillery shall be appointed until all the companies in his regiment or battalion shall be organized, and orders for the election of company officers of cavalry and artillery shall issue from the adjutant general. Officers whose appointments are to be submitted to the senate for confirmation shall not be commissioned until their appointments are confirmed, but in the mean while shall be deemed commissioned. No general or field officer of the militia shall be mustered into service with less than the following number of non-commissioned officers and privates in his command: A major general, 4,000; a brigadier general, 2,000; a colonel or lieutenant colonel, 500; a major, 250. Where a company in actual service shall have for three months continuously less than fifty non-commissioned officers and privates, it shall be incorporated with other companies in the same regiment or battalion, and the commissions of the officers shall be revoked. If there be two or more companies in the same regiment or battalion, with less than the said number of non-commissioned officers and privates, they shall be consolidated; the commissions of the officers shall be revoked, and the requisite number be re-elected.

Musters and training.

8. Musters and trainings of the reserve shall continue as heretofore. Those for the active class shall be prescribed by the governor. He may furnish camp equipage to the active class, or such portion of them as may be ordered into encampments for military exercises, and to the reserve when mustered into service.

Calling the militia into service.

9. When the militia are needed for active service, the governor shall first call out the active class, or such portion of it as may be necessary, unless the exigency is such as to require both the active class and the reserve; but he need not call out the entire active class before calling out any portion of the reserve. In all cases where the reserve is called out, it shall be relieved as speedily as possible by the active class.

Term of service.

10. The term of service of the reserve shall be as heretofore; that of the active class shall be as follows: All under 26 years of age, three years; and the rest two years. Service as a volunteer, as well heretofore as hereafter, shall be estimated as service in the active class, but shall not shorten the aggregate service which would otherwise have been due from such volunteer. But if such volunteer be in service at the time of the passage of this ordinance, and shall serve continuously two years, no further service shall be required from him in the active class, and he shall be deemed in the reserve. If the term of service due from a member of the active class be not rendered continuously, he may again be called out for the remainder of the term, but not longer.

Volunteers.

11. The organization of the volunteers shall remain as heretofore. When the term of service for which a volunteer has been mustered in is about to expire, and

the militia company in which he has been or ought to be enrolled is mustered in, or about to be mustered into service, he shall have the option of volunteering for one year more, or of being mustered into the service with the militia company of which he is a member. If he prefer to be discharged from the volunteer service, he shall receive his discharge, and the fact of such discharge shall of itself be deemed a mustering into service as a member of the militia company to which he belongs, if such company be in service. In either case, such furlough shall be granted to him as the public safety permits, but it shall specify the company of which he is a member. A volunteer may elect, at any time before the expiration of his term of service, to re-enter the volunteer service, and thereupon his furlough may be granted if the public safety permits it.

Furloughs, absences and failures to enroll.

12. All persons, whether volunteers or militia, who overstay their time after a furlough or leave of absence, or who shall absent themselves from their company without permission, or fail to enroll themselves in the militia company in which they should be enrolled, for thirty days after notice requiring enrollment to be made has been posted at three places of public resort in the company district, shall, in addition to such other punishment as the law may inflict, have their term of service lengthened three days for every day they have overstayed their furlough or leave of absence, absented themselves without permission, or failed to enroll, unless they show good cause before a court of enquiry for such absence or failure to enroll.

Repeal of militia law.

13. The militia laws and the laws concerning volunteers shall continue in force except so far as they may be in conflict with the foregoing ordinance, and the militia law shall apply to both classes of militia. The existing organization shall continue in each regimental and battalion district until the company officers of the active companies in the district are elected. The authority of all officers, regimental and company, under the existing laws, shall then cease, except for the purpose of organizing the reserve. General and staff officers shall remain in commission until their successors are appointed. All acts and parts of acts in conflict with the foregoing ordinance, are hereby repealed.

This ordinance shall take effect from its passage, and may be repealed or amended by the general assembly.

No. 94.—An ORDINANCE authorising that ordinances may be enrolled otherwise than now required by law.

Passed December 4, 1861.

It having been made known to the convention that it is impossible to procure parchment for the enrollment of the ordinances, according to the requirements of existing laws:

Be it therefore ordained, that the secretary be and he is hereby authorized to enroll the ordinances which have been or may be passed by this convention, on substantial paper.

ORDINANCES OF THE VIRGINIA CONVENTION.   9

No. 95.—An ORDINANCE authorizing the General Assembly to fill Vacancies in that body in certain cases.

Passed December 4, 1861.

Whereas vacancies may have occurred or may occur in the general assembly, and by reason of the presence of the public enemy, it may be impossible to fill such vacancies in the mode now provided by the constitution and laws: Therefore,

Be it ordained, that in all such cases now existing, or that may hereafter occur during the present war, the senate and the house of delegates shall each have power to elect members to fill such vacancies in its own body, or such vacancies may be filled in such other manner as the general assembly may prescribe by law.

No. 96.—An ORDINANCE concerning Treasury Notes.

Passed December 4, 1861.

Whereas, by ordinances of this convention, number thirty-five, entitled an ordinance to authorize the issue of treasury notes, passed April 30th, 1861, and an ordinance number seventy-one, entitled an ordinance authorizing treasury notes, and concerning the banks, passed June 28th, 1861, authority was given to issue treasury notes to an amount not exceeding in the aggregate the sum of six millions of dollars, of which four millions were to bear interest at the rate of six per centum per annum, and the remaining two millions were to be without interest; and it being desirable to relieve the treasury from the payment of interest on the treasury notes used and circulated as a currency:

Be it ordained, that the auditor of public accounts be and he is hereby authorized to issue treasury notes, which shall bear no interest, to an amount not exceeding four millions of dollars, for the purpose of redeeming at maturity, or at such other time as they may be presented for payment, the interest bearing treasury notes which were issued under the ordinances of this convention, passed as aforesaid, respectively, on the 30th day of April 1861, and on the 28th day of June 1861. The said notes shall be of denominations not less than five dollars; be payable to bearer at the treasury, on demand; and when presented for payment in sums of five hundred dollars, or any multiple of one hundred dollars above that sum, they may be converted into registered bonds of the state, bearing six per centum per annum interest. All the provisions of said ordinances numbers thirty-five and seventy-one, in this ordinance referred to, and the ordinance entitled an ordinance requiring the banks to receive the treasury notes of this commonwealth, passed July 1st, 1861, shall be held to apply to the notes authorized to be issued by this ordinance, except so far only as they may be inconsistent therewith. And to enable the auditor of public accounts to execute the provisions of this ordinance, he is authorized to employ, for the purpose of dating, numbering, clipping and registering said notes, such clerical force, in addition to that now in his office, as may be necessary for the object, at an expense not exceeding the rate of nine hundred dollars per annum for the time so employed. All expenses incurred in the execution of this act, shall be defrayed out of any money in the treasury not otherwise appropriated.

This ordinance shall be in force from its passage.

No. 97.—An ORDINANCE enabling the Bank of the Old Dominion at Pearisburg and the Northwestern Bank at Jeffersonville to issue Small Notes.

Passed December 5, 1861.

Be it ordained, that the provisions of the ordinance passed on the 26th day of April 1861, permitting the issue of notes of a less denomination than five dollars, by the banks of this commonwealth, be and the same are hereby extended to the Bank of the Old Dominion at Pearisburg and to the Northwestern Bank at Jeffersonville.

No. 98.—An ORDINANCE concerning Returned Natives.

Passed December 6, 1861.

Be it ordained, that natives of Virginia who were residents of any other states or countries, prior to the 4th day of March last, and who since that time have returned hither, with the intention of permanently resuming their citizenship, or who are now here with such intention, shall have and enjoy all the rights and privileges of citizens of Virginia, as fully as if they had never resided elsewhere.

This ordinance shall take effect from its passage.

No. 99.—An ORDINANCE to authorize the qualified Voters of the Commonwealth, who may be in the Military Service of the State or the Confederate States, to vote for Members of the General Assembly within their Encampments; and authorizing the General Assembly to make such laws as may be requisite to give the qualified voters, in the Military Service of the State or the Confederate States, on the day of any election under the Constitution, the right to vote within their Encampments at such elections, and authorizing the citizens of any County or Corporation absent therefrom because of the presence of the Public Enemy, who would be qualified to vote for Members of the General Assembly, in such County or Corporation, to vote at any general or special Election for Members of the General Assembly for their counties or corporations.

Passed December 6, 1861.

1. Be it ordained, that the qualified voters of this commonwealth, who may be in the military service of the state or of the Confederate States on the day of any general or special election for the general assembly, may vote in said elections at such place or places within their encampment as the commander at such encampment shall designate, whether the said encampment shall be within the limits of this state or not.

2. For each place of voting the commander of the encampment shall appoint a superintendent, three commissioners, and as many clerks as shall be necessary, who, after being first duly sworn by him, shall perform the duties required of, and be liable to the penalties imposed upon, such officers, by the election laws of the state. The said commissioners shall open polls for the counties and corporations of the state from which there may be voters in the said encampment desiring to vote. The qualified voters who present themselves to exercise the right of

suffrage, shall be each asked to name the county or corporation of his residence, and shall be allowed to vote to represent the county in which he resides, and his name shall be headed in the poll book opened for his county or corporation. When the polls taken as aforesaid shall be closed, the commissioners holding said election shall make a certified statement of the result of the election in such encampment, for each county for which a poll was opened, and shall deliver the statement so made and the poll book to the commander of the encampment, who shall forthwith appoint some person whose duty it shall be to take the poll book and the statement of the result to the courthouse of the county for which said election was held, and to deliver the same to the officer conducting the election at the courthouse of said county; but if said county is in possession of the public enemy, then to deliver the same to the secretary of the commonwealth. All other proceedings shall be the same as prescribed by the election laws of the state.

3. Power is hereby given the general assembly to make such laws during the existing war between the Confederate States and the president of the United States, as may be requisite to authorize the qualified voters of the commonwealth, who may be in the military service of the state on the day of any election under the constitution, to vote within their encampment at such elections.

4. The citizens of any county or corporation absent therefrom because of the presence of the public enemy, who would be qualified to vote for members of the general assembly in such county or corporation, may, during the continuance of the present war, vote at any general or special election for members of the general assembly for their counties or corporations at the courthouse of any county or corporation in the state where they may happen to be on the day of said election: and returns shall be made and certificates given in the mode now prescribed by law.

THE

CONSTITUTION

OF THE

CONFEDERATE STATES OF AMERICA,

ADOPTED MARCH 11, 1861.

CONSTITUTION.

We, the people of the Confederate States, each state acting in its sovereign and independent character, in order to form a permanent federal government, establish justice, insure domestic tranquillity and secure the blessings of liberty to ourselves and our posterity—invoking the favor and guidance of Almighty God—do ordain and establish this constitution for the Confederate States of America.

ARTICLE I.

Section 1.

All legislative powers herein delegated shall be vested in a congress of the Confederate States, which shall consist of a senate and house of representatives.

Section 2.

1. The house of representatives shall be composed of members chosen every second year by the people of the several states; and the electors in each state shall be citizens of the Confederate States, and have the qualifications requisite for electors of the most numerous branch of the state legislature; but no person of foreign birth, not a citizen of the Confederate States, shall be allowed to vote for any officer, civil or political, state or federal.

2. No person shall be a representative who shall not have attained the age of twenty-five years, and be a citizen of the Confederate States, and who shall not, when elected, be an inhabitant of that state in which he shall be chosen.

3. Representatives and direct taxes shall be apportioned among the several states, which may be included within this Confederacy, according to their respective numbers, which shall be determined by adding to the whole number of free persons, including those bound to service for a term of years, and excluding Indians not taxed, three-fifths of all slaves. The actual enumeration shall be made within three years after the first meeting of the congress of the Confederate States, and within every subsequent term of ten years, in such manner as they shall by law direct. The number of representatives shall not exceed one for every fifty thousand, but each state shall have at least one representative: and until such enumeration shall be made, the state of South Carolina shall be entitled to choose six; the state of Georgia ten; the state of Alabama nine; the state of Florida two; the state of Mississippi seven; the state of Louisiana six; and the state of Texas six.

4. When vacancies happen in the representation from any state, the executive authority thereof shall issue writs of election to fill such vacancies.

5. The house of representatives shall choose their speaker and other officers; and shall have the sole power of impeachment; except that any judicial or other federal officer, resident and acting solely within the limits of any state, may be impeached by a vote of two-thirds of both branches of the legislature thereof.

Section 3.

1. The senate of the Confederate States shall be composed of two senators from each state, chosen for six years by the legislature thereof, at the regular session next immediately preceding the commencement of the term of service; and each senator shall have one vote.

2. Immediately after they shall be assembled, in consequence of the first election, they shall be divided as equally as may be into three classes. The seats of the senators of the first class shall be vacated at the expiration of the second year; of the second class at the expiration of the fourth year; and of the third class at the expiration of the sixth year; so that one-third may be chosen every second year; and if vacancies happen by resignation, or otherwise, during the recess of the legislature of any state, the executive thereof may make temporary appointments until the next meeting of the legislature, which shall then fill such vacancies.

3. No person shall be a senator who shall not have attained the age of thirty years, and be a citizen of the Confederate States; and who shall not, when elected, be an inhabitant of the state for which he shall be chosen.

4. The vice-president of the Confederate States shall be president of the senate, but shall have no vote, unless they be equally divided.

5. The senate shall choose their other officers; and also a president pro tempore in the absence of the vice-president, or when he shall exercise the office of president of the Confederate States.

6. The senate shall have the sole power to try all impeachments. When sitting for that purpose, they shall be on oath or affirmation. When the president of the Confederate States is tried, the chief justice shall preside; and no person shall be convicted without the concurrence of two-thirds of the members present.

7. Judgment in cases of impeachment shall not extend further than to removal from office, and disqualification to hold and enjoy any office of honor, trust or profit, under the Confederate States; but the party convicted shall, nevertheless, be liable and subject to indictment, trial, judgment and punishment according to law.

Section 4.

1. The times, places and manner of holding elections for senators and representatives, shall be prescribed in each state by the legislature thereof, subject to the provisions of this constitution; but the congress may, at any time, by law, make or alter such regulations, except as to the times and places of choosing senators.

2. The congress shall assemble at least once in every year; and such meeting shall be on the first Monday in December, unless they shall, by law, appoint a different day.

Section 5.

1. Each house shall be the judge of the elections, returns and qualifications of its own members, and a majority of each shall constitute a quorum to do business; but a smaller number may adjourn from day to day, and may be authorized to compel the attendance of absent members, in such manner and under such penalties as each house may provide.

2. Each house may determine the rules of its proceedings, punish its members for disorderly behavior, and with the concurrence of two-thirds of the whole number expel a member.

3. Each house shall keep a journal of its proceedings, and from time to time publish the same, excepting such parts as may in their judgment require secrecy; and the yeas and nays of the members of either house, on any question, shall, at the desire of one-fifth of those present, be entered on the journal.

4. Neither house, during the session of congress, shall, without the consent of the other, adjourn for more than three days, nor to any other place than that in which the two houses shall be sitting.

Section 6.

1. The senators and representatives shall receive a compensation for their services, to be ascertained by law, and paid out of the treasury of the Confederate States. They shall, in all cases, except treason, felony, and breach of the peace, be privileged from arrest during their attendance at the session of their respective houses, and in going to and returning from the same; and for any speech or debate in either house, they shall not be questioned in any other place.

2. No senator or representative shall, during the time for which he was elected, be appointed to any civil office under the authority of the Confederate States, which shall have been created, or the emoluments whereof shall have been increased during such time; and no person holding any office under the Confederate States shall be a member of either house during his continuance in office. But congress may, by law, grant to the principal officer in each of the executive departments a seat upon the floor of either house, with the privilege of discussing any measures appertaining to his department.

Section 7.

1. All bills for raising revenue shall originate in the house of representatives; but the senate may propose or concur with amendments, as on other bills.

2. Every bill which shall have passed both houses, shall, before it becomes a law, be presented to the president of the Confederate States; if he approve, he shall sign it; but if not, he shall return it, with his objections, to that house in which it shall have originated, who shall enter the objections at large on their journal, and proceed to reconsider it. If, after such reconsideration, two-thirds of that house shall agree to pass the bill, it shall be sent, together with the objections, to the other house, by which it shall likewise be reconsidered, and if approved by

two-thirds of that house, it shall become a law. But in all such cases, the votes of both houses shall be determined by yeas and nays, and the names of the persons voting for and against the bill shall be entered on the journal of each house respectively. If any bill shall not be returned by the president within ten days (Sundays excepted) after it shall have been presented to him, the same shall be a law, in like manner as if he had signed it, unless the congress, by their adjournment, prevent its return; in which case it shall not be a law. The president may approve any appropriation and disapprove any other appropriation in the same bill. In such case he shall, in signing the bill, designate the appropriations disapproved; and shall return a copy of such appropriations, with his objections, to the house in which the bill shall have originated; and the same proceedings shall then be had as in case of other bills disapproved by the president.

3. Every order, resolution or vote, to which the concurrence of both houses may be necessary (except on a question of adjournment), shall be presented to the president of the Confederate States; and before the same shall take effect, shall be approved by him; or being disapproved by him, shall be repassed by two-thirds of both houses, according to the rules and limitations prescribed in case of a bill.

SECTION 8.

The congress shall have power—

1. To lay and collect taxes, duties, imposts, and excises, for revenue necessary to pay the debts, provide for the common defence, and carry on the government of the Confederate States; but no bounties shall be granted from the treasury; nor shall any duties or taxes on importations from foreign nations be laid to promote or foster any branch of industry; and all duties, imposts, and excises shall be uniform throughout the Confederate States:

2. To borrow money on the credit of the Confederate States:

3. To regulate commerce with foreign nations, and among the several states, and with the Indian tribes; but neither this, nor any other clause contained in the constitution, shall ever be construed to delegate the power to congress to appropriate money for any internal improvement intended to facilitate commerce; except for the purpose of furnishing lights, beacons, and buoys, and other aids to navigation upon the coasts, and the improvement of harbors and the removing of obstructions in river navigation; in all which cases, such duties shall be laid on the navigation facilitated thereby, as may be necessary to pay the costs and expenses thereof:

4. To establish uniform laws of naturalization, and uniform laws on the subject of bankruptcies, throughout the Confederate States; but no law of congress shall discharge any debt contracted before the passage of the same:

5. To coin money, regulate the value thereof and of foreign coin, and fix the standard of weights and measures:

6. To provide for the punishment of counterfeiting the securities and current coin of the Confederate States:

7. To establish post-offices and post-routes; but the expenses of the post-office department, after the first day of March in the year of our Lord eighteen hundred and sixty-three, shall be paid out of its own revenues:

8. To promote the progress of science and useful arts, by securing, for limited times to authors and inventors, the exclusive right to their respective writings and discoveries:

9. To constitute tribunals inferior to the supreme court:

10. To define and punish piracies and felonies committed on the high seas, and offences against the law of nations:

11. To declare war, grant letters of marque and reprisal, and make rules concerning captures on land and water:

12. To raise and support armies; but no appropriation of money to that use shall be for a longer term than two years:

13. To provide and maintain a navy:

14. To make rules for the government and regulation of the land and naval forces:

15. To provide for calling forth the militia to execute the laws of the Confederate States, suppress insurrections, and repel invasions:

16. To provide for organizing, arming, and disciplining the militia, and for governing such part of them as may be employed in the service of the Confederate States; reserving to the states, respectively, the appointment of the officers, and the authority of training the militia according to the discipline prescribed by congress:

17. To exercise exclusive legislation, in all cases whatsoever, over such district (not exceeding ten miles square) as may, by cession of one or more states and the acceptance of congress, become the seat of the government of the Confederate States; and to exercise like authority over all places purchased by the consent of the legislature of the state in which the same shall be, for the erection of forts, magazines, arsenals, dockyards, and other needful buildings: and

18. To make all laws which shall be necessary and proper for carrying into execution the foregoing powers, and all other powers vested by this constitution in the government of the Confederate States, or in any department or officer thereof.

SECTION 9.

1. The importation of negroes of the African race from any foreign country other than the slaveholding states or territories of the United States of America, is hereby forbidden; and congress is required to pass such laws as shall effectually prevent the same.

2. Congress shall also have power to prohibit the introduction of slaves from any state not a member of, or territory not belonging to, this Confederacy.

3. The privilege of the writ of habeas corpus shall not be suspended unless when in cases of rebellion or invasion, the public safety may require it.

4. No bill of attainder, ex post facto law, or law denying or impairing the right of property in negro slaves, shall be passed.

5. No capitation or other direct tax shall be laid, unless in proportion to the census or enumeration herein before directed to be taken.

6. No tax or duty shall be laid on articles exported from any state, except by a vote of two-thirds of both houses.

7. No preference shall be given by any regulation of commerce or revenue to the ports of one state over those of another.

8. No money shall be drawn from the treasury, but in consequence of appropriations made by law; and a regular statement and account of the receipts and expenditures of all public money shall be published from time to time.

9. Congress shall appropriate no money from the treasury, except by a vote of two-thirds of both houses, taken by yeas and nays, unless it be asked and estimated for by some one of the heads of departments, and submitted to congress by the president, or for the purpose of paying its own expenses and contingencies; or for the payment of claims against the Confederate States, the justice of which shall have been judicially declared by a tribunal for the investigation of claims against the government, which it is hereby made the duty of congress to establish.

10. All bills appropriating money, shall specify in federal currency the exact amount of each appropriation and the purposes for which it is made; and congress shall grant no extra compensation to any public contractor, officer, agent or servant, after such contract shall have been made or such service rendered.

11. No title of nobility shall be granted by the Confederate States; and no person holding any office of profit or trust under them, shall, without the consent of the congress, accept of any present, emolument, office, or title of any kind whatever, from any king, prince, or foreign state.

12. Congress shall make no law respecting an establishment of religion or prohibiting the free exercise thereof: or abridging the freedom of speech, or of the press; or the right of the people peaceably to assemble, and petition the government for a redress of grievances.

13. A well regulated militia being necessary to the security of a free state, the right of the people to keep and bear arms shall not be infringed.

14. No soldier shall, in time of peace, be quartered in any house without the consent of the owner; nor in time of war, but in a manner to be prescribed by law.

15. The right of the people to be secure in their persons, houses, papers and effects, against unreasonable searches and seizures, shall not be violated; and no

warrants shall issue but upon probable cause, supported by oath or affirmation, and particularly describing the place to be searched, and the persons or things to be seized.

16. No person shall be held to answer for a capital or otherwise infamous crime, unless on a presentment or indictment of a grand jury, except in cases arising in the land or naval forces, or in the militia, when in actual service in time of war or public danger; nor shall any person be subject for the same offence to be twice put in jeopardy of life or limb; nor be compelled in any criminal case to be a witness against himself; nor be deprived of life, liberty, or property, without due process of law; nor shall private property be taken for public use, without just compensation.

17. In all criminal prosecutions, the accused shall enjoy the right to a speedy and public trial, by an impartial jury of the state and district wherein the crime shall have been committed, which district shall have been previously ascertained by law, and to be informed of the nature and cause of the accusation; to be confronted with the witnesses against him; to have compulsory process for obtaining witnesses in his favor; and to have the assistance of counsel for his defence.

18. In suits at common law, where the value in controversy shall exceed twenty dollars, the right of trial by jury shall be preserved; and no fact so tried by a jury shall be otherwise re-examined in any court of the Confederacy, than according to the rules of the common law.

19. Excessive bail shall not be required, nor excessive fines imposed, nor cruel and unusual punishments inflicted.

20. Every law, or resolution having the force of law, shall relate to but one subject, and that shall be expressed in the title.

SECTION 10.

1. No state shall enter into any treaty, alliance, or confederation; grant letters of marque and reprisal; coin money; make any thing but 'gold and silver coin a tender in payment of debts; pass any bill of attainder, or ex post facto law, or law impairing the obligation of contracts; or grant any title of nobility.

2. No state shall, without the consent of the congress, lay any imposts or duties on imports or exports, except what may be absolutely necessary for executing its inspection laws; and the net produce of all duties and imposts, laid by any state on imports or exports, shall be for the use of the treasury of the Confederate States, and all such laws shall be subject to the revision and control of congress.

3. No state shall, without the consent of congress, lay any duty on tonnage, except on sea-going vessels, for the improvement of its rivers and harbors navigated by the said vessels; but such duties shall not conflict with any treaties of the Confederate States with foreign nations; and any surplus revenue, thus derived, shall, after making such improvement, be paid into the common treasury. Nor shall any state keep troops or ships of war in time of peace, enter into any agreement or compact with another state, or with a foreign power, or engage in war,

unless actually invaded, or in such imminent danger as will not admit of delay. But when any river divides or flows through two or more states, they may enter into compacts with each other to improve the navigation thereof.

ARTICLE II.

Section I.

1. The executive power shall be vested in a president of the Confederate States of America. He and the vice-president shall hold their offices for the term of six years; but the president shall not be re-eligible. The president and vice-president shall be elected as follows:

2. Each state shall appoint, in such manner as the legislature thereof may direct, a number of electors equal to the whole number of senators and representatives to which the state may be entitled in the congress; but no senator or representative, or person holding an office of trust or profit under the Confederate States, shall be appointed an elector.

3. The electors shall meet in their respective states, and vote by ballot for president and vice-president, one of whom, at least, shall not be an inhabitant of the same state with themselves; they shall name in their ballots the person voted for as president, and in distinct ballots, the person voted for as vice-president, and they shall make distinct lists of all persons voted for as president, and of all persons voted for as vice-president, and of the number of votes for each, which lists they shall sign and certify, and transmit, sealed, to the seat of the government of the Confederate States, directed to the president of the senate; the president of the senate shall, in the presence of the senate and house of representatives, open all the certificates, and the votes shall then be counted; the person having the greatest number of votes for president, shall be the president, if such number be a majority of the whole number of electors appointed; and if no person have such majority, then, from the persons having the highest numbers, not exceeding three, on the list of those voted for as president, the house of representatives shall choose immediately, by ballot, the president. But in choosing the president, the votes shall be taken by states—the representation from each state having one vote. A quorum for this purpose shall consist of a member or members from two-thirds of the states, and a majority of all the states shall be necessary to a choice. And if the house of representatives shall not choose a president, whenever the right of choice shall devolve upon them, before the fourth day of March next following, then the vice-president shall act as president, as in case of the death, or other constitutional disability of the president.

4. The person having the greatest number of votes as vice-president, shall be the vice-president, if such number be a majority of the whole number of electors appointed; and if no person have a majority, then, from the two highest numbers on the list the senate shall choose the vice-president. A quorum for the purpose shall consist of two-thirds of the whole number of senators, and a majority of the whole number shall be necessary to a choice.

5. But no person constitutionally ineligible to the office of president, shall be eligible to that of vice-president of the Confederate States.

6. The congress may determine the time of choosing the electors, and the day on which they shall give their votes; which day shall be the same throughout the Confederate States.

7. No person except a natural born citizen of the Confederate States, or a citizen thereof at the time of the adoption of this constitution, or a citizen thereof, born in the United States prior to the 20th of December 1860, shall be eligible to the office of president; neither shall any person be eligible to that office who shall not have attained the age of thirty-five years, and been fourteen years a resident within the limits of the Confederate States, as they may exist at the time of his election.

8. In case of the removal of the president from office, or of his death, resignation or inability to discharge the powers and duties of the said office, the same shall devolve on the vice-president; and the congress may by law provide for the case of removal, death, resignation, or inability, both of the president and vice-president, declaring what officer shall then act as president; and such officer shall act accordingly, until the disability be removed or a president shall be elected.

9. The president shall at stated times receive for his services, a compensation, which shall neither be increased nor diminished during the period for which he shall have been elected; and he shall not receive within that period any other emolument from the Confederate States, or any of them.

10. Before he enters on the execution of his office, he shall take the following oath or affirmation:

"I do solemnly swear (or affirm) that I will faithfully execute the office of president of the Confederate States, and will, to the best of my ability, preserve, protect, and defend the constitution thereof."

SECTION 2.

1. The president shall be commander-in-chief of the army and navy of the Confederate States, and of the militia of the several states, when called into the actual service of the Confederate States; he may require the opinion in writing of the principal officer in each of the executive departments, upon any subject relating to the duties of their repective offices; and he shall have power to grant reprieves and pardons for offences against the Confederate States, except in cases of impeachment.

2. He shall have power, by and with the advice and consent of the senate, to make treaties, provided two-thirds of the senators present concur: and he shall nominate, and by and with the advice and consent of the senate shall appoint ambassadors, other public ministers and consuls, judges of the supreme court, and all other officers of the Confederate States whose appointments are not herein otherwise provided for, and which shall be established by law. But the congress may, by law, vest the appointment of such inferior officers as they think proper in the president alone, in the courts of law, or in the heads of departments.

3. The principal officer in each of the executive departments, and all persons

connected with the diplomatic service, may be removed from office at the pleasure of the president. All other civil officers of the executive department may be removed at any time by the president, or other appointing power, when their services are unnecessary, or for dishonesty, incapacity, inefficiency, misconduct, or neglect of duty; and when so removed, the removal shall be reported to the senate, together with the reasons therefor.

4. The president shall have power to fill all vacancies that may happen during the recess of the senate, by granting commissions which shall expire at the end of their next session; but no person rejected by the senate shall be reappointed to the same office during their ensuing recess.

Section 3.

1. The president shall, from time to time, give to the congress information of the state of the Confederacy, and recommend to their consideration such measures as he shall judge necessary and expedient; he may, on extraordinary occasions, convene both houses, or either of them; and in case of disagreement between them, with respect to the time of adjournment, he may adjourn them to such time as he shall think proper; he shall receive ambassadors and other public ministers; he shall take care that the laws be faithfully executed; and shall commission all the officers of the Confederate States.

Section 4.

1. The president, vice-president, and all civil officers of the Confederate States shall be removed from office on impeachment for and conviction of treason, bribery, or other high crimes and misdemeanors.

ARTICLE III.

Section 1.

1. The judicial power of the Confederate States shall be vested in one supreme court, and in such inferior courts as the congress may from time to time ordain and establish. The judges, both of the supreme and inferior courts, shall hold their offices during good behavior, and shall, at stated times, receive for their services a compensation which shall not be diminished during their continuance in office.

Section 2.

1. The judicial power shall extend to all cases arising under this constitution, the laws of the Confederate States and treaties made, or which shall be made, under their authority; to all cases affecting ambassadors, other public ministers and consuls; to all cases of admiralty and maritime jurisdiction; to controversies to which the Confederate States shall be a party; to controversies between two or more states; between a state and citizen of another state, where the state is plaintiff; between citizens claiming lands under grants of different states; and between a state or the citizens thereof, and foreign states, citizens or subjects; but no state shall be sued by a citizen or subject of any foreign state.

2. In all cases affecting ambassadors, other public ministers and consuls, and

those in which a state shall be a party, the supreme court shall have original jurisdiction. In all the other cases before mentioned, the supreme court shall have appellate jurisdiction both as to law and fact, with such exceptions and under such regulations as the congress shall make.

3. The trial of all crimes except in cases of impeachment, shall be by jury, and such trial shall be held in the state where the said crimes shall have been committed; but when not committed within any state, the trial shall be at such place or places as the congress may by law have directed.

Section 3.

1. Treason against the Confederate States shall consist only in levying war against them, or in adhering to their enemies, giving them aid and comfort. No person shall be convicted of treason unless on the testimony of two witnesses to the same overt act, or on confession in open court.

2. The congress shall have power to declare the punishment of treason; but no attainder of treason shall work corruption of blood, or forfeiture, except during the life of the person attainted.

ARTICLE IV.

Section 1.

1. Full faith and credit shall be given in each state to the public acts, records, and judicial proceedings of every other state. And the congress may, by general laws, prescribe the manner in which such acts, records and proceedings shall be proved and the effect thereof.

Section 2.

1. The citizens of each state shall be entitled to all the privileges and immunities of citizens in the several states; and shall have the right of transit and sojourn in any state of this Confederacy, with their slaves and other property; and the right of property in said slaves shall not be thereby impaired.

2. A person charged in any state with treason, felony, or other crime against the laws of such state, who shall flee from justice, and be found in another state, shall, on demand of the executive authority of the state from which he fled, be delivered up, to be removed to the state having jurisdiction of the crime.

3. No slave or other person held to service or labor in any state or territory of the Confederate States, under the laws thereof, escaping or lawfully carried into another, shall, in consequence of any law or regulation therein, be discharged from such service or labor; but shall be delivered up on claim of the party to whom such slave belongs, or to whom such service or labor may be due.

Section 3.

1. Other states may be admitted into this Confederacy by a vote of two-thirds of the whole house of representatives and two-thirds of the senate, the senate voting by states; but no new state shall be formed or erected within the jurisdic-

tion of any other state; nor any state be formed by the junction of two or more states, or parts of states, without the consent of the legislatures of the states concerned, as well as of the congress.

2. The congress shall have power to dispose of and make all needful rules and regulations concerning the property of the Confederate States, including the lands thereof

3. The Confederate States may acquire new territory; and congress shall have power to legislate and provide governments for the inhabitants of all territory belonging to the Confederate States, lying without the limits of the several states; and may permit them, at such times, and in such manner as it may by law provide, to form states to be admitted into the Confederacy. In all such territory, the institution of negro slavery, as it now exists in the Confederate States, shall be recognized and protected by congress and by the territorial government; and the inhabitants of the several Confederate States and territories shall have the right to take to such territory any slaves lawfully held by them in any of the states or territories of the Confederate States.

4. The Confederate States shall guaranty to every state that now is, or hereafter may become, a member of this Confederacy, a republican form of government; and shall protect each of them against invasion; and on application of the legislature (or of the executive, when the legislature is not in session), against domestic violence.

ARTICLE V.

SECTION 1.

1. Upon the demand of any three states, legally assembled in their several conventions, the congress shall summon a convention of all the states, to take into consideration such amendments to the constitution as the said states shall concur in suggesting at the time when the said demand is made; and should any of the proposed amendments to the constitution be agreed on by the said convention—voting by states—and the same be ratified by the legislatures of two-thirds of the several states, or by conventions in two-thirds thereof—as the one or the other mode of ratification may be proposed by the general convention—they shall thenceforward form a part of this constitution. But no state shall, without its consent, be deprived of its equal representation in the senate.

ARTICLE VI.

1. The government established by this constitution is the successor of the provisional government of the Confederate States of America, and all the laws passed by the latter shall continue in force until the same shall be repealed or modified; and all the officers appointed by the same shall remain in office until their successors are appointed and qualified, or the offices abolished.

2. All debts contracted and engagements entered into before the adoption of this constitution shall be as valid against the Confederate States under this constitution as under the provisional government.

3. This constitution and the laws of the Confederate States made in pursuance thereof, and all treaties made or which shall be made under the authority of the Confederate States, shall be the supreme law of the land; and the judges in every state shall be bound thereby, any thing in the constitution or laws of any state to the contrary notwithstanding.

4. The senators and representatives before mentioned, and the members of the several state legislatures, and all executive and judicial officers, both of the Confederate States and of the several states, shall be bound by oath or affirmation to support this constitution; but no religious test shall ever be required as a qualification to any office or public trust under the Confederate States.

5. The enumeration, in the constitution, of certain rights, shall not be construed to deny or disparage others retained by the people of the several states.

6. The powers not delegated to the Confederate States by the constitution, nor prohibited by it to the states, are reserved to the states, respectively, or to the people thereof.

ARTICLE VII.

1. The ratification of the conventions of five states shall be sufficient for the establishment of this constitution between the states so ratifying the same.

2. When five states shall have ratified this constitution, in the manner before specified, the congress under the provisional constitution shall prescribe the time for holding the election of president and vice-president, and for the meeting of the electoral college, and for counting the votes, and inaugurating the president. They shall also prescribe the time for holding the first election of members of congress under this constitution, and the time for assembling the same. Until the assembling of such congress, the congress under the provisional constitution shall continue to exercise the legislative powers granted them; not extending beyond the time limited by the constitution of the provisional government.

EXTRACT FROM THE JOURNAL OF THE CONGRESS.

CONGRESS, March 11, 1861.

On the question of the adoption of the constitution of the Confederate States of America, the vote was taken by yeas and nays; and the constitution was unanimously adopted, as follows:

Those who voted in the affirmative being Messrs. Walker, Smith, Curry, Hale, McRae, Shorter, and Fearn, of Alabama (Messrs. Chilton and Lewis being absent); Messrs. Morton, Anderson, and Owens, of Florida; Messrs. Toombs, Howell Cobb, Bartow, Nisbet, Hill, Wright, Thomas R. R. Cobb, and Stephens, of Georgia (Messrs. Crawford and Kenan being absent); Messrs. Perkins, de Clouet, Conrad, Kenner, Sparrow, and Marshall, of Louisiana; Messrs. Harris, Brooke, Wilson, Clayton, Barry, and Harrison, of Mississippi (Mr. Campbell being absent); Messrs. Rhett, Barnwell, Keitt, Chesnut, Memminger, Miles, Withers, and Boyce, of South Carolina; Messrs. Reagan, Hemphill, Waul, Gregg, Oldham, and Ochiltree, of Texas (Mr. Wigfall being absent).

A true copy:

J. J. HOOPER,
Secretary of the Congress.

CONGRESS, March 11, 1861.

I do hereby certify that the foregoing are, respectively, true and correct copies of "the constitution of the Confederate States of America," unanimously adopted this day, and of the yeas and nays on the question of the adoption thereof.

HOWELL COBB,
President of the Congress.

www.ingramcontent.com/pod-product-compliance
Lightning Source LLC
Chambersburg PA
CBHW031739230426
43669CB00007B/405